LAW AND AUTHORITY
IN EARLY
MASSACHUSETTS

LAW AND AUTHORITY
IN EARLY
MASSACHUSETTS

A Study in Tradition and Design

By

GEORGE LEE HASKINS

ARCHON BOOKS
1968

SBN: 208 00685 0
LIBRARY OF CONGRESS CATALOG CARD NUMBER: 68-26932
PRINTED IN THE UNITED STATES OF AMERICA

B

NOVA · ANGLIA · FILIAE

EIVSQVE · CONDITORIBVS · PRIMIS

ORTAE

Preface

AMERICAN legal history has only begun to receive from scholars the attention it deserves. There is no history of American law' corresponding to the works of Maitland and Holdsworth for England, and this lack has long been a subject of lament on the part of those who have appreciated that our legal traditions are at least as much a part of American culture as are our political traditions. Yet only the smallest beginnings have been made toward reconstructing the story of the development of American law. Substantial materials for the undertaking are available, and the impediment is less a lack of implements than of workers. Over the course of the last thirty years important studies and monographs have appeared, but extensive gaps remain, and practically no attempt at synthesis has been made. Few historians have attempted to relate legal development to the social and economic pattern of each period; fewer still have sought to go behind the law of the early period to inquire into its sources in English and even in Continental law. In consequence, serious misconceptions about the nature of our law before 1800 continue to prevail, and concerted effort to correct them in the broad perspective of history is long overdue. Those misconceptions become significant when it is recalled that the constitutions or statutes of several states specifically incorporated the law of the colonial period into the law of their respective jurisdictions.

The beginnings of American law are to be sought in the colonial period, the formative era during which the needs of a new civilization molded traditional ideas and practices into thirteen distinct legal systems. The search, however, is neither easy nor simple. The colonies differed greatly in background, in the conditions of settlement, and in the forms of government they adopted. Moreover, the social and political development of each proceeded, for the most part, along different lines. Hence, it is essential that the character and growth of the several colonial legal systems be studied individually and be separately described. An eminent legal historian has declared:

Not until we have a series of state histories by authors solidly grounded in English legal history and in their own state archives, and treating the history of every state with minute accuracy and exhaustiveness, can any attempt be fruitfully made to write American legal history as a whole. When each state has had its Reeves, then in the fulness of time there may come a Maitland.[1]

This book is intended as an introduction to the history of Massachusetts law.

The task of the historian of law is not merely one of recounting the growth and jurisdiction of courts and legislatures or of detailing the evolution of legal rules and doctrines. It is essential that these matters be related to the political and social environments of particular times and places. Broadly conceived, legal history is concerned with determining how certain types of rules, which we call law, grew out of past social, economic, and psychological conditions, and how they accorded with or accommodated themselves thereto.[2] The sources of legal history therefore include not only the enactments of legislatures and the decisions of courts and other official bodies, but letters, diaries, tracts, and the almost countless varieties of documents that reveal how men lived and thought in an earlier day. Law is not simply a body of rules for the settlement of justiciable controversies; law is both a product of, and a means of classifying and bringing into order, complex social actions and interactions. As Savigny has written, the phenomena of law, language, customs, government are not separate: "There is but one force and power in a people, bound together by its nature; and only our way of thinking gives these a separate existence."[3]

Unfortunately the domain of the law is terrain upon which the historian without formal legal education has been reluctant to intrude. One reason for this reluctance has been the traditional isolation of the law from other disciplines as a result of the professionalization of legal study in this country. Moreover, the complexities of legal doctrine and the intricacies of legal procedure have understandably tended to deter those without professional legal training from investigating the sources and the operation of law even in a past civilization. Yet, because law is a social product, reflecting not only social organization but the incidence of political and economic pressures, the discovery of its past particularly requires the techniques and insights of the social scientist. Unhappily, as Professor Mark Howe has said, "lawyers consider the historians incompetent and irresponsible, and the historians consider the lawyers unimaginative and narrow." [4] If the history of American law is to be written, this mutual distrust must be dispelled, and the outlooks of both disciplines combined.

It must again be emphasized that this book is intended only as an introduction to the history of Massachusetts law in the colonial period. It is confined to the first twenty years of the colony of Massachusetts Bay, from 1630 to 1650. So conceived, the present undertaking may appear narrow and limited, and it is accordingly appropriate to make some explanation for confining these studies to so short a period of time. In the first place, the initial decades of the Bay Colony's existence were the formative years during which, under the pervasive influence of Puritan doctrine, and with virtually no outside interference, the structure of the civil government took shape and was completed. Within the framework of that structure and of the social life which developed in its interstices, the laws of the colony were shaped and brought together in 1648 in a code which became the basic legislation for the remainder of the seventeenth century. During the same years, church doctrine and ecclesiastical polity, which premeated every aspect of colony life, were carefully developed and likewise codified in 1648 in the Cambridge Platform of Church Discipline, which became the constitution of the Congregational churches. In the second place, the first twenty years are relatively distinct from those which followed. During the 1640's, the colonial economy went through a drastic change, from one that was predominantly agrarian and self-sufficient to one that came to be based to a substantial extent upon foreign trade. The early social and political structure was to endure for several decades, but it gradually crumbled as primitive zeals began to wane and the religious aspects of life were subordinated to commercial interests. Increasing wealth and a growing population forced the religiously inspired minority to retreat and to consolidate, so that after 1650 that element no longer had the same assured control; indeed, the outbreak of religious persecutions in the late 1650's should be viewed as part of an effort of that minority to reassert its position. On the legal side, a new period also began in the 1650's. Once the law had been embodied in a code, the principal problem came to be "the enforcement of that Code by the judicial process," [5] with the result that the ensuing years witnessed the development of the law chiefly through the decisions of the courts rather than through legislation.

This volume seeks, first, to trace the evolution of the colony's institutions and instruments of government, and, second, to describe in broad outline certain aspects of the substantive law that developed in the first two decades. Its purpose is to emphasize, on the one hand, the role of tradition—social, political, legal, religious, and intellectual—and, on the other, the role of design, that is, the conscious effort to construct a system of government and law consonant with the purposes and ideas which had inspired the founding of the colony. The book seeks, further, to illustrate that law, in its general sense, is much more than the sum of the rules administered by the courts and that it consists of the formal and informal understandings of people as socially organized. Hence, it is concerned not only with legislation and with the decisions and orders of the courts but with such agencies of social control as the family and the church. In this way, the Massachusetts legal system emerges as a regime both for the ordering of men's lives and conduct and for securing and adjusting their competing interests.

The book is therefore not intended to present a comprehensively detailed legislative and judicial history of Massachusetts Bay between 1630 and 1650; by the same token, it does not purport to give a systematic account of the state of the law in that period. These matters will be developed in further volumes, for which

extensive materials have already been assembled, and which, with
a companion study for Plymouth, will carry the legal history of
Massachusetts down to the Revolution.

Consistent with the purpose and plan of this introductory volume, the opening chapters recount, first, the genesis of the Massachusetts enterprise in terms of Puritan doctrines and aspirations,
and they go on to describe the institutions of central and local
government, the development of civil and ecclesiastical orthodoxy,
legal and political theory, and the role of the family and of the
churches as sources of positive law. Much of the material upon
which the first seven chapters are based will be familiar to colonial
historians; to others, however, it will be *terra incognita*, and that
fact of itself has seemed to justify an extended introduction. However, the material in those chapters has been developed from a standpoint entirely different from that employed in standard political
and institutional histories, which have had other purposes in view.
All the topics dealt with in the opening chapters are used as vehicles
for tracing the sources and evolution of a substantial segment of
what may be termed the public-law aspect of the colonial legal
system, to the end that this area of the law may appear in the context of the social and institutional arrangements which were its
matrix. Thus, these chapters provide not only the historical introduction which most readers will expect but extensive illustrations
of the interplay of tradition and design in early Massachusetts law.

The last five chapters deal more particularly with substantive
law, such as crime, wrongdoing, inheritance, property, domestic
relations, and civil liberties. However, these topics are not treated
either systematically or comprehensively, but are used to illustrate
the sources from which legal rules were drawn and the conditions
that developed them. Massachusetts law in the colonial period was
a syncretization of biblical precedent and a complex English heritage which included not only the common law and the statutes, but
practices of the church courts, of the justices of the peace, and of
the local courts of manors and towns from which the colonists
came. Parts of that heritage were deliberately incorporated into the
colony's legal system, but other parts were rejected or adapted as
Puritan ideals and the conditions of settlement might require. It is
thus the purpose of the last five chapters to identify, and to demon-

strate the influence of, the varied inheritance upon which the colonists drew in developing the early legal system of Massachusetts, and
also to indicate areas in which they departed from English traditions and their reasons for so doing.

The materials upon which the book is based include original
English and colonial legal records, both printed and unprinted, as
well as secondary texts, law reports, special studies, and papers
contained in the proceedings of learned societies. Few periods of
history, with the exceptions of Greece and Rome, have been the
subject of so many books and monographs dealing with nearly every
phase of social, political, and intellectual life as has that of colonial
Massachusetts. So extensive are these sources, and so scattered, that
they are seldom all accessible except in the largest libraries. It has
therefore seemed desirable, for the benefit of those who are not
specialists in the colonial field, to provide extensive footnote citations for statements in the text. This is especially important in the
case of English legal records, which have rarely been utilized to
demonstrate the extent to which the colonists drew upon practices
with which they had been familiar in the localities from which they
had come.[6]

It should be emphasized that particular difficulties beset anyone
who attempts to utilize colonial court records before 1650. The
entries are so sketchy and incomplete that they can hardly be termed
case law, and next to no pleadings or other court papers survive to
supplement them, with the result that even the trained lawyer is
frequently at a loss to determine the final outcome of a suit. Moreover, the printed records have been prepared, condensed, and in-
dexed chiefly from the standpoint of the interests of the social historian and the genealogist, so that from the lawyer's standpoint
essential matter is often unavailable or difficult to find.

Since this book is intended only as an introduction to the early
history of Massachusetts law, it is worth remarking upon a feature
of that history which it has not been possible adequately to develop
in these studies but which should nevertheless be borne in mind.
Separate and distinct though the Massachusetts legal system was
from those of other British colonies, there are numerous points of
similarity among them all which are not attributable merely to their
common background and heritage. Certain of these similarities were

the result of intercolonial borrowing; the extent thereof, together with the processes by which patterns of life and thought were carried from colony to colony, should not be overlooked.[7] Other similarities appear to have been the consequence of common problems which it is a function of law to resolve. Political scientists have long been aware that the legal systems of widely differing societies and cultures have many common features, and it is beginning to be recognized that these are often associated with recurrent patterns in legal development which reflect uniformities in human drives and conduct. It has become a special function of what is called comparative jurisprudence to investigate these general patterns with a view to identifying their characteristics and, more especially, to understanding their influence at particular stages of legal growth. Recurring forms of law—for instance, codification—reflect persistences in human sentiments and attitudes which make more intelligible the course of legal development and, at the same time, help to explain some of the influences and pressures responsible for social and political growth and change within particular societies.[8] Comparative law has thus acquired an assured and important position in jurisprudence generally and in legal history in particular. Its lessons deserve to be remembered in writing even of the first years of the legal history of Massachusetts Bay, which in several respects parallels that of the early Greek colonies in Sicily and southern Italy.[9] Such instances of uniformities in human behavior in differing civilizations give continuing reality to history and help to reveal it as a coherent whole.

Acknowledgments

THE studies upon which this book are based were begun several years ago while I held an appointment in the Society of Fellows at Harvard University. The coming of war interrupted them, but they were resumed under a Demobilization Award from the Social Science Research Council and later pursued under a research grant from the Council and under a fellowship awarded me by the John Simon Guggenheim Memorial Foundation. To these institutions I express my very deep appreciation.

To Dean Jefferson B. Fordham, of the University of Pennsylvania Law School, I express my thanks for his continuing interest in this work and for his efforts to arrange my teaching duties so as to ensure its early completion. I am also grateful to Professor Roscoe Pound and to the late President A. Lawrence Lowell, of Harvard University, as well as to my late colleague Professor Edwin R. Keedy, for their warm personal encouragement.

Several friends have been kind enough to read one or more chapters of the manuscript. Chiefly, I wish to thank Professor Perry Miller, of Harvard University, who reviewed and criticized with great care an early draft of the first seven chapters and offered invaluable suggestions. I also thank my colleague Professor Clarence Morris for many helpful comments.

Through the kind permission of a number of learned journals, I have drawn upon several of my published articles, particularly in connection with parts of Chapters VIII and X. For that permission I thank the editors of the *American Quarterly*, the *Boston Univer-*

sity Law Review, the *University of Pennsylvania Law Review*, the *William and Mary Quarterly*, and the *Yale Law Journal*. A portion of Chapter VIII enlarges upon a paper delivered in Paris in 1954 before the Académie Internationale du Droit Comparé and published in the *Revue d'histoire du droit* and, in translation, in the *Indiana Law Journal*. Most of the book, however, is based upon research not hitherto published; much of it will be developed in greater detail in a series of projected studies of Massachusetts law in the seventeenth and eighteenth centuries.

Inevitably, the preparation of the book has been greatly facilitated by the many scholarly works and studies relating to the political, social and religious life of the colony of Massachusetts Bay. Principally, I acknowledge my indebtedness to the writings of Professors Perry Miller and S. E. Morison, of Harvard University, and to the work of Professor Julius Goebel, Jr., and of the late Professor Herbert L. Osgood, of Columbia University. The debt owed to the scores of others, historians and antiquaries, whose work has made accessible the legal and other records of early Massachusetts, is greater than any list of names could indicate.

The research upon which the greater part of this book is based was conducted in the source collections of the Library of Congress. For the many courtesies there extended to me over the last two years I am deeply grateful to Mr. L. Quincy Mumford, Librarian of Congress, and to Colonel Willard Webb, Chief of the Stack and Reader Division of the Library. I am also appreciative of the helpfulness of my colleague Professor Carroll C. Moreland, and of Mr. Paul Gay and Miss Nancy I. Arnold, of the Biddle Law Library, in procuring through interlibrary loans numerous books and periodicals not readily available.

Two friends, Mr. Ralph H. Clover and Mr. Lawrence B. Custer, students at the University of Pennsylvania Law School, rendered invaluable assistance, particularly during the later stages of the completion of the book, and for their earnest labors and unfailing help I express my warmest thanks and appreciation. Mrs. William P. Gilbert assisted in preparing the final draft of the manuscript for the printer, and to her also I express deep appreciation.

G. L. H.

Philadelphia
September, 1959

Contents

I

〜

Their Highest Inheritance

IN A small quarter of the Western world, in the year 1630, a small Puritan community was established along the shores and tidewater in the general vicinity of what is today Boston Harbor. This was the colony of Massachusetts Bay, which within a short time became one of the most renowned of the British settlements in North America. Founded by men dedicated to ideals as exalted as any that have ever inspired those of the Christian faith, the colony began a record of accomplishments which the passing of time has never obliterated. Few others equaled its contributions to theology, letters, and education; none paralleled its early achievements in government and law. Building upon and purifying its English heritage, the colony constructed within less than two decades a commonwealth in which the religious and social goals that had inspired its founding were achieved. Those goals were realized within an impressive framework of laws and institutions created and molded to meet the needs and purposes of a new civilization.

The achievements of the Bay colonists are hardly to be measured merely in terms of their having established a permanent settlement on the bleak New England coast. The dangers and the hardships of the wilderness were many, but those adversities were not unique, and the physical courage with which they were met was not exceptional; conditions at Plymouth and in Virginia had been more severe. It was the great achievement of the colonists of Massachusetts Bay that they founded and developed a new type of community in which they were able to purify their religious and political heritage. This they accomplished under a government not only of laws but of men—men who were dedicated to live, and cause others to live, in accordance with the word of God and the teachings of Christ.

Of the colony leaders who led and inspired the enterprise it may be said without exaggeration, and in the words which Henry Adams applied to the ruling class of Virginia after the Revolution, that they "were equal to any standard of excellence known to history. Their range was narrow, but within it they were supreme."[1] If their aims in time became tarnished, their outlook intolerant, their attitudes glacialized, the greatness of their early effort remained unimpaired. In law, their accomplishments were even more enduring, for they had a continuing influence on American legal history throughout both the colonial period and that of the Republic which followed.

In 1648 the colony laws were brought together into a comprehensive legal code which was an authoritative compilation not only of constitutional guarantees, provisions for the conduct of government, trade, military affairs, and the relations between church and state, but of the substantive law of crime, tort, property, and domestic relations. The Code was no mere collection of English laws and customs, but was a fresh and considered effort to order men's lives and conduct in accordance with the religious and political ideals of Puritanism. Traditional elements there were, but these were consciously reworked into a carefully thought-out and integrated pattern. Many of its provisions were notable improvements on the law of contemporary England in the sense that judicial procedure was simplified, criminal penalties mitigated, primogeniture abolished, debtors accorded humane treatment, and rules of due process instituted to safeguard men's lives from the arbitrary exercise of governmental power. The first compilation of its kind in the English-speaking world, the Code of 1648 stands as a monument to the elements of tradition and design from which the early law of Massachusetts was fashioned.[2]

In 1630 Massachusetts Bay was only one of several colonies which had been planted along the shores of the western Atlantic. To the north the French had occupied parts of what is now Canada; to the southwest the Dutch had established permanent settlements along the Hudson; and the Swedes were soon to secure footholds along the Delaware. As the century progressed, the British colonies became more numerous than those of other nations. Virginia had been founded in 1607 and Plymouth in 1620; Maryland, Connecticut, New Haven, and the plantations of Rhode Island were settled in the 1630's. Hardly less important were the island colonies of Bermuda, St. Kitts, Nevis, and Barbados, which were established before 1650. Although modern interest in the antecedent history of the United States tends to focus attention on the British colonies of the mainland, it is well to remember that the settlement of the latter was but one aspect of the vast colonizing movement which was a major event of the seventeenth century. At least as many colonists settled on the islands as on the mainland. It has been estimated that by 1640 the population of the British colonies was probably in excess of 64,000, of which more than one-half were in Bermuda and the West Indies.[3] Even by that year, the fraction of those in New England appears not to have been much larger than a quarter of the whole, and of that quarter probably no more than 14,000 or 15,000 were in Massachusetts Bay.[4]

These various settlements resulted from an extensive stream of migration out of England which had begun in the reign of James I and which had had its origins in the "voyages, traffiques and discoveries" of the early navigators. Gathering momentum, the tide reached unprecedented heights in the 1630's. "Never," writes Churchill, "since the days of the Germanic invasions of Britain had such a national movement been seen." [5] The opening up of the New World seemed to offer limitless possibilities for profit and wealth, as well as for escape from conditions in politics and religion which, under the Stuarts, had for many become intolerable. Widely differing in aims and purposes, in which the hopes of the godly and the self-interest of the materialists were nearly always commingled, the colonies were all subjected to a greater or less degree of supervision on the part of the entrepreneurs who financed them and of the crown which authorized them. Relations with the homeland were therefore in some instances close and in others distant, depending on the type of colony, the purpose of settlement, and the character of its inhabitants. For example, independence of outlook and action was more typical of the New England than of the Middle Atlantic colonies, partly because of the primarily religious reasons which had inspired their settlement and partly because the English authorities exercised little or no supervision over them. Massachusetts Bay was accordingly freer to depart from English ways in developing its laws and instruments of government than were Maryland and Virginia.

The history of American law begins, at least in a geographic sense, with the establishment of the first permanent settlements and colonies along the Atlantic seaboard in the seventeenth century. Each of them, whatever the nationality of its inhabitants, of necessity established, or had established for it, some system of laws immediately upon settlement. This was inevitable, since the first colonies were settled not by individual frontiersmen but by groups of men and by families. No social group, not even the family unit, can long subsist without rules of some sort to order and regulate its conduct. In politically organized society those rules, which we call law, are the product of, or a response to, complex social and psychological pressures. Their purpose is to secure, limit, and adjust the demands and desires of men with respect to things, to one another, and to the community.[6] Law, in this sense, consists partly of received precepts and ideals and partly of legislative enactments, judicial decisions, and the orders of public officials. So viewed, the law of a particular civilization is a compound of past as well as of present forces; it is both an anchor to tradition and a vehicle for change. Hence the wisdom of the ancient maxim which spoke of the law as the highest inheritance by which the people are preserved.[7]

Two distinct but related assumptions about early American law have interposed serious obstacles to a comprehensive study of its development. The first is the view, which has become encysted in the tissue of judicial precedents, that the law of the colonies was essentially the common law of England, brought over to the extent applicable to colonial conditions. As early as 1798, a United States Circuit Court announced that the colonists "brought hither, as a birth-right and inheritance, so much of the common law, as was applicable to their local situation, and change of circumstances;"[8] and a generation later the Supreme Court stated that they brought with them the general principles of the common law but "adopted only that portion which was applicable to their situation." [9] More recently, it has been asserted that "As soon as the Colonies reached a stage where there was need of any developed system of law, the whole of the English law was introduced in its system of common law and equity, with exceptions that are not important." [10] Nothing could be more misleading than sweeping statements of this kind, which in effect deny any native legal achievements in the colonial period. It is true, of course, that the colonial charters customarily provided that the laws established should not be contrary to the laws of England.[11] Those provisions undoubtedly established a standard to be observed, but what were the "laws of England" in the seventeenth century? Certainly they included more than the statutes of parliament, more than the law of the king's courts which we call the common law. In the days before the common law had achieved its later ascendancy, the laws of England included the customs of the merchants, the local and divergent customs of towns and manors, as well as the laws enforced by the ecclesiastical tribunals and by numerous other courts and commissions of specialized jurisdiction. Hence, the charters did not prescribe the wholesale introduction of any one form of English law. Indeed, they usually authorized the colony governments specifically to establish their own laws and ordinances, provided they did not violate the announced standard.[12] What constituted a departure from that standard, and what consequences resulted therefrom, depended on the administrative policies of the English government and its relationship at particular times with particular colonies. Clearly, the standard did not describe what laws were in effect in the colonies. Indeed, in Massachusetts Bay, a number of laws were enacted and remained in force which were entirely foreign to any laws known in England.

Equally misleading and inaccurate is the official theory of American courts that all English statutes enacted prior to the founding of Jamestown were in force in the colonies, and all statutes enacted thereafter were applicable only insofar as expressly extended.[13] English statutes of both periods were in some instances rejected, in others adopted in whole or in part by colonial enactment or judicial decision.[14] Whether, therefore, an English statute was part of the colony's law at a particular time is a question to be answered by research and inquiry, not by assumptions. As the Chief Justice of Pennsylvania observed in 1813:

It required time and experience to ascertain how much of the English law would be suitable to this country. By degrees, as circumstances demanded, we adopted the English usages, or substituted others better suited to our wants, till at length, before the time of the revolution, we had formed a system of our own. . . .[15]

The truth is that American law in the colonial period drew upon a complex legal heritage which included not only many of the English statutes and the rules applied by common-law courts but various customs of particular localities—all of which were supplemented by colonial enactments and decisions. Unquestionably, as the eighteenth century progressed, a substantial amount of English common law was absorbed into the local product as English lawbooks and reports found their way into colonial libraries and as a number of the colonists went over to the Inns of Court for legal training. Nevertheless, the extent of the reception of English law remains a fact to be proved in particular instances.[16]

The second mistaken assumption about early American law is an extension of the first. It presupposes that, because the law of the colonies was essentially that of England, colonial law was basically the same everywhere. This assumption is wholly without foundation. There was no uniform growth of an "American" law throughout the colonies beginning with the founding of Jamestown in 1607. On the contrary, the conditions of settlement and of development within each colony meant that each evolved its own individual legal system, just as each evolved its individual social and political system. Geographical isolation, the date and character of the several settlements, the degree or absence of outside supervision or control—all had their effect in ultimately developing thirteen separate legal systems. The divergences between English and colonial practices had become so marked by the end of the seventeenth century that an *Abridgement* was published in 1704 of the laws of several of the American settlements, including colonies on the continent of North America and in the West Indies.[17] Even at the end of the eighteenth century, when there had been a substantial reception of much common-law doctrine, Thomas Jefferson, writing in Virginia, could properly refer to the law of Massachusetts, along with that of Bermuda and Barbados, as "Foreign Law." [18] Whatever the impact of Blackstone's *Commentaries,* not only in accelerating the reception of English doctrines but in helping to bring about uniformity by eliminating many local divergences fostered by independent growth, the experience of the colonial period was neither jettisoned nor forgotten. That period remains the essentially formative era of the law of the several American states.

Even among scholars who have not been misled by these two assumptions but have recognized the separate and independent legal developments of the colonies, there have arisen substantial misconceptions as to the nature and sources of their laws. This has been notably true with respect to the colony of Massachusetts Bay in the seventeenth century, which has been characterized both as "a period of rude, untechnical popular law" [19] and as an era in which "the Scriptures were an infallible guide for both judge and legislator." [20] Neither of these positions can be sustained, and the Code of 1648 bears eloquent testimony to the developed nature of the Massachusetts legal system. Although a number of the colony's laws were based upon the Old Testament, and although several laws were enacted to meet the needs of a wilderness community, there was also a very substantial reception of various forms of English law during the early period. Yet to assert that much of the law of the colony was substantially English provides no answers to the further and vital questions: how much, of what sort, and why?

The process of importation and rejection of law and legal institutions with which the colonists had been familiar in England is illustrative of one phase of the general problem of survival and adaptation in the colonies of English patterns of thought and habits of life. The ensuing chapters emphasize how extensively the colonists drew upon their English experience in developing their political institutions, their family and social life, their institutions of government. In law, too, they availed themselves of their antecedent heritage, and a consideration of their reasons for accepting or rejecting or improving upon parts of that heritage enlarges our understanding of the alchemy of cultural transformation. More than any other aspect of colonial life, the Massachusetts legal system emerges as the product of tradition and of conscious design through which countless aspects of individual and social behavior were molded to comport with the conditions of settlement and, above all, to achieve the ideals which had inspired the founding of the colony.

II

Creeds and Platforms

THE Massachusetts Bay Company owed its legal existence to a royal charter which passed the seals in March, 1629. [1] The charter granted and confirmed to the company a tract of land which was bounded on the south by a line three miles south of the Charles River and on the north by a line three miles north of the Merrimack River; on the erroneous supposition of crown officials that those streams ran parallel to each other, the grant extended from the Atlantic on the east "to the south sea on the west." [2]

Similar in most respects to contemporary English trading organizations, and analogous to a modern business corporation, the company created was a joint stock company managed by a governor, a deputy-governor, and a board of eighteen assistants, all of whom were to be chosen annually by the stockholders, or "freemen," of the company. The board and its officers, together with the freemen, were to meet quarterly in a General Court for the purpose of admitting new members and to make laws and ordinances "for the good and welfare of the saide Company, and for the government and ordering of the saide landes and plantacion, and the people inhabiting and to inhabite the same . . . Soe as such lawes and ordinances be not contrarie or repugnant to the lawes and statutes . . . of England." [3] The governor, the deputy-governor and the assistants were to meet each month, or oftener, in what may be called executive session, as a board or "court" of assistants, which

9

was roughly the equivalent of the board of directors of a modern business corporation.[4]

Like other trading companies of the day, the Massachusetts Company was, in form, a land and trading association, organized for profit. To that end it was expected to send out colonists or "planters" who would be governed from England by the officers and shareholders. Familiar prototypes were the London Company, which governed Virginia, and the East India Company, in both of which the management remained in England distinct from the colony which it controlled. The Massachusetts Company also began in this way. Even before the charter had been procured, Captain John Endecott, a soldier from Devon, was appointed governor of the plantation and sent out with a small body of colonists, together with cattle and provisions and supplies. This group settled at what is now Salem, joining forces with the remnants of a fishing community which had been established on Cape Ann under an earlier but superseded grant.[5]

Several of the instructions which the company sent out to Endecott during 1629 related to the export of fish, or other local products, and thus suggest that the purpose of the undertaking, at its inception, was primarily commercial.[6] Other instructions, however, referred to the work of the Lord and to the propagation of the gospel, and one letter stated that the "cheifest ayme" of the company was the glory and honor of God.[7] Endecott was also enjoined to supervise his colonists' personal conduct,[8] and three ministers were appointed to sit on his council of thirteen.[9] These instructions indicate that religious purposes played at least a subsidiary part in the founding of the colony. The circumstances under which the enterprise was developed, however, provide convincing evidence that, far from being subsidiary, religious objectives were in fact paramount.

Prompted initially though it may have been by financial motives, the project of establishing a colony in New England had attracted the attention of a number of prominent and well-to-do Puritans in the eastern counties of England. Much of the inspiration for the undertaking unquestionably came from one of the most powerful of Puritan divines, John White, rector of the Church of Holy Trinity at Dorchester, who had been a chief promoter of the early colony on Cape Ann and who had continued to urge the founding of a refuge for God's oppressed people.[10] One of his warm admirers, and an associate in the earlier enterprise, was John Humfry, son-in-law of the Earl of Lincoln. The earl was one of the most earnest Puritans in England, and, stirred by Humfry's interest, his household became a center for the discussion of plans for establishing in America a form of commonwealth in which the teachings of Puritanism might be fully realized. Among other Puritans to whom the project also appealed were John Winthrop, lord of the manor of Groton in Suffolk; Isaac Johnson, a wealthy landowner in Rutland and another son-in-law of the earl; Thomas Dudley, sometime steward of the earl's estates and a parishioner of the distinguished Puritan clergyman John Cotton; Richard Bellingham, recorder of Boston and another parishioner of Cotton. The latter were all ultimately to emigrate and, with the exception of Johnson, to become principal and energetic leaders in the Massachusetts Bay Colony.

These men, and others such as Sir Richard Saltonstall of London, associated themselves at one stage or another with the early entrepreneurs of the Massachusetts Company,[11] and in the summer of 1629 a number of them decided upon emigration to New England with a view to achieving beyond the seas religious and political objectives which seemed progressively more difficult of attainment in England. Those objectives had by then almost entirely displaced the original commercial purposes, and a plan was conceived for establishing a new type of corporate colony in which the management of the company would be transferred from London to New England and there merged with the government of the colony. Whether the plan was in fact formulated before or after the charter was obtained is not wholly clear. The fact that the charter omitted, either by design or through oversight, the usual requirement as to the residence of the corporation in England has been thought to provide evidence of an early intention to transfer the corporation itself across the Atlantic.[12] Certainly, the omission helped to overcome what would otherwise have been a serious legal obstacle. Undoubtedly, the decision to move the headquarters of the company was prompted in part by the awareness of its members of the difficulties experienced by the Virginia colonists, who had been continually plagued by meddlesome orders from the London Company in England and whose charter, readily accessible in London, had been revoked by the crown in 1624. In any event, the Massachusetts entrepreneurs must have realized that, with three thousand miles between the seats of the colonial and ·of the royal governments, they could carry out their religious mission more effectively than if the management of the corporation remained in England subject to the crown's immediate control.

The merger of the company management with the colonial government was voted at a meeting of the General Court in the summer of 1629.[13] In October, John Winthrop, who had become associated with the company during the summer, was elected governor of both the company and the colony.[14] Active preparations for emigration were immediately initiated, and arrangements were instituted for concluding the company's financial affairs in England.[15] It remained only to recruit colonists, to charter vessels, to collect supplies and provisions, and to embark on the long voyage across the western sea.

The expedition was unprecedented in the history of English colonization. Neither the founding of Virginia nor that of the Pilgrim colony at Plymouth afforded a parallel. The men who carried out the Massachusetts enterprise were neither adventurers nor victims of persecution: they were persons of wealth and ability, brought together by the ties of marriage and friendship and by a sense of common purpose.[16] They were energetic, resourceful, and intelligent; most of them were well educated, many of them university graduates.[17] Above all, they were dedicated to the progressive, even radical, cause of Puritanism, which not only motivated the colonial undertaking but had profound consequences upon the structure and form of the colonial government which they were to establish. Accordingly, it becomes necessary to outline the main features of the Puritan doctrines to which they were committed.

Misconceptions as to who the Puritans were and what they stood for are legion, and these misconceptions have multiplied in the shadows of the ignorance or of the prejudice of later generations, prone always to reading back into history the attitudes or values of a later day. The words "Puritan" and "Puritanism" not only have, but have had, many meanings, varying with the context in which they are used. Efforts to define those terms are complicated by the fact that Puritanism was both a religious phenomenon and a political movement. Beginning as a way of life, it became a sect and later a political party. Thus, at one stage, the Puritans were the reformers of the Anglican Church; at another, they were the makers of the Revolution of 1642. Moreover, Puritanism took various forms which passed through numerous phases in inception, growth, and decline, and those forms had at all times their right and left wings and their centers. Precise definition is accordingly impossible. Nevertheless, for present purposes, it will not be incorrect to say that, viewed in its religious aspect, Puritanism advocated replacing the ecclesiastical hierarchy of the Established Church of England with a system approximating the Reformed polity of Scotland and Geneva.[18] More specifically, Puritan doctrine prescribed that God must be worshiped by inner feeling and outward conduct, not by mere ritual or doctrinal conformity. Hence, the Puritans regarded it as their mission to purge the Anglican Church of the forms and ceremonies for which they found no warrant in the Bible and which, despite the compromises of Elizabeth, had persisted from England's Catholic days.

The early Puritans were convinced that the Church should be reformed from within, rather than by separating from it. They did not, therefore, regard themselves as schismatics; indeed, they subscribed to the Elizabethan principles of enforced religious uniformity and of compulsory church attendance. Likewise, in their own eyes at least, the Puritans were not rebels against the state, and the accepted principles of political loyalty and of civil supremacy over the Church were among the essential ingredients of their creed. The difference between the Anglicans and the Puritans was therefore less a differing as to fundamental principles than it was a differing as to the application thereof. Apart from such doctrinal divergencies, they were Englishmen of their time, and their culture and thinking were primarily those of their contemporaries, with whom they shared the religious and political heritage of the Middle Ages and of the Protestant Reformation. Indeed, many attitudes and points of view which are commonly ascribed to the Puritans were essentially those of the great majority of their countrymen of the seventeenth century.

Numerous gradations and refinements grew out of the core of Puritan doctrine, and these in time became the nuclei from which various sects developed. Among the earliest of such sects was a group which coalesced in the second decade of the seventeenth century and became a principal inspiration of the leaders in the Massachusetts enterprise. That group, of whom the most important was the theologian William Ames, although advocating the reform of the Church of England from within rather than by separation from it, nevertheless espoused at least two of the major tenets of the sect which came to be known as Congregationalist and which actively supported the principle of separation.[19] The first of these tenets was the belief that the national Church should not be all-inclusive but should consist only of those "visible saints" who could prove that they were redeemed; the second was the belief that each church was a self-constituted, self-sufficient unit, independent of external supervision. Both tenets ran counter to those two basic Elizabethan principles accepted by orthodox Puritan doctrine—compulsory religious uniformity and state supremacy in Church affairs. However, recognizing the ineffectiveness of Separatist Congregationalism because of the political disabilities which its doctrines entailed, the non-Separatist Puritans, instead of declaring that the Church of England was a false church, took the position that that Church was a true one but that it needed to be purged both of its ceremonies and rituals and of its extensive "reprobate" membership.[20] Thus, although they went beyond orthodox Puritan doctrine in condemning centralized church government, the non-Separatists did not altogether impugn the principle of uniformity, but instead asserted that it should be restricted to the elect; at the same time, they subscribed to conventional political philosophy in accepting traditional ideas of obedience to political rulers.

The close alliance of the non-Separatist movement with the Massachusetts emigration has been demonstrated by Professor Perry Miller,[21] who has adduced convincing evidence that the removal from England was thought to provide the answer to the difficult and ambivalent position in which non-Separatists found themselves in 1629, when hopes of reform were shattered and the Puritan parliamentary cause to which they had rallied seemed to have failed. They appear to have concluded that if a group which had never separated from the Church could remove to America, under the authority of the crown, it would be possible to realize legitimately their profound hopes for a reformed church and state which they believed could never be brought about in England.[22] The bitter disillusionments which had accompanied over fifty years of controversy would thus be dispelled by constructive achievement made possible by setting open a "wide doore . . . of liberty." [23]

Although the leaders in the Winthrop group, both lay and clerical, professed to be intent upon reformation without separation,[24] careful analysis of their writings supports the conclusion that, in fact, a chief reason why they decided to emigrate to Massachusetts was put into effect certain of the teachings of Congregationalism.[25] That conclusion is further demonstrated not only by their adoption in New England of the ecclesiastical discipline of the schismatics but by the form and organization of government which they established in the colony upon their arrival. The fact that the leading men in the company sought out as ministers for the colony churches such men as John Cotton, Thomas Hooker, and Hugh Peter provides additional evidence of their strong Congregationalist leanings.[26] This alliance between members of the Congregational clergy and such laymen as Winthrop, Dudley, and others is basic to understanding the purposes of emigration and the reasons for establishing the colony. Their wish to realize many of the creeds and platforms of Congregationalism helps to explain why they believed it advantageous that the usual clause prescribing the residence of the company in England had been omitted from their charter. Without that provision, they were in a position to remove the seat of government to New England with formal legality and there elude the watchful eye of crown officials and ecclesiastical authorities. In New England, as Professor Miller has said, they were convinced that they could perform all the acts pertaining to a commonwealth and an established church, maintain orthodox uniformity, and at the same time define heresy to suit themselves. This reasoning "may have been sophistry, but Massachusetts was founded on it." [27] Proclaiming that they were His Majesty's loyal subjects, and professing that they were not schismatics but only departing from the corruptions of the English churches, Winthrop and his associates could plausibly assert that the churches of Massachusetts were legitimate offshoots of the Church of England.[28] From a political standpoint, this position was astute, for, by emphasizing the legitimacy of their undertaking, the Winthrop group could differentiate themselves from acknowledged Separatists like the Pilgrims, who, lacking legal standing in England, had been harried out of the land and had ultimately settled at Plymouth in 1620.

It must be emphasized that Puritanism involved more than mere opposition to the forms, rituals, and ceremonies of the ecclesiastical hierarchy which had survived from Roman Catholic England; it involved more than a wish to restore the primitive apostolic church in accordance with biblical precept. Puritanism was also a way of life, a rigoristic ethic, prescribing strictness of living as well as simplicity of worship, affecting the mind and the heart. It sprang, in Ralph Barton Perry's words, "from the very core of the personal conscience—the sense of duty, the sense of responsibility, the sense of guilt, and the repentant longing for forgiveness." [29] Intense belief in all these underlying assumptions of Puritanism was a driving force not only in the emigration to Massachusetts but in the political and ecclesiastical organization that was there evolved. The deep spiritual conviction that the colonists could carry these ideals into practice is fundamental to an understanding of their new society.

Because Puritanism was a way of life, it had social and political implications of great magnitude. It assumed that its disciples would regulate not only their own conduct but that of others, so that the world could be refashioned into the society ordained by God in the Bible. Pursuant to this assumption, the Puritans placed great reliance upon religious dogma as the basis for reforming social and governmental institutions. In its earlier stages, Puritanism looked to the Bible as containing all the precepts—however few or brief—by which man should be governed. God had spoken in the first instance through His word, and hence extended study of the Bible and logical deductions from its texts were thought to provide the primary means of discovering the purposes of God. All parts of the Scriptures were thought to be explicable by study and dialectical deduction, and dogma and text were therefore continually expounded in tracts and sermons which the faithful read or listened to with rapt attention, both for the practical guidance which they provided and for the solemn joy and inspiration which they afforded. Yet, although the Bible as so expounded was believed to provide a complete and unamendable constitution, God's word as therein contained did not inhibit, but rather gave impetus to, progress and reform. The Puritan conception of the kingdom of God was not a static one, confined by the injunctions of the Decalogue and the lapidary counsels of the prophets; it was equally inspired by the life of Christ and by the spirit of the Sermon on the Mount. Thus, a zeal to reform both the individual and society is one of the very notable features of Puritanism, which was active rather than contemplative.[30] "It is action," wrote Richard Baxter later in the century, "that God is most served and honoured by." [31]

The impulse to reform, though idealistic, was not utopian but was directed to the promotion and realization of what the Puritans referred to as Christian liberty. This was not liberty in the modern sense, a freedom to pursue individual wishes or inclinations; it was a freedom from any external restraint "to [do] that only which is good, just, and honest." [32] Christ had been born to set men free, but the liberty so given was a freedom to walk in the faith of the gospel and to serve God through righteousness in conduct and devoutness in worship. Liberty of this kind, as John Winthrop said in 1645, "is the proper end and object of authority" and could only be exercised and maintained by subjection to authority.[33] Hence the insistence in Puritan thinking on the twin necessities of obedience to duly constituted civil authority and of subordination of the individual to the group of which he was a part. Religious objectives were accordingly intimately connected with political institutions.

The close bond that existed between religious and political thought in the seventeenth century has often been remarked upon, but it was not by any means restricted to Puritan thinking. As Prothero has observed, "In England, as well as on the continent, religion was the chief motive power of the age." [34] The Puritans were Englishmen of their day, and they subscribed, as did their contemporaries, to theories about law and government which were still essentially mediaeval. They believed, as the Schoolmen of the Middle Ages had taught, that God had instituted government to save men from their own depravity, and hence that civil rulers must be obeyed. More importantly, they believed that the welfare of the whole was more significant than individual advantage, that society was an organism in which each part was subordinate to the whole, but to which each part contributed a definite share. At the same time, they accepted the principles of contemporary political philosophy which prescribed that religion and politics were one, and that, as a matter of religious duty, men must submit to their governing superiors, who had full powers to lead, to discipline, and to coerce.[35] Orthodoxy in matters of religion and politics was accepted as axiomatic, and hence there was no room for diversity of belief or for toleration, which was viewed nearly everywhere, in Europe as well as in England, as subversive to morals, to national independence, and to the compulsory uniformity essential to preserve both church and state.[36] Individual liberty, therefore, was viewed as permissible only within the limits of conformity as prescribed by civil and ecclesiastical authority.

This adherence to the mediaeval conception of uniformity, in the face of the diversities of belief which had in fact come about through the Protestant Reformation, is "the key to the political thought of the time."[37] Inevitably, as Professor McIlwain has observed, diversity in an age of uniformity results in persecution because acceptance of uniformity as a principle means that each religious or political group demands the supremacy of its own doctrines.[38] Each group regarded its own doctrines and beliefs as true and all others as false. This fact goes far to explain the intolerance of which the Puritans have commonly been accused and also what often appears as their self-righteous attitude of superiority. Puritan theories of government were therefore not mere self-vaunting rationalizations but were complex responses to intricate social and intellectual challenges brought on by the breaking up of the assumptions of the mediaeval world. Within the ambit of their endeavors, and in the face of these challenges, they were seeking to frame the kind of philosophic explanations and syntheses which Bacon and Descartes were then attempting in science and politics.[39]

Although the leaders of the Winthrop group accepted generally current assumptions with respect to the purposes of government, there were divergences when it came to applying them. Thus, although this group adhered to the principle that civil rulers were ordained of God and must be obeyed, they were opposed to those who they believed were misusing governmental power. To assure the maintenance of that principle, they felt compelled to remove from England, to conditions under which they could select rulers who would properly and faithfully carry out their duties. This aspect of their political beliefs parallels their religious thinking with respect to purifying the church. Separatism in civil as well as in ecclesiastical affairs was one of the direct consequences of their efforts to put their doctrines into effect.

Other conceptions helped to give new direction to contemporary political thought. Although the Puritans' theory of government was authoritarian, it was also consensual, for they drew upon and developed the theory of social covenant which was well known in the last quarter of the sixteenth century and which viewed government as a compact between ruler and subjects.[40] In the seventeenth century these contractual ideas had been given impetus and general currency in England as a means of combatting the prerogative pretensions of James I, but the New England Puritans also found them useful to justify the subordination of individuals to the state.[41] In their view, the state was the embodiment of the collective will, and the covenant was the means whereby submission to the collective will was expressed. However, divine approval of the Christian purposes of the state made the state an emanation of God, and obedience to the common will was therefore also obedience to God. The older idea of obedience to civil rulers was thus enlarged and strengthened by the idea, fostered by the conception of covenant, that in obeying the civil ruler the people were also obeying God. Hence, the covenant was more than a social compact between men: it was a compact to live righteously and according to God's word. God was therefore viewed as a party to the covenant, as He had been in ancient Israel.

With the foregoing religious and political theories most men who espoused the Puritan cause were not only familiar but in general accord. Although few but the well educated could have understood them in any philosophic sense, it must be remembered that the issues to which they gave rise were at least as vital to them, and as hotly debated, as are issues of civil liberty in our own time. Moreover, there were not wanting Puritan ministers and lecturers who had the capacity to express, and to reduce to relatively simple terms, exceedingly sophisticated ideas, especially through their sermons, which were not only eagerly attended but were the medium of communication among those to whom learned religious tracts were not accessible. John Winthrop, although a layman, was particularly capable of explaining complex ideas in simple form. In an address which he prepared on the outward voyage he emphasized the consensual aspects of the enterprise and the strong bonds of social solidarity upon which it was founded:

> wee are a Company professing our selues fellow members of Christ . . . for the worke wee haue in hand, it is by a mutuall consent through a speciall overruleing providence . . . to seeks out a place of Cohabitation and Consorteshipp. . . . In such cases as this the care of the publique must oversway all private respects. . . . The end is to improue our liues to doe more seruice to the Lord. . . .[42]

Here, in concise phrases, are expressed the fundamental principles which guided Winthrop and his associates not only in undertaking the colonial enterprise but in establishing in Massachusetts what he described as a "due forme of Goverment both ciuill and ecclesiasticall." [43]

Such was the appeal of their creeds and platforms that the leaders of the company were able within a matter of months to rally to the idea of a Puritan commonwealth a substantial group of persons who were prepared to remove permanently from England to Massachusetts. Word of the venture got about not only on market and lecture days, but through personal solicitation and letters on the part of Winthrop, Saltonstall, and others.[44] Much of the recruiting was accomplished by vicars and curates in various parts of England. John White, to whom reference has already been made, was one of the most energetic promoters of Puritan emigration.[45] Another was John Cotton, vicar of St. Botolph's in Boston, Lincolnshire, who held out to his parishioners the promise of a new Canaan in the wilderness that awaited the new children of Israel.[46]

For the majority of those who determined upon joining in the Massachusetts enterprise religious motives were paramount. Many of them came from the eastern counties of England which had long been a stronghold of Puritanism,[47] and there, particularly, the belief was widespread that "in the great opening up of the world

. . . God had reserved a place for his elect." [48] Men were firmly convinced that at long last it would be possible to live and worship according to the word of God as they understood it, in a holy community where they would be free from the interference of outsiders and nonbelievers. Unlike those who escaped from religious persecution in the Bohemia of Ferdinand or the France of Louis XIV, the Puritan emigrants to Massachusetts were primarily concerned with purifying and perfecting their religion and with realizing its full implications in their daily lives. Nothing could be more clear than that religious persecution was not a cause of their leaving England. Certainly, many had been disciplined for refusing to obey the canons of the Church, and others had been prosecuted for defying the law of the land, but there is practically no evidence that any in the Massachusetts group had been subjected to persecution.[49]

Contemporary conditions also provided a strong stimulus to the decision to leave England, not only in 1630 but in the ensuing years as well. A sense of impending calamity in religion and domestic affairs pervaded men's thinking. Winthrop sadly wrote to his wife that he was "veryly perswaded, God will bringe some heauye Affliction vpon this lande, and that speedylye." [50] Not only were Puritan clergymen being silenced and deprived of their benefices, but the outlook for Protestantism generally was gloomy, and Thomas Hooker could preach that "God is packing up his Gospell, because no body will buy his wares, nor come to his price." [51] The new school of Anglicans, known as Arminians, were in the ascendant and were encouraged by the king in their efforts to force an elaborate sacerdotalism upon the country.[52] Queen Henrietta was a Roman Catholic, and the laws against Catholics were largely suspended in order to please her. Anxious eyes were turned upon Europe where, too, the cause of the reformed faith was faltering. With the Huguenots crushed in the fall of La Rochelle, and the course of the Thirty Years' War favoring the Catholic cause, Winthrop could write that the churches of Europe were smitten and brought to desolation by the Lord, who "hath made them to drinke of the bitter cuppe of tribulation, euen vnto death." [53]

Politics in England had become progressively unsettled by 1629. The sanguine enthusiasm with which men had greeted the accession of the debonair young Charles had all but dissipated. Disgraceful failures had been the lot of English military endeavors abroad, while at home waste, corruption, and flagrant incompetence characterized the entire government. Forced loans and illegal exactions were being demanded of the rich, and mutinous troops billeted across the countryside. Even education seemed to many to be going the way of politics and religion. Winthrop wrote that the "Fountaines of Learning and Religion are soe corrupted as (besides the vnsupportable charge of there education) most children . . . are perverted, corrupted, and vtterlie ouerthrowne by the multitude of euill examples . . . of those Seminaries." [54] When parliament was dissolved in 1629, not only did the last hope of reforming the Anglican Church seem to have gone, but with it the political aspirations of the entire Puritan party. Under such circumstances, men might well think of forsaking the land of their birth for a New England that promised salvation.

Economic motives for migration there were, but they were subsidiary to the religious. John White had emphasized economic opportunities in his tract, *The Planters Plea*,[55] and, unquestionably, many of the prospective colonists, including Winthrop himself,[56] were influenced by hopes of material betterment. Excessive regulation by government had cramped industry, and the low level of wages, which had not kept pace with advancing prices, had reduced thousands to beggary. The rise in rents, and the progress of the enclosure movement, had been driving men from agricultural pursuits. Agrarian and industrial distress were especially severe in Puritan East Anglia, where during the 1620's a depression in the textile industry had caused widespread unemployment and poverty.[57] "This land," wrote Winthrop, "growes weary of her Inhabitantes, soe as man whoe is the most praetious of all creatures, is here . . . of lesse prise among vs then an horse or a sheepe. . . . all townes complaine of the burthen of theire poore." [58] Moreover, there was a growing, though erroneous, conviction that England had become overpopulated.[59] Economic opportunity was urged by all the early promoters of colonization, not only to bring profit and self-sufficiency to the individual but to provide strength and greatness to the nation.[60] Economic opportunity was also urged by Winthrop as a reason for emigration, but he emphasized its connection with religious purposes. The whole earth, he said, was the Lord's garden, and had been given to the sons of men with a commandment to replenish and subdue it.[61] Yet while advocating such opportunity, the leaders were at pains—not only at the outset but during the ensuing years as well—to discourage emigration merely for the prospect of gain.[62]

Other motives also inclined the minds of those who decided upon emigration. The prospect of owning land, as well as the lure of the unknown, played some part in the decision, according to individual temperament. Such prospects were, of course, conspicuous in the thinking of those who were not Puritan. Of these there were a considerable number among the colonists,[63] chiefly servants and men having special skills who were recruited to ensure the practical success of the undertaking.[64] To many of such persons Puritanism did not appeal, and for them adventure, material gain, or the hope of greater personal freedom were among the principal inducements.

Concurrently with the recruitment of colonists, Winthrop and his associates took steps to fit out vessels and to obtain the provisions, supplies, and equipment which would be needed both for the Atlantic voyage and in the colony. Cattle, seed, furniture, clothing, food, beer and wine, household utensils, nails and tools, firearms, and articles for trading were among the many types of articles collected.[65] Concluding arrangements were made for settling the English affairs of the company, and those of the assistants who decided to remain in England resigned their places on the board.[66]

In the spring of 1630, the company, consisting of the governor, the deputy-governor, and ten assistants,[67] was ready to set sail for New England with some seven hundred colonists.[68] With them they had the precious charter, to which they clung both as a shield of their religion and as a weapon of defense against possible encroachments of king and parliament.[69] Genuinely sad though they were at departing, their aims were clear: the founding of a "united, cohesive body politic, led by the saints, shepherded by the clergy and regulated by energetic governors, . . . fully prepared to use the lash of authority upon stragglers or rugged individualists." [70] These were purposes that they could hardly openly avow, for it was essential that they not attract the unfavorable attention of either

Charles or Archbishop Laud. Not long before, the company had urged Governor Endecott not to "render yourselfe or vs distastefull to the state heere, to which (as wee ought) wee must and will haue an obsequious eye." [71] Accordingly, in a farewell letter, written aboard Governor Winthrop's flagship, the *Arbella*, and addressed to their "Brethren in and of the *Church of* ENGLAND," the leaders were at pains to enunciate their allegiance to the land of their birth and to seek to correct any "misreport of our intentions" —presumably with respect to Separatism.[72] In April the eleven vessels of the Winthrop Fleet, seven carrying passengers and the rest freighted with livestock and supplies,[73] weighed anchor at Cowes. By June they began to drop anchor, one by one, in Massachusetts Bay, joining forces with the few hundred colonists who were already established at Salem under the former governor, John Endecott. Other vessels crossed over during the summer, and before winter the total number of settlers in the Bay Colony was well over a thousand.[74]

This handful of men and women, inspired by the creeds and platforms of Puritanism, and believing themselves children of Israel bent on the achievement of a mission that was divinely inspired and protected, was the nucleus not of a colony but of an American commonwealth. Thousands were to come after them during the ensuing decade of the great migration, but the ideals of the firstcomers continued to inspire and permeate the enlarging community. Little did Winthrop know how accurately would be fulfilled his prophecy that his "Citty vpon a Hill" should be made "a prayse and glory." [75] Separating first from the English Church, later from English ways, they and their children began slowly to form the matrix of a new and indigenous American civilization.

III

Foundations of Power

ALMOST the first task that faced the colony leaders upon their arrival in Massachusetts was the adaptation of the machinery of a simple business organism to the requirements of a body politic. As they viewed the task, it involved the institution of legal and political arrangements which would most effectually control and shape the social and religious life of the colonists in accordance with the purposes for which the enterprise had been undertaken. That those purposes were primarily social and religious, rather than commercial, is clear not only from the creeds in which their hopes were sown but from the courses of action upon which they immediately embarked.

From the outset, for example, the new government adopted land and trading policies which were entirely different from those usual in trading companies of the day. By the time of Winthrop's arrival, the company had ceased to act as an organization seeking profit from its landholdings. It began at once to grant land to the various communities as they were established, and these in turn distributed allotments to individual colonists.[1] Trade, likewise, was encouraged on a private and individual, rather than on a corporate, basis, so that by the close of 1630 the commercial element in the enterprise had virtually disappeared. Moreover, within a matter of months the admission of new freemen into the company came to be based on religious qualifications rather than on a capacity and willingness to pay for shares in the enterprise.[2] These radical departures from normal trading-company practice demonstrate that the leaders viewed the enterprise as anything but commercial in character. Above all, however, the organization of the colony government, developed in association with the churches, provides objective proof that the chief aim of the undertaking, as declared by Winthrop, was to build "a Citty vpon a Hill" where it would be possible not only to worship and live as Christians but to set the world an example of godliness.[3]

The most striking feature of the organization of Massachusetts government during the first two decades of its history was the "concentration of influence, power, offices, functions of every kind, in a small and compact group of leaders." [4] As stated earlier, the charter had placed the general management of the company in the hands of the General Court, consisting of the freemen, or stockholders, and of the officers and assistants. However, it appears that although the company consisted of something over a hundred freemen, practically none of them who was not also an assistant or an officer emigrated to the colony,[5] and of these there were no more than ten or eleven in Massachusetts in 1630.[6] From the standpoint of composition, therefore, the General Court and the Court of Assistants were virtually identical at this date, and hence from that standpoint it made little practical difference by which body the affairs of the company were managed. However, since seven of the assistants constituted a quorum under the charter, and since a majority of those seven were empowered to act, it was obviously advantageous that the governing body should be the Court of Assistants rather than the General Court, in which the concurrence of the governor and at least six assistants was essential to action.[7]

It may be inferred with some confidence that it was partly for this reason that the General Court, at its first meeting of only eight members in October, 1630, gave to the assistants the power to select the governor and deputy-governor from among themselves, to make laws and to select officers for carrying them out.[8] A more compelling reason was the likelihood that a number of the colonists would, in due course, be admitted as freemen, and that, consequently, the assistants would be in a better position to control the life of the colony if the power of legislation were entirely in their hands. To this first meeting of the General Court the assistants, as the constituent members, invited a large number of the colonists. Although none of the latter was a freeman and entitled to participate in the proceedings, Winthrop and his colleagues undoubtedly perceived that their power would be strengthened if existing as well as future arrangements had the approval of those who were to be governed thereunder. Probably this consideration explains why so many of the inhabitants were invited to the meeting. In any event, the advisability of the transfer of the General Court's functions was put to the assemblage, which assented thereto by "ereccion of hands." [9]

At the first meeting of the Court of Assistants, held two months before, that body had conferred upon six of its members the powers of English justices of the peace.[10] Hence, the effect of the October meeting of the General Court was to concentrate in the hands of the "magistrates" (as all members of the Court of Assistants were hereafter referred to) all legislative, judicial, and executive powers of the government. It seems not to have concerned these few men that the assumption of the powers of the General Court was a clear violation of the charter. If pressed, they might have agreed with Milton that "Men of most renowned virtue have sometimes by transgressing most truly kept the law." [11]

Among the powers which the charter had conferred on the General Court was the power:

from tyme to tyme to make, ordeine, and establishe all manner of wholesome and reasonable orders, lawes, statutes, and ordinances, direccions, and instruccions not contrarie to the lawes of this our realme of England, aswell for setling of the formes and ceremonies of government and magistracy fitt and necessary for the said plantacion and the inhabitantes there, and for nameing and stiling of all sortes of officers, both superior and inferior, which they shall finde needefull for that governement and plantacion, and the distinguishing and setting forth of the severall duties, powers, and lymyttes of every such office and place, . . . and for imposicions of lawfull fynes, mulctes, imprisonment, or other lawfull correccion, according to the course of other corporacions in this our realme of England. . . .[12]

Pursuant to these powers, now transferred to the Court of Assistants, the latter proceeded to grant lands, establish town boundaries, vote taxes, appoint officers, and issue orders designed to supervise and control the social, political, and religious life of the settlers. In September, 1630, they ordered that no one should settle within the limits of the patent without their consent.[13] In the following March, six persons were sent back to England as "vnmeete to inhabit here"; [14] and before the autumn of 1636 as many as twenty persons were reportedly banished from the colony.[15] Contempt of authority was summarily punished. One Phillip Ratcliffe, for uttering "scandulous speeches" against the government and the church of Salem, was ordered whipped, to have his ears cut off, to be fined £40, and banished.[16] Another colonist was sentenced to the bilboes for threatening to take an appeal to the English courts.[17] The assistants also proceeded to regulate trade and industry by fixing prices and wages, as well as to deal judicially with such matters as manslaughter, theft, fraud, breach of contract, and the administration of estates.[18] Orders reflecting typically Puritan concern about personal conduct were issued to punish idleness, to exact fines for drunkenness, and to proscribe tobacco, dice, and cards.[19]

This concentration of all governmental power in the hands of a dozen or less men substantially endured until 1634. Prior thereto, several efforts on the part of some of the colonists to limit that power and to obtain a share in the government made little headway, largely because of the keen political insight of Governor Winthrop, who, like the other magistrates, had no wish to see the colony's objectives jeopardized by allowing its management to fall into the hands of those who might not be sympathetic with the leaders' views. However, at the October, 1630, meeting of the General Court above referred to, about a hundred colonists expressed a desire (whether by invitation or otherwise is not clear) to be admitted as freemen, presumably in order to obtain some voice in the conduct of colony affairs.[20] Inevitably, complete exclusion from a share in the government was bound, sooner or later, to arouse resentment, at least on the part of the earlier settlers. Prior to Winthrop's arrival, the colonists under Endecott had had the express right to choose two members of the governor's council.[21] Whether a formal demand, political expediency, or even the Puritan conception of the social compact [22] explains the step, Winthrop and his colleagues nevertheless decided to admit as freemen a substantial number of colonists in the spring of 1631.[23] As a result, the membership of the General Court and the Court of Assistants ceased to be substantially identical.

At the same session in 1631, an order of far-reaching implications provided that thereafter no one should be admitted as a freeman unless a member of one of the colony churches.[24] Since only a portion even of those who were devout Puritans could qualify for church membership,[25] the order imposed a drastic limitation on the franchise and constituted another flagrant violation of the charter, which neither authorized nor contemplated any religious or political qualification for membership in the General Court. The significance of the order becomes clear when it is realized that between 1631 and 1641 only about thirteen hundred adult males are listed as having become freemen.[26] Assuming that the total population by 1641 was about fifteen thousand,[27] the proportion of those who had any voice in the colony government cannot, even by that date, have been much more than 7 or 8 per cent. The effect of the 1631 order was thus to put the colony government on a narrow religious basis and to ensure that the composition of the General Court, as now enlarged, should be limited to those "visible saints" who were members of the churches and shared the views of their leaders as to the dominantly religious purposes of the enterprise. Since the General Court began forthwith to elect the assistants [28] and, after 1632, the governor and deputy-governor as well,[29] and since in 1634 it also assumed from the latter their legislative functions,[30] it is plain that the order was one of the foundation stones upon which the new commonwealth was built. Yet, narrow and oligarchical as the basis of the government may appear, it was hardly more so than the government of an English chartered borough in which, typically, only a small, although differently selected, portion of the inhabitants participated.[31]

The movement on the part of the colonists to obtain a stronger voice in the government, and to restrict the power of the governor and assistants, continued to express itself in various ways and with varying degrees of success throughout most of the first twenty years of the colony's existence. In 1632 the levy of a tax by the Court of Assistants met with resistance when the minister of the church at Watertown assembled his flock and warned them that it was not safe to pay taxes to which they had not consented, lest they bring themselves and posterity into bondage.[32] It may be observed that the charter had no more given to the Court of Assistants power to levy taxes and assessments on nonfreemen than it had given the General Court power to delegate legislation to the assistants. Yet the protestants were summoned before Winthrop for admonishment, and they confessed their error, and submitted. Winthrop counseled that the government of the colony was not like that of a corporation but was "in the nature of a parliament" in which the assistants, now the elected representatives of the freemen, had full power both to legislate and to levy taxes.[33] Nevertheless, the government apparently felt obliged to concede that thereafter two from every town should be appointed "to advise with the governor and assistants about the raising of a public stock, so as what they should agree upon should bind all, etc." [34]

The Watertown protest thus had an important result in that it led to the institution of representative government for the limited purpose of taxation. Two years later, however, the principle was extended, and brought about what amounted to a constitutional revolution.[35] In the spring of 1634, the freemen appointed two deputies from each town to consider what matters might be brought before the May meeting of the General Court. An important result of their discussions was a request to see the charter, from which they learned that all laws were to be made in the General Court. Forthwith they repaired to Winthrop, who had no choice but to concede that this was so. However, he told them, the freemen were now so numerous that "it was not possible for them to make or execute laws, but they must choose others for that purpose." [36] Accordingly, deputies from the towns appeared at the May meeting of the court, but they proceeded to pass resolutions which went far beyond the limited purposes envisaged by Winthrop in his conference and voted that only the General Court should have the power to admit freemen, the power to make laws, and the power to dispose of lands.[37] At the same session the establishment of a general representative system was ordered: those in each town who had become freemen were empowered to choose two or three representatives to prepare business for the General Court and to act therein on behalf of all the freemen in the making of laws, the granting of lands, and in dealing with "all other affaires of the commonwealth wherein the freemen haue to doe," elections excepted.[38] The General Court thereby became a wholly elective body, which thereafter consisted typically of some twenty or so deputies in addition to the governor and the deputy-governor and the assistants.[39] The order applied to only three of the four yearly sessions of the General Court. At the fourth, or election, session every freeman was expected to be present and to "gyve his owne voyce." [40]

As a result of this session, the General Court resumed the powers granted to it under the charter and displaced the Court of Assistants as the chief organ of the governmental system. Its activities were not limited to legislation, but included judicial and administrative functions as well; indeed, in conformity with ideas then current, little distinction was perceived between those functions.[41] Much business came before it through petitions, many of which were of a public character and resulted in legislative or executive orders.[42] Others were of a private nature—requests for licenses, for grants of land, for remission of fines—so that the action required was essentially judicial or administrative.[43]

The task of dealing with these various matters was now shared in the General Court by the deputies and assistants, but the latter still retained extensive powers when meeting separately either as the Court of Assistants or as an executive board during the recess of the General Court. In 1636 there was created an elite standing council for life which was to have certain nonjudicial powers, including direction of military affairs.[44] Winthrop and Dudley were named to the council initially, later Endecott.[45] Soon afterward, the principle of life tenure came under fire from the deputies and was repudiated, but the council itself, with an enlarged membership of magistrates, continued to perform important functions in directing public affairs.[46] Thus, throughout the early period, the magistrates not only continued to play a major role in the enactment of laws and in the decision of cases but performed most of the administrative and directive work of the government. Indeed, as Osgood says, the "continuous executive work of the colony was done as fully by the governor and assistants . . . as it was by the king and council in England." [47]

The judicial powers of the governor and the assistants were in many ways more extensive than the legislative and other functions which they exercised. Not only did they have, individually, wide summary jurisdiction, but they sat in, or controlled appointments to, every court in the colony. Thus, most of the cases that arose during the early years of the colony's existence were decided by them, in one capacity or another. Sitting singly, they had, under the early order of August, 1630, the "like power that justices of peace hath in England for reformacion of abuses and punishing of offenders." [48] Under an act of 1638 a single magistrate was further authorized to decide in his discretion and without a jury, in the town where he lived, all suits in which the debt or damage was twenty shillings or less.[49] He might also punish for drunkenness, profane swearing, lying, and petty theft, as well as for such offenses as contempt toward ministers and absence from church.[50] Sitting together as the Court of Assistants, the magistrates exercised judicial powers which initially were as broad as those of the three great English common-law courts, as well as of Chancery, the High Commission, and the Court of Star Chamber.[51] Subsequently, the jurisdiction of the Court of Assistants was narrowed as a result of the creation of new courts of first instance.

These new courts were established in 1636. In March of that year it was ordered that the assistants should hold four judicial sessions annually at Boston.[52] This provision was made necessary partly by the pressure of judicial business consequent on the increase in population and partly by a recognition that the General Court, which by then included deputies of the towns, was ill suited in composition to determine judicial matters. These new judicial sessions of the assistants were known as Great Quarter Courts. The concurrent establishment of four Inferior Courts for Ipswich, Salem, Newtowne (Cambridge), and Boston, which were likewise to be held every quarter, also reflected the increase in the number of suits and at the same time presaged the division of the colony into counties.[53] That division was accomplished in 1643,[54] and shortly thereafter it became customary to refer to the Inferior Quarter Courts as the County Courts. The establishment of these lower courts had the effect of limiting the number of cases heard in the first instance by the Court of Assistants, whose original jurisdiction thereafter was limited to civil suits involving more than £ 10,[55] to cases of divorce,[56] and to all capital and criminal cases extending to life, member, or banishment.[57] The Court of Assistants also heard appeals from the County Courts,[58] and concurrent jurisdiction of the two courts was authorized in certain types of suits.[59] In 1649 it was expressly ordered that the Court of Assistants should take cognizance of no case triable in the County Court except by appeal.[60]

Under the act of 1636 it was provided that the Inferior Quarter (or County) Courts should be held by the assistants who resided in or near the particular towns named,[61] or by any other magistrate who could attend them, or by any whom the General Court should designate to be joined as associates to the magistrates. Five were to sit, but three constituted a quorum, provided that at least one was a magistrate. The records disclose that prominent freemen regularly sat with the magistrates.[62]

The jurisdiction of the County Courts at the end of the period under consideration extended to all civil and criminal causes not expressly reserved to the Court of Assistants or to some other inferior court or to a single magistrate.[63] Assault, battery, debt, defamation, drunkenness, fornication, Sabbath-breaking, theft, and trespass were among the most frequent types of suits that came before them.[64] Like the Court of Assistants, the County Courts normally employed jury trial for questions of fact. They also had extensive administrative jurisdiction, broadly summarized as follows:

. . . They appointed . . . persons to lay out highways, . . . searchers of money, and viewers of fish. They confirmed the nomination of military officers, apportioned charges for the repair of bridges; they licensed innkeepers, and packers of sturgeon, and punished violation of licenses; they ordered the removal of obstructions on highways, punished idle persons, punished excess of apparel, compelled restitution of overcharge by merchants, determined rates of wages in case of dispute, provided for the poor; . . . fixed ministers' allowances, saw that they were paid, inquired into the publication of heretical doctrines, . . . saw that Indians were civilized and received religious instruction, did all varieties of probate business, punished those who carried on unlicensed trade with the Indians.[65]

Two other sets of courts supplemented the work of these courts of first jurisdiction—Commissioners' Courts and Strangers' Courts.[66] In 1638 it was enacted that in towns where no magistrate lived, the General Court might appoint three freemen to hear and determine suits in which the debt or damage involved did not exceed twenty shillings.[67] Later, the County Courts and the Court of Assistants were given this appointive power.[68] Commissioners were empowered to send for parties and witnesses by summons or attachment and to administer oaths; but they had no power to commit to prison, and, when a party refused to give bond for satisfaction and had no property in the town, the case was remitted to a magistrate or to the County Court.[69] The jurisdiction of the Commissioners' Courts was therefore less extensive, particularly in criminal matters, than that of the single magistrate. The several towns had no courts of their own other than the Commissioners' Courts, but the town selectmen usually had power to punish offenses against the town by-laws, and under specified circumstances they were required to determine "small causes" and to enforce certain of the colony laws.[70]

Strangers' Courts were instituted by an act of 1639.[71] Strangers who could not conveniently await the next session of the County Court were entitled to have summoned a special court consisting of the governor or deputy-governor, together with any two magistrates, who were empowered to try any civil or criminal cause triable in the County Court by jury or otherwise.[72]

As already indicated, important judicial functions were also exercised by the General Court, which in due course became the supreme court of judicature in the colony. Initially, that Court was seldom convened, so that during the first four years the entire judicial administration was conducted by the Court of Assistants.[73] After the General Court was resuscitated in 1634 and enlarged by the inclusion of deputies from the towns, numerous suits began to come before it. However, its size and composition was not suited to the trial of ordinary suits, and these were discouraged,[74] particularly after the institution of the Inferior Quarter Courts in 1636.[75] In 1642 a law declared that all causes between parties should first be tried in an inferior court.[76] Thereafter, although a few suits continued to come before the General Court as a court of first instance,[77] its principal judicial function became one of hearing appeals from the Court of Assistants.[78] Since, as will be explained, the assistants successfully insisted in 1644 that they had the final or "negative vote" in both judicial and legislative matters before the General Court, they had the power for several years to defeat appeals from their own decisions.[79] In 1649 that practice was altered insofar as judicial matters were concerned, and thereafter cases in the General Court were decided by majority vote.[80]

For a supposedly simple frontier community, the colony's judicial system was both elaborate and comprehensive. The numerous courts made justice conveniently accessible to litigants. Procedures were simple compared with those of the English courts of common law, but they afforded the parties involved adequate notice, hearing, trial, and appeal. Although the magistrates controlled the judicial process, several were legally trained or had had experience as justices of the peace in the English quarter sessions. The judicial system, like the political system, was thus developed largely out of traditional ideas and practices.

Notwithstanding the union of the deputies and assistants in the General Court, the embers of earlier discontent flared up from time to time into open conflicts between those component parts. Essentially, the cause of these conflicts was the determination of the magistrates to retain in their hands a maximum amount of governmental power in order to promote and ensure the success of the colony mission as they conceived it. Three of those conflicts deserve special emphasis: the question of the magistrates' exercise of discretionary justice, the question of their final or "negative" vote in the General Court, and the question of the extent of their executive powers.

An early and persistent source of complaint against the magistrates was the wide discretion which they exercised in the courts in the imposition of punishments. The freemen were dissatisfied with the manner in which penalties for similar crimes varied from case to case, and they did not believe that the magistrates could be counted upon to do justice in particular situations unless penalties were openly fixed by law. Both the magistrates and the clergy were, as a group, opposed to having penalties so fixed. "I would knowe," asked Winthrop, "by what Rule we may take vpon vs to prescribe penaltyes, where God prescribes none." [81] Nevertheless, objections to discretionary justice were voiced with increasing insistence, and they not only brought about the prescription of clearly defined punishments for certain types of crime,[82] but, more importantly, they stimulated a movement to reduce the colony laws to writing.[83]

As early as 1635 Winthrop noted that the deputies were fearful of the dangers which could result from the "want of positive laws" whereby the magistrates "in many cases, might proceed according to their discretions," and he went on to say that it was therefore agreed by the General Court that "some men should be appointed to frame a body of grounds of laws, in resemblance to a Magna Charta, which . . . should be received for fundamental laws." [84] In the following year the court "intreated" Winthrop, Dudley, and others "to make a draught of lawes agreeable to the word of God, which may be the Fundamentalls of this commonwealth. . . . And . . . in the meane tyme the magistrates & their assosiates shall proceede in the courts to heare & determine all causes according to the lawes nowe established, & where there is noe law, then as neere the law of God as they can." [85] These excerpts clearly attest the deputies' desire to limit the magistrates' judicial powers through a written constitution, but they also bring out the standards to which the magistrates were expected to adhere: on the one hand, the traditional and fundamental rights of Englishmen, as embodied in Magna Carta and the common law; on the other hand, the clear and unamendable word of God as embodied in the Bible.

The magistrates, however, were opposed to having the laws reduced to writing, partly because they believed that to do so would call to the attention of the crown colonial divergences from English law, but more particularly because a written code would put a bridle upon their own power and discretionary authority, which they regarded as necessary for the accomplishment of their tasks and as belonging to them by virtue of their office.[86] Nevertheless, despite their opposition and continued resistance, the movement for written laws gradually made headway. By 1641 an extensive bill of rights, known as the Body of Liberties, had been prepared and published.[87] Its provisions contained important constitutional rules and standards, many of which were intended to inhibit the exercise of arbitrary justice, but the deputies were not content. They wanted a complete codification of the colony laws, including, particularly, precise statements of punishments and penalties.[88] This the Body of Liberties had not accomplished for any but the capital crimes, and hence it failed to meet a primary ground of complaint against the magistrates. Accordingly, the preparation of a complete code was soon consigned to a series of committees,[89] and at the same time the whole problem of discretionary justice was again brought before the General Court as one of a number of broad issues relating to the powers of the magistrates in the colony.[90]

During the summer of 1644, and in anticipation of the differences which were certain to arise between the magistrates and the deputies at the autumn meeting of the General Court, Winthrop prepared a "Discourse on Arbitrary Government."[91] In it he argued for flexible penalties, partly on the basis of the discretion permitted English judges and juries in certain types of cases, but principally on the ground that the Bible prescribed few fixed penalties except for capital crimes. He also argued that, since the magistrates resorted to God's word as the guide for their decisions, the administration of justice could not be arbitrary. The issue of discretionary justice was submitted to the clergy, who substantially supported the magistrates' position but who nevertheless set forth with care and finality the circumstances under which latitude and discretion were properly to be exercised.[92] At the end of the session, it was resolved that certain penalties ought to be prescribed, and that such as were prescribed might not be departed from without the consent of the General Court.[93] In other situations, it must be presumed *a silentio* that the magistrates' discretion was to remain unimpaired. After this session of the Court, the work of codification again proceeded, and it was accompanied by extensive revision and elaboration of the existing laws, including those which prescribed penalties. By 1648 the long-awaited comprehensive code of laws had been completed and was approved by the General Court.[94]

The second phase of the controversy between the deputies and the magistrates related to the latter's right to exercise, through the standing council which had been established in 1636, executive and consultative powers when the General Court was not sitting.[95] In the spring of 1644, a bill was carried through the deputies empowering a committee consisting of seven magistrates and three deputies to order the affairs of the colony during the approaching recess of the Court.[96] Essentially, it was the theory of the bill that the General Court was supreme in the colony and that when that Court was not in session the assistants had no power other than that given them by the Court. The assistants, on the other hand, took the position that, although the charter authorized the General Court to direct the exercise of their power, there was no authority therein to deprive them of it. The scheme was temporarily defeated by the refusal of the named magistrates to serve; but the question was again raised in the autumn meeting of the Court, the same session at which the question of discretionary justice was taken up.[97] In this matter, too, the clergy were called upon for advice, and struck hard at the assertion of the deputies that the General Court was by itself the supreme power in the colony.[98] Again, as in the resolution of the question of penalties, Winthrop's discourse on arbitrary government undoubtedly carried great weight.[99] In any event, as Osgood says, "the position of the assistants as an executive board was never again questioned." [100]

A third, though chronologically second, phase of the struggle between the magistrates and the deputies was the attack on the magistrates' asserted right to exercise a "negative vote" in assenting to or rejecting all matters—judicial as well as legislative—brought before the General Court. The controversy had its origin in a statute of 1636 enacted at the time of a dispute arising out of the emigration of Thomas Hooker and others to the banks of the Connecticut River.[101] The statute had apparently been intended to give the magistrates the prevailing voice in the settlement of disputed questions in the General Court, but the issue did not become crucial until 1642 as a result of *Sherman* v. *Keayne*, the celebrated case of the missing sow.[102] In 1640 a County Court had acquitted the defendant, Robert Keayne, of taking and killing a stray sow belonging to the plaintiff's husband. Two years later, the case came on original petition to the General Court, where a majority of the assistants voted for the defendant and a majority of the deputies for the plaintiff, who was thus defeated by the rule of the "negative vote." Thereupon, the constitutional issue involved in the rule became the subject of heated debate. Winthrop prepared the defense of the magistrates' position and argued on the basis of English precedents that the assistants, as a distinct body within the General Court, had an original and fundamental authority to reject all matters brought before that Court.[103] This view prevailed, and the question was resolved, for a few years, by an act of 1644 providing for the separation of the assistants and the deputies into two bodies and for the concurrence of both in the adoption or resolution of any measure.[104] Although the issue at the time was that of ultimate judicial authority, the 1644 act had important consequences in other directions in that it resulted in establishing a bicameral legislature in Massachusetts.[105]

These conflicts were all aspects of the same source of difference between the deputies and the magistrates, namely, the problem of the basis of political power and of the allocation of spheres of authority within the colony. Underlying the position of the deputies, and of the two or three assistants who from time to time sided with them,[106] was the belief that the composition of the General Court as a representative body made it supreme in the colony, whereas Winthrop and a majority of the magistrates took the position that under the charter, and in accordance with contemporary political thinking, the magistrates had final authority in all matters. The issue was raised in final and dramatic form in 1645 in a case involving the propriety of Winthrop's having committed and bound over for trial two defendants who had slighted the authority of the colony government in the course of a dispute over confirming the lieutenant of the militia at Hingham.[107] A majority of the deputies were of the opinion that the excessive power of the magistrates was jeopardizing the liberties of the freemen. The remainder of the deputies, along with the magistrates, saw in the issue the danger that, unless the authority of the magistrates was sustained, the government would fast degenerate into a popular democracy.[108] The deadlock lasted for several months, and the issue became primarily political. Those who had been thwarted in the issue of the "negative vote" and in their wish to see an early enactment of written laws, appear to have resolved to make an example of Winthrop. The latter was determined that the issue of censure or acquittal be squarely faced, and a majority of the magistrates thereupon decided to refer the matter to the arbitration of the clergy—always their strong supporters. At that point, the opposing deputies, "finding themselves now at the wall," gave in and agreed that Winthrop should be publicly exculpated.[109] When the sentence of acquittal had been pronounced in the General Court, Winthrop delivered himself of a "little speech" which is one of the clearest and most concise statements ever made of the magistrates' position as to the foundations of power in the colony government:

The great questions that have troubled the country, are about the authority of the magistrates and the liberty of the people. It is yourselves who have called us to this office, and being called by you, we have our authority from God. . . . I entreat you to consider, that when you choose magistrates, you take them from among yourselves. . . . Therefore when you see infirmities in us, you should reflect upon your own . . . when you have continual experience of the like infirmities in yourselves and others. We account him a good servant, who breaks not his covenant. The covenant between you and us is the oath you have taken of us . . . that we shall govern you and judge your causes by the rules of God's laws and our own, according to our best skill . . . when you call one to be a magistrate . . . you must run the hazard of his skill and ability. . . .
   "Concerning liberty, . . . There is a twofold liberty, natural . . . and civil or federal. The first is common to man with beasts and other creatures. By this, man . . . hath liberty to do what he lists; it is a liberty to do evil as well as to good. This liberty is incompatible and inconsistent with authority, and cannot endure the least restraint of the most just authority. The exercise and maintaining of this liberty makes men grow more evil . . . The other kind of liberty I call civil or federal, it may also be termed moral. . . . This liberty is the proper end and object of authority, and cannot subsist without it; and it is a liberty to that only which is good, just, and honest. This liberty you are to stand for, with the hazard (not only of your goods, but) of your lives, if need be. Whatsoever crosseth this, is not authority, but a distemper thereof. This liberty is maintained and exercised in a way of subjection to authority; it is of the same kind of liberty wherewith Christ hath made us free. . . . [S]o shall your liberties be preserved, in upholding the honor and power of authority amongst you." [110]

Here Winthrop was going beyond the accepted seventeenth century doctrine that men must submit to their rulers because God orders them to submit. He was making the further point that by joining in a covenant men renounce their liberty to do anything but that which has been agreed to, and, further, that the duty to do that which is "good, just and honest" extends beyond the field of moral law and is the basis of political authority in the state. In other words, none might have the benefit of the law except those who subject themselves to it, and none have the protection of authority except those who obey it.[111]

These conceptions of law and government were cornerstones upon which the political institutions of the colony had been built, and the freemen were continually reminded of them not only by the exhortations of the magistrates and the clergy but by the oath in which all freemen—including even the magistrates [112]—undertook to support the commonwealth and to submit themselves "to the wholesome lawes & orders made & established by the same." [113]

Thus, despite the broadening of the basis of government through the extension of the franchise, the management of the colony government remained, and in several respects became more strongly entrenched, in the governor, the deputy-governor, and the assistants. The right of the magistrates to exercise the broad powers which they had arrogated to themselves in 1630 and in the years immediately following had been effectively challenged and to some extent curtailed; but they had been successful in limiting the franchise to church members who subscribed to their own creeds and platforms. The magistrates had also succeeded in resolving the controversy over the "negative vote" in a way that made them supreme in legislative and, temporarily at least, judicial matters. When their executive and consultative powers had come under fire, they had again emerged triumphant.

For two decades, and more, the Massachusetts system worked, and it worked well. In the first place, the magistrates, to whom ultimate power was entrusted, were as a group united in their outlook and purpose and energetic in their leadership. Composed though that group was of men of strong personalities and differing temperaments, there was remarkably little dissension among them as to the policies to be pursued.[114] Another reason the system worked well was that the freemen who shared political power with the magistrates were essentially in agreement with them as to the basic mission of the colony. Moreover, as will appear, many of the institutions of government established to carry out that mission were, to a subtantial extent, reproductions or adaptations of what the colonists had known in England.[115] Hence the system also worked because little violence was done to their inherited sentiments and traditions.

IV

A Due Form of Government

THE foundations of power in the government of Massachusetts Bay did not rest, and could not have rested, solely on its civil institutions and on the political arrangements which were established in the course of the first twenty years. Religious doctrine, political theory, church organization, social institutions, community sentiment and, above all, the substantive law were the principal strands which held together the web of government.

The preceding sketch of the Massachusetts civil government during the first two decades of its history reveals that, despite the development of a system of representative government, the dominating influence which shaped the course of colonial life was that of the magistrates. More importantly, it discloses how religious doctrine was translated into action through political and legal institutions. That translation had been a primary purpose of the migration, and credit for its successful accomplishment belongs to the colony leaders who inspired and directed its course. Inevitably, the Puritan conception of the enterprise determined their political thinking and hence the form and structure of the government. However, as already explained, Puritanism itself had emerged from and built upon traditional English political ideas, and those ideas had not been forgotten. Among them were the beliefs that government exists to regulate man's corruption, that civil rulers must be obeyed, and that the welfare of the whole is more important than that of the individual.[1] Out of these older ideas there was evolved a new political theory in which the conception of covenant was used to strengthen the authority of the state.[2] Under that conception, government was viewed as originating in a compact among the people, but the government which they had joined in creating was one to whose authority they must submit not only because of the terms of their compact but because it was a Christian government conforming to what God had decreed. Thus, in subjecting themselves to a state that was divinely approved, the people also subjected themselves to obedience to God.[3] Although they might choose their rulers, the office to which the latter were elected was ordained by God. Once chosen, the magistrates were thus the essence of lawfully and divinely constituted authority to which the people must submit in order that the covenant be kept. Hence Winthrop could state that magistrates "are Gods vpon earthe."[4]

Carried into practice in Massachusetts, these doctrines resulted in a government in which authority was jealously held by the magistrates, intent upon carrying out the holy purposes of God's word as expressed in the Bible. To that end, they determined that society must be regimented. Insistence upon religious orthodoxy and uniformity emerged from the realm of theological doctrine and was prescribed as a civil necessity. Concentration of power, and the freedom to use it, were axiomatic principles to the magistrates, who were convinced that the state should be "an active instrument of leadership, discipline, and, wherever necessary, of coercion."[5] Hence the colony government undertook not merely to regulate misconduct but "to inspire and direct all conduct."[6] Its leaders were not concerned that the major part of the colonists had no political rights, for not only were the latter outside the covenant and the engagements represented by the freeman's oath, but, as the Code of 1648 recites, those coming into the colony "doe tacitly submit to this Government and to all the wholesome lawes thereof."[7] Moreover, every nonfreeman was required to take a special oath acknowledging himself lawfully subject to the authority of the colony government and submitting his person, family, and estate to the laws, orders, sentences, and decrees published or to be published for the welfare of "this body pollitique."[8] The government of Massachusetts was thus a dictatorship of a small minority who were unhesitatingly prepared to coerce the unwilling to serve the purposes of society as they conceived it.

These ideas and practices can hardly be described as democratic in a modern sense, but Puritan doctrine, like that of the mediaeval Church from which it ultimately derived, was little concerned about the equality of men. Even Roger Williams, always a liberal in theological matters, believed that anarchy would result if all were politically equal.[9] In the eyes of the Massachusetts leaders, not only was the right to share in the government restricted to those few "visible saints" who were the proven elect, but the supreme power in that government belonged only to the magistrates. The latter accordingly objected to the concessions wrung from them by the "people," for they viewed them as evidence of an unfortunate "democraticall spirit." When Roger Ludlow was informed that the "people" intended to elect the assistants and the governor in 1632, he "grew into passion" and said that "then we should have no government, but . . . every man might do what he pleased." [10] Winthrop, who expressed this attitude in more general, even philosophical, terms, asserted that the best part of a community "is always the least, and of the best part the wiser part is always the lesser." [11] At the same time, he condemned democracy as "the meanest and worst of all formes of Goverment . . . and fullest of troubles." [12] This attitude was fully endorsed by such eminent ministers as John Cotton, who pointedly inquired: "If the people be governors, who shall be governed? As for monarchy, and aristocracy, they are both of them clearly approved, and directed in scripture. . . ." [13]

Read literally, these expressions suggest that the leaders' conceptions about government were more authoritarian than in fact they were. To all of them, the term "democracy" had a different meaning from what it has today—largely perhaps, as a result of their familiarity with the political writers of antiquity. Thus, to Cotton, for instance, a government administered by the people is a democracy, whereas one in which the people choose those who administer the government he refers to as an aristocracy.[14] Interpreted in the light not only of what the word "democracy" then connoted but of the political system which had resulted from the participation of the deputies in the government, these expressions take on a different meaning. The magistrates conceded that political power must be shared, yet they were determined that it should not be divided equally but on a basis appropriate to the superior and inferior conditions, respectively, of the magistrates and the deputies. John Norton, writing in support of the magistrates, declared that it was "not an Arithmeticall equality but a Geometricall that is to be attended to; that is, not the equality of number, but of vertue." [15]

When Winthrop and Cotton condemned democracy they were not impugning the principles of the political system which had been evolved in Massachusetts, but supporting what they conceived to be constitutionalism against the extremes of popular government. "I see," wrote Nathaniel Ward, "the spirits of people runne high and what they gett they hould." [16] In conformity with contemporary political thinking, the magistrates believed that they had an authority which belonged only to them and with which no one could interfere. Ward could therefore logically protest against submitting the colony laws to the freemen, and at the same time state that they could not be deprived of their lawful liberties. [17] In this connection it is worth observing that there is no inconsistency between present-day conceptions about the rule of law and Puritan insistence that officials, once elected, must be obeyed and that the laws, once made, must likewise be obeyed until changed. [18]

The magistrates' views as to the ends and purposes of government were not merely siphoned out of arid political and theological tracts. They were living ideals, translated into viable political and legal institutions in the light of what were conceived to be the colony's needs. From the outset, Winthrop, who was a political realist, recognized the importance of patience and flexibility in the process. Repeatedly, when confronted with crises which threatened to tear the colony asunder, he dealt with them by negotiation and persuasion, always recognizing that harsher measures would have been self-defeating in terms of preserving community solidarity. Largely because of his personal influence, the colony authorities, with few exceptions, displayed a distinct and politic reluctance to make martyrs of the dissident. [19] They preferred to exact obedience and enforce standards of conduct by persuading the recalcitrant elements not only that the course of the magistrates was right and honest in itself but that, by entering into the covenant, everyone

had voluntarily bound himself to accept their rule. Reform and
regeneration were among the magistrates' chief objectives, but
when neither appeared possible they did not hesitate to apply the
most serious sanctions at their command.

Winthrop's instinctively pragmatic bent was encouraged by his
personal success in dealing with various crises on an *ad hoc* basis,
and his capability in this direction helps to explain why he consistently advocated that the magistrates be vested with wide discretionary powers. Although that position could be justified on the
basis of expediency, it conformed, as has been pointed out, with
Puritan beliefs about the social covenant, Christian calling, and
divine providence. If God was pleased, through the agency of the
social covenant, to call a man to rule over His people, He would
afford him the judgment and insight needed to understand the
divine purpose. Thus the magistrate, in Puritan thinking, could be
assured of arriving by logical processes at the "matter of the scripture," which, in Winthrop's words, "be always a Rule to vs, yet not
the phrase." [20]

The principal illustrations of the regimentation of society in accordance with God's revealed purposes are to be found in the
government's insistence on religious orthodoxy and in its regulation
of personal conduct. With respect to the first, it should be pointed
out that, from the beginning, a chief source of danger to the new
colony was the Separatist tendencies inherent in Puritanism, particularly in its Congregational form, which prescribed that the
churches were not subject to external supervision and that each was
wholly independent of the others. The danger was twofold. On the
one hand, there was the possibility that the principle of independence would result in splintering the colony into a number of
separate holy communities, each convinced of the sanctity of its
own form of doctrine, so that the unity of the colony would be
shattered. On the other hand, there was the related danger that even
if the unity of the churches were maintained, the same principle
could lead to an open separation of the Massachusetts churches from
the Church of England and thus bring down upon the colony government the wrath of Archbishop Laud and the English crown.

As explained earlier, it was the intention of the Massachusetts
leaders to find a middle way whereby doctrinal and other reforms

could be accomplished without open separation.[21] To this end, it was imperative that their own brand of religious orthodoxy be strictly enforced and maintained. Ordinarily, argument and admonition on the part of the magistrates and the ministers sufficed to cause errant strays to see the folly of their ways.[22] However, the celebrated cases of Roger Williams and Anne Hutchinson vividly illustrate not only the firmness with which the colonial government was prepared to meet departures from orthodoxy, when the situation required, but the rapidity with which the churches could be aroused by an attack on the civil power.

Williams was a stubborn man, but courageous. He was an avowed Separatist who believed, and taught, that the New England churches should separate completely from the English Church, defiled as it was with the corruption of "whores and drunkards." [23] He preached that a truly reformed group, such as the Massachusetts Puritans professed to be, should express repentance for ever having had connection with the Church of England, and he specifically counseled the Salem church to withdraw from the other Massachusetts churches. As Williams' zeal increased, he went even further and denied that the magistrates had any authority in religious matters. Earlier, he had been rash enough to question the legality of the land titles in Massachusetts and to pronounce that the king's authority to grant land to the company rested on "a solemn public lie." Present-day admiration for the proponent of religious toleration, which Williams later became, must not be permitted to obscure the fact that he presented an obvious and dangerous threat to the non-Separatist principles on which the colony churches were founded and consequently to the whole foundation of the colony's existence. The authorities therefore felt compelled to bring him to heel. Immune to persuasion, spurning all opportunities to recant, he was finally banished from the colony by the General Court in 1635.[24]

The Hutchinson affair was far more serious than that of Roger Williams because, although it began as a theological dispute, it developed into the political issue known as the Antinomian controversy, which came close to splitting the colony asunder.[25] Anne Hutchinson began her short and brilliant career in Boston by teaching the doctrines of Antinomianism, which not only fostered egalitarianism but embraced the belief that man's conduct in this world is no proof of what he may expect in the next.[26] In proclaiming the truth of these doctrines, and in announcing to her disciples that most of the Massachusetts clergy were not under a "covenant of grace" and hence unable properly to interpret or expound the Bible, she struck a deep blow at principles upon which both the Massachusetts churches and the civil government were based. After prolonged debates among the magistrates and the clergy, she was charged before the General Court with "traduceing the ministers."[27] At the legislative hearing, she so handled her defense that, despite solicitous statements made on her behalf, she antagonized the entire Court, magistrates and deputies alike. In her supreme self-assurance, she flung out a challenge which, on top of the Williams affair, posed the gravest of threats to God's special commission to Massachusetts. "For this you goe about to doe to me," she proclaimed, "God will ruine you and your posterity, and this whole State."[28] The sentence of banishment was pronounced upon her as "a woman not fit for our society."[29] Shortly afterward, in 1638, she was brought to trial before the Boston church, by which she was also convicted and solemnly excommunicated.[30]

Looking back a year later on the Hutchinson episode, Winthrop congratulated himself and the colony on the successful outcome of the episode by writing: "The Lord brought about the hearts of all the people to love and esteem them more than ever before, and all breaches were made up, and the church was saved from ruin beyond all expectation."[31] When she was slain by Indians five years later in another colony, the event was hailed as a special manifestation of divine justice.[32]

Criticisms of the Massachusetts leaders for their conduct of the Hutchinson trial tend to be unduly harsh because their actions have commonly been judged by modern rather than by contemporary standards.[33] Seventeenth century English law provided few of the safeguards that are presently regarded as essential to the fair conduct of a criminal trial. Many of the practices commonly associated with the courts of Star Chamber and High Commission were characteristic of English criminal procedure generally at that time. In common-law felony or treason proceedings, the prisoner enjoyed no right to counsel;[34] he was not entitled to a copy of the indictment; [35] and, if he was allowed to call witnesses, their testimony was unsworn.[36] Moreover, the rules of evidence were strongly weighted against him. He had no right that prosecution witnesses be produced for his cross-examination; [37] hearsay evidence against him was freely admitted; [38] and he could not refuse to answer questions on the ground of self-crimination.[39] In criminal trials generally, but particularly in trials of persons accused of offenses threatening the safety of the state, the accused had "a very slender opportunity of making an effective defence." [40] By contrast, Mrs. Hutchinson, whose heresies threatened everything that her judges and accusers held most dear, was in fact allowed considerable freedom in making her defense. If the heated disputation that permeates the Hutchinson trial is shocking to modern notions of proper judicial demeanor, it should be emphasized that in the early seventeenth century, no less than in the sixteenth, the ordinary English criminal trial was basically "an altercation between the accused, and the prosecutor and his witnesses." [41] In state trials, such as that of Sir Walter Raleigh for treason, the "altercation" was typically between the prisoner, the court, and king's counsel. Not only was the prisoner at a disadvantage from the standpoint of procedure; he was often subjected to vilification and abuse by the court and the prosecutor.[42] If Winthrop and the other magistrates were occasionally peremptory in their questioning, and if, thwarted by the astuteness of Mrs. Hutchinson's answers, they displayed their anger, her trial did not involve anything like the judicial badgering that often characterized the English state trial.

To accuse the colony government of religious intolerance because of its handling of the Williams and Hutchinson affairs is idle. The mind rebels at the lack of historic sense in accusations that in the Bay Colony free speech and free inquiry were suppressed and that the voices pleading for toleration and civil liberty were silenced.[43] In the first place, the idea of toleration was hardly known, certainly not understood, in England or Europe at this time; indeed, it ran counter to those mediaeval principles of unity and uniformity which were accepted nearly everywhere. To the Puritans, Jesuits, in particular, and later Quakers, were anathema, whereas the very name Anabaptist was synonymous with anarchist and was suggestive of the excesses of John of Leyden at Münster in the sixteenth century.[44] In the second place, if the Massachusetts leaders were deaf to the "new voices being raised on behalf of justice and humanity," [45] it may be remarked that separation and departures from orthodoxy were utterly subversive of the whole purpose for which the Winthrop group had come to New England. The extirpation of any dissent was essential to the survival of the enterprise. Indeed, the royal charter had expressly authorized the colony government to expel any who might endanger the under-taking, and banishment from the country was a regularly employed penalty in seventeenth century England.[46] Winthrop, as a political scientist, unquestionably understood that, if any element in a community persists in opposing the basic premises of government and its purposes, the psychological attitudes on which its effective-ness as an agency of social control depends are broken down.

The magistrates, as well as the ministers, were convinced that to tolerate many religions in a state would destroy the peace of the churches and dissolve the continuity of the state.[47] Hence they were forced to brand competing religions as heresies. Nearly every-one in the colony government was in agreement with Winthrop when he said that the cause against Anne Hutchinson was "not their cause but the cause of the whole country." [48] Thomas Weld, the eminent divine, wrote that if the New England Way were "*our way* and not Christs," suppression would be "our great sinne." [49] This view was to their minds merciful as well as necessary, for it was firmly believed that the faithful would be corrupted and destroyed by the toleration of other groups. "It is a mercilesse mercy," wrote John Cotton, "to pitty such as are incureably con-tagious, and mischeivous, and not to pitty many scores or hundred of the soules of such, as will be infected and destroyed by the toleration of the other." [50] Weld was not alone in proclaiming that "to forebeare giving priviledges to such as submit not to the rules of participation, is no rigour, but such a thing as Christ himselfe would doe if in our places. . . . It is no more than all other so-cieties in the world doe, who first require conformity before they permit to any the injoyment of their liberties." [51]

The colony government's supervision of the moral welfare of the community was not confined to the prescription of religious ortho-doxy, but extended to countless aspects of personal conduct and behavior. Wages and prices were fixed, gaming for money was proscribed, and heavy penalties were imposed for excesses in dress and for idleness, disobedience, tippling, drunkenness, profanity, and the telling of lies.[52] Puritanism, it will be recalled, was a way of life, prescribing strictness of living as well as of worship, and God must be worshiped by outward as well as by inner conduct.[53] Moreover, the world was viewed as the scene of open and actual warfare between God and the devil, and the magistrates therefore conceived that, as divinely appointed agents of God, it was their duty to shield the colonists from the temptations of greed and idleness, for "Where God hath a Temple, the Devil will have a chapel."[54] If the divine commission was fully to be carried out, sin in all its forms must be sought out and strictly punished so that the community might remain pure and undefiled by human waywardness.

It is therefore idle to castigate the Massachusetts Puritans for the restrictions which they imposed on personal liberty. The regulation of prices and wages was not only imperative under conditions of scarcity in the colony but entirely consonant both with currently accepted theories with respect to the "just price"[55] and with the Puritan belief that high wages promoted "vaine and idle wast of much precious tyme."[56] Extensive regulation of economic life was also a well recognized feature of contemporary England, which demanded that activities affected with a public interest be supervised and that deceits and abuses in manufacturing be stamped out.[57] Moreover, Puritan ideas as to the realization of God's bounty meant that the production of wealth could not be left to man's volition but must be controlled by government in accordance with social and religious standards.[58] The same kind of paternalism, also reflective of English practices but strongly infected with religious ideals, is apparent in the regulation of personal conduct.[59] Thus, if the community was to function as a unit and carry out the precepts of God's word, it was essential that human conduct in all its aspects be regulated in the interest of promoting the welfare of the whole community.

It would be a mistake, and a grave one, to suppose that the control exercised by the magistrates over the affairs of the colony and its inhabitants was either arbitrary or despotic. It is frequently overlooked that the charter had not only given the company broad powers to determine the form of the colony government but, as emphasized above, had authorized them to expel any persons who proved a source of annoyance.[60] Although at the outset the magistrates assumed certain powers for which there was no warrant in the charter, most of those that they subsequently exercised or acquired were confirmed to them, or conferred upon them, by orders of the General Court in which the freemen of the colony participated. Designated freemen regularly sat with the magistrates in the County Courts and, through committees of their deputies, participated in assembling the colony laws in the Code of 1648.[61]

Despite sporadic efforts to narrow the extent of certain of the magistrates' powers, there can be little doubt that the freemen of the colony reposed great confidence in the small group of magistrates whom, year after year, they returned to office. Political authority, writes John Dickinson, "rests on obedience, whether produced by reverence, habit, rational conviction, or the fear of compulsory sanctions. . . . [T]he use of force against recalcitrant individuals will not be effective unless acquiesced in, and if need be supported, by the preponderance of the impartial elements in the community not directly concerned with the controversy." [62] In Massachusetts the magistrates had to go before the voters once a year, and this requirement provided a potential check on their exercise of arbitrary power. Yet the check was seldom applied. Winthrop was governor or deputy-governor for fifteen of the years between 1630 and 1649, when he died, and in the remaining years he served as an assistant. After 1630 and until 1650, only thirteen new names are found in the lists of assistants.[63] In this connection it is noteworthy that the full complement of eighteen assistants was never filled, and that in no year until 1680 were there more than twelve.[64]

The confidence displayed in these few men was, generally speaking, continuous despite the fact that the colony population, numbering scarcely more than a thousand at the outset, grew to something in the neighborhood of fifteen thousand within approximately ten years.[65] That confidence resulted in part from the magistrates' conspicuous qualities of leadership and of sound judgment in handling colony affairs; but it also resulted from their political astuteness, for they took advantage of every opportunity to consolidate their power and to justify its exercise—often after the fact—by ingenious and frequently dialectical arguments. Their casuistry, however, was not attended by a cynical rejection of moral values but resulted from a conscientious effort to relate fundamental tenets of Puritan theology to political realities.[66]

The magistrates enjoyed the advantages that accrue to a clique in power, and their individual temperaments and sense of invincible rectitude were such that they exercised that power without hesitation. All of those who served as governor during the early years were born commanders or trained to a kind of leadership that the colonists were willing to accept. Endecott was a soldier, tactless, impatient, and aggressive. His severity was such that a colonist remarked (to his immediate regret) that "its better to goe to hell gate for mercy then to mr. Endecott for iustice." [67] Dudley, too, had been a soldier, not long since a captain of English volunteers under Henry of Navarre. He was a hard man, opposed to leniency in any form [68] and hence appealing to the fanatically Puritan element among the colonists. Bellingham, though impetuous and disinclined to moderation, was perhaps less a leader than he was an experienced administrator who was periodically prepared to take the side of the deputies against the other magistrates.[69] The great man among them was Winthrop, a man of natural humanity, the "purest, gentlest, and broadest-minded of all who were to guide the destinies of the Bay Colony." [70] Lenient to a degree that at times earned him the censure of his colleagues,[71] he was nevertheless practical-minded and never expected perfection however much he sought it. These qualities, together with his passionate dedication to the welfare of his beloved commonwealth, helped to make him the leader that he was, as well as the most powerful figure in early Massachusetts.

Government normally enlists obedience by deriving its purposes and the standards it applies from forces and tendencies at work within the community.[72] Much of the strength of the magistrates' position was therefore a consequence of the fact that the Puritan elements were in general agreement as to the colony's mission, which it was realized must be carried out through forceful and centralized leadership. To men of that time a primary concern of government was thought to be the effective maintenance of order in the community,[73] and general acceptance of the basic postulates of contemporary English political thought, which viewed government as a power existing independently of the people, clearly reinforced the magistrates' power. Moreover, it was an age in which the mediaeval belief was still current that men are appointed by God to different stations in life and have a duty to cleave to those stations and carry out the responsibilities attaching thereto.[74] Hence in orthodox Puritan thinking the "rights of the people" were far less important than were the advancement of God's glory and the achievement of true liberty through fulfilling the ordinances of Christ.[75] When Dr. Robert Child and others petitioned the General Court in 1646 to enlarge the circle of church membership and secure for all colonists—Puritan and non-Puritan—"civil liberty and freedom," their efforts were resisted and successfully obstructed by an overwhelming majority of the Court.[76] In effect, Child was advocating the establishment of a presbyterian system under which both saints and sinners would have been eligible for membership in the churches and the religious basis of political rights entirely removed.[77] Magistrates and deputies alike saw in these proposals the gravest of threats not only to the New England Way but to the independence of the colony. The Child petition was unequivocally denied, and he and his fellow remonstrants were forthwith brought to trial and convicted in 1646 of defaming the government, slandering the churches, and denying the jurisdiction of the General Court; in the following spring they were again brought to trial and convicted on a new charge of conspiring against the government.[78]

The rigor of the rule of the magistrates was tempered, however, by certain doctrines which were deeply rooted in English political tradition and which helped to prevent the government from becoming a tyranny. Chief among them was one which had been given special impetus in the seventeenth century and which the colonists were hardly likely to forget. This was the ancient principle that the government of kings and civil rulers is limited by the concept of a "fundamental law," made up of immemorial usages which, through lapse of time, had acquired a character of permanence and inviolability. This view of law gave it a transcendental

force from which emanated a protective power existing independently of any human agency and immune from interference either by
men or their civil rulers.[79] With this concept of fundamental law
many of the Massachusetts colonists were entirely familiar, and
among the principal safeguards which it was thought to provide
were long-accepted judicial procedures that protected the people
from arbitrary governmental acts.[80] Indeed, the freemen's concern
about such safeguards was a primary reason for their wish to have
prepared a declaration of rights "in resemblance to a Magna
Charta," which resulted in the constitutional guarantees of the
Body of Liberties.[81]

Unlike the Stuarts, the colony leaders never pretended to be
above the law. On the contrary, they felt entirely bound thereby,
but they insisted that the fundamental law to which they and the
colonists must conform was the law of God as revealed in the
Bible. Thus, the Preamble to the Code of 1648 recites:

So soon as God had set up Politicall Government among his people
Israel hee gave them a body of lawes for judgement both in civil and
criminal causes. These were breif and fundamental principles, yet withall so full and comprehensive as out of them clear deductions were to
be drawne to all particular cases in future times.[82]

Of this law the magistrates considered themselves the sole exponents
and interpreters by virtue of the divinely ordained office to which
they had been called. Because they regarded themselves as account-
able to God, as their oath prescribed,[83] they believed that they were
under a duty to find biblical authority or justification for all their
actions. Thus, to a substantial extent, and despite their insistence
on the right to interpret the word of God, the idea of a rule of law
imposed curbs upon the magistrates' authority. However, although
they insisted that the law of God was the primary standard by which
the affairs of the colony were to be regulated, the existence of that
standard did not in any way preclude the enactment or adoption
of positive laws which were not inconsistent therewith. In other
words, the Bible was by no means the only source of colonial law.[84]

Although the freemen accepted the Puritan premise as to the
force of the law of God, to them the "Fundamentalls" of the com-

monwealth also included the traditional rights and liberties of Englishmen.[85] Indeed, the charter had expressly assured that all the colonists "and every of their children which shall happen to be borne there . . . shall have and enioy all liberties and immunities of free and naturall subiects . . . as yf they and everie of them were borne within the realme of England." [86] Any act or policy of the magistrates which appeared to the freemen as violative of such rights at once aroused their opposition: for example, the imposition of taxation without consent in 1632, the effort to establish a standing council for life, and above all, the magistrates' insistence on discretionary justice.[87] It is significant, however, that all these major constitutional issues were approached by both sides in orderly debate and were discussed in a legalistic fashion which presupposed the existence of constitutional standards which are characteristic of a government under law.[88]

If the individual was regimented and coerced in the interest of forming a community which would be able to walk in the ways of godliness, the magistrates were nevertheless responsive to inherited political traditions. Unlike the democracies of the Greek city-states, or of Italian cities such as Florence in the Middle Ages, in which government was substantially viewed as the agency or protagonist of the poor and the underprivileged, the government of Massachusetts Bay was not concerned with material dissatisfactions. If the lives of individuals were under continual surveillance in accordance with the policies which had developed out of the purposes of settlement, the individual remained for many purposes the basic postulate of rights and obligations. To this the traditions of the English common law and political liberty contributed. Political freedom grew up in England not through popular government as we now know it but through the evolution of the principle of legal limitations on the power of government. Moreover, one of the notable features of the common law, as it came to maturity, was its concern for the individual. In Massachusetts Bay, the individual's position was not constantly shifted and molded to suit the changing purposes of the government, for the purpose was unchanging in that the Bible provided the divine and unamendable constitution which guided it. To the extent that regimentation and restrictions were a marked feature of colonial life, the individual was not entirely free to plan his own conduct. Yet there were wide areas wherein he was left free. "No humane power," says the Code of 1648, "be Lord over the Faith & Consciences of men, and therfore may not constrein them to beleive or professe against their Consciences," [89] and any minority unable to assent to the majority vote in "any Court, Council or civil Assemblie" was expressly given the right to make a counter-remonstrance and have it recorded.[90] Extensive economic legislation enacted in the 1640's encouraged individual initiative and enterprise.[91] In such attitudes and policies lay the genesis of the economic and political freedom of later days.

It seems doubtful whether the colonists' acceptance of Puritan doctrines would have enabled the leaders to carry out their objectives in the way they did had it not been for the social solidarity existing and continually promoted within the colony. That solidarity resulted from a strong sense of common purpose, from a vivid community spirit engendered by Puritan beliefs, and from the fact that a substantial number of the colonists had come from the same parts of England, frequently in groups from the same parish. Solidarity also grew out of certain ingrained, traditional ideas and practices which had their origin in the English background.

Among these traditional ideas were those that underlay the organization of the English trading companies, which were the lineal descendants of the mediaeval guilds.[92] The early guilds were fellowships marked by a close analogy to the family. Within them every effort was made to develop a sense of community of membership.[93] Many of the characteristics of the guild were carried over into the trading companies, which not only fostered close cooperation but developed a spirit of exclusiveness toward outsiders. Frequently, they also undertook to regulate the details of the family and social life of the members.[94] The fact that the members, or freemen, of the trading companies were not merely the owners of shares in the enterprise, but were aggregations of individuals associated for business purposes and regulated by exacting standards in the interest of the whole group, tended further to foster a sense of social solidarity among them. These characteristics of the guild and of the trading company were present at the outset in the organization of the Massachusetts Company, and the success of the magistrates in pursuing their central objectives undoubtedly owed something to those traditions which provided them with precedents known to and accepted by at least some elements in the population.[95]

Another feature of the colonists' background which played a part in the development of solidarity was their inherited political experience. Englishmen of the day had become accustomed to extensive participation in local government, in both town and village life. They were also accustomed to a large degree of governmental control on the part of Tudor and Stuart kings who, through the justices of the peace and other local officials, closely supervised the details of local activities and personal conduct and knit the country together by compelling men to cooperate in the work of government. This political inheritance was reinforced by acceptance of the doctrine, already referred to as a legacy of the mediaeval Church, that society was not a mere aggregation of individuals but a unitary organism in which all parts were contributory and subordinate to the welfare of the whole.

The conditions of settlement likewise promoted a sense of unity within the community and helped the leaders to carry out their religious and political mission. At the outset, the colony population was small, relatively free of the threat of outside interference, and concentrated in a few compact settlements about the bay and close to the seat of government in Boston. This feature of settlement enabled the magistrates not only to supervise closely all aspects of colony life but to make their personal influence felt in every community, particularly through the colony courts. At the same time, they were astute to envisage the potential dangers to which dispersed settlements might give rise, and they perceived that the institutions of local government could be made to contribute to the solidarity of the colony in something of the way that the towns and parishes of England had, as agencies of the central government, contributed to the strength of the Tudor and Stuart kings. To this end, the towns were not only carefully supervised by the magistrates but were made the colony's units of local administration and used for carrying out legislation with respect to numerous aspects of colony life, such as agricultural arrangements, education, and domestic relations.[96] Extensive regulation of this sort was facilitated by the fact that the Massachusetts towns reproduced the same kind of common life with which the colonists had been familiar in England and which stemmed from the localism of the Middle Ages. Strong local ties, based on the social, religious, and economic associations of daily living, shaped the towns into closely knit organisms. Inevitably, a sense of unity at the local level fostered a sense of unity in colony life generally.

A potential threat to the colony's solidarity was the continuous influx of new immigrants during the first decade of its existence. In 1633 William Laud became Archbishop of Canterbury, and he proceeded with energy and determination to force ritualism on every parish, to silence Puritan lecturers and to suppress their tracts. This was the year in which the full tide of emigration set in. A number of the new colonists brought with them doctrines which, if not wholly heretical, were at best not consonant with those approved by the Massachusetts magistrates and clergy. Others had had not a little personal experience with arbitrary government at the hands of Charles I and were something less than pleased with the form of government they found in Massachusetts. Control over newcomers was facilitated by the resident's oath required of nonfreemen and by the laws requiring the magistrates' consent to the establishment of new towns and plantations,[97] but the reality of the threat which new settlers could present is illustrated by the Williams and Hutchinson affairs and by the Child Remonstrance.[98] That threat, however, was somewhat abated by the events in England in 1640, when the likelihood of civil war slowed down to a trickle the flood of emigration as men decided to remain at home to fight for the parliamentary cause. The economic depression which followed in the wake of this turning of the tide also made emigration less attractive to those whose interests were primarily material. At the same time, the colony's growing reputation for intolerance caused many to leave Massachusetts and settle elsewhere.[99] The result of these various developments was to consolidate the group that remained and further to entrench the position of their leaders.

Probably the most important single force contributing to the solidification of the power of the magistrates in the government and in the life of the colony was the influence of the clergy. From its inception, the Massachusetts enterprise was characterized by the active cooperation of lay and ecclesiastical elements; indeed, without the close union that developed, the oligarchy that constituted the Massachusetts civil government might well have failed.[100] The teachings of Calvin had emphasized the mediaeval belief in the organic relation between church and state, and, as interpreted by the Massachusetts Puritans, it was the duty of both to create and foster a perfect Christian society. The ministers continually gave direct support to the policies of the magistrates, and, through their sermons and otherwise, they regularly exhorted their congregations to keep the magistrates in office and likewise to support those policies.[101] The handling of the controversies with Roger Williams and Anne Hutchinson provides two notable instances of the cooperation of church and state.[102] In these as in other controversies the influence of individual ministers, such as Hooker, Cotton, and Shepard, was very great, and they could be counted on to form public opinion by explaining and justifying to their congregations important issues of policy. As Winthrop said, the "Ministers have great power with the people, wherby throughe the good correspondency between the magistrates and them, they are the more easyly gouerned." [103] The efficient functioning of the system was virtually guaranteed by the requirement that the electorate be members of the churches.[104]

Thus the churches were important agencies of social control not only because they fostered solidarity within the community but because they had extensive powers over individual conduct and behavior.[105] As a group, moreover, the ministers performed an especially valuable function in the resolution of difficult public questions, especially those which related to the allocation of power between the magistrates and the deputies. When such questions were submitted to the clergy for advice, their responses were nearly always favorable to the magistrates' position.[106] In fact, the clergy acted as a kind of board of referees or supreme court on constitutional issues. In their turn, the magistrates as "nursing fathers" [107] of the churches were expected to, and did, support the ministers in the rigorous enforcement of punishments for moral and religious offenses.[108]

In principle, the partnership between the magistrates and the clergy was an equal one. The civil government and the churches were planted and grew up together "like two twinnes." [109] Both had the same general objective—the establishment and maintenance of a divinely ordered commonwealth—and through both it was achieved. In 1640 Thomas Lechford wrote that "The Magistrates, and Church-leaders, labour for a just and equall correspondence in jurisdictions, not to intrench one on the other." [110] Thus, although the magistrates were under a duty to reform corrupt worship, they had in theory no authority to interfere with the election of church officers, to perform any ecclesiastical function, or to establish any but a "pure" form of worship. In practice, however, although they continually supplemented one another's efforts, the civil arm was the superior of the two. [111] For example, the magistrates were able to uphold Winthrop's belief in their immunity from church censure [112] contrary as this position was to Puritan thinking of the time. [113] After 1636 permission to establish new churches had to be obtained from the magistrates, [114] and the prospective members were examined by them for proof of the work of God's grace. [115] Similarly, approval of the selection of church officers by the magistrates was customary, [116] and ministers whose remarks displeased the magistrates were subject to censure and rebuke. [117] Even the ministers took the position that any limitation of the magistrates' jurisdiction to nonreligious questions was sinful as well as dangerous. [118] Accordingly, the Cambridge Platform of Church Discipline, which crystallized in 1648 once and for all the standards of Puritan orthodoxy, expressly proclaimed it the duty of the magistrates

to take care of matters of religion, and to improve his civil authority for the observing of the duties commanded in the first, as well as for observing of the duties commanded in the second table. They are called gods. The end of the magistrates' office, is not only the quiet and peaceable life of the subject in matters of righteousness and honesty, but also in matters of godliness, yea, of all godliness. [119]

The Cambridge Platform stands both as a symbol and as a manifesto of the united and cohesive body politic which Winthrop and his associates had intended to create and had succeeded in establishing. The form of government evolved entirely belies the characterization of Massachusetts as a "theocracy," which connotes a government in which a priestly class has the controlling voice of authority. In Massachusetts, church and state were separate, however much the two strove for the same goals, and the final voice was not in the clergy. No church could depose a man from public office, and excommunication, though a powerful sanction, did not result in civil disabilities.[120] It should also be noted that in Massachusetts the civil authorities assumed jurisdiction over many matters which in contemporary England were within the province of ecclesiastical authority, for example, the recording of births, marriages, and deaths, the performance of the marriage ceremony, and the granting of divorces.[121]

History presents numerous illustrations of the force and effectiveness of an ideal upon the behavior of men. Yet the force of an ideal, whether of justice, of liberty, or of freedom, frequently spends itself leaving little but memory to survive unless it is accepted as a principle of conduct by the group which it inspires. The high purpose of the leaders of the Bay Colony could easily have given way to the materialism or the failures of everyday living had not those leaders, through the "due forme of Goverment," which they established, been able to transform their ideals into the practical realities of a commonwealth in which God's word and Christ's way were the central principles of both church and state.

Within the first two decades of its history, the Bay Colony had assumed the form which it was substantially to retain for the greater part of the seventeenth century. The structure of its civil government, its ecclesiastical organization, as well as the relationship between the two, had been formed and settled in a way that seemed to assure for posterity the fulfillment of the mission for which the enterprise had been undertaken. Orthodoxy in civil and ecclesiastical affairs was the central characteristic of this community in which religion was a living, emotional force. Every phase of political and social life was made to contribute to the maintenance of the Puritan system of belief. The electorate had been narrowed to church members who could be expected to support their leaders' policies. Heresies and even differences of opinion were quickly and sharply repressed. Outsiders were discouraged or denied permission to settle. Relations with other colonies were determined by the colonists' growing sense of self-righteousness and their fear of contamination by nonbelievers. Winthrop, for example, did not scruple to calumniate Virginia as a place where drunkenness customarily prevailed.[122] "These people," wrote the Dutch De Vries of the Bay colonists, "Give out that they are Israelites, and that we at our colony are Egyptians." [123] At the same time, the Massachusetts government did not hesitate to bring under its jurisdiction new territory to the north and also to attempt to dominate the neighboring Puritan colonies.[124]

Outwardly the Massachusetts colonists professed that they remained loyal to the Established Church and to the royal government in England. At the outset the leaders were sensitive both to accusations of Separatism and to any expression of hostility on the part of the English government. It was partly for this reason that they were reluctant either to publish a code of their laws [125] or to frame a written statement of church discipline.[126] Any aspersion on the royal grant, wrote Winthrop, might "have provoked our Kinge against vs, and putt a sworde into his hande to destroy vs." [127] Yet slowly and unobtrusively, and aided by geographical isolation, they set about establishing the New England Way. Judicial appeals to England were quashed or frustrated,[128] and every effort on the part of the English government to interfere with the colony's independence was promptly and strenuously resisted. When, in 1634, at the instance of Sir Ferdinando Gorges, *quo warranto* proceedings were instituted against them and it seemed that they might lose their charter,[129] the leaders began to fortify Boston Harbor,[130] and a committee was appointed to "consulte, direct, & giue command for the manageing & ordering of any warr." [131] Subsequently, when the Child Remonstrance seemed to threaten the abrogation of the charter and the overthrow of the government, the petition was summarily denied and its authors convicted of sedition.[132]

The onset of the English Civil War in 1642 removed much of the necessity for continued lip service to the English Church and state, and the colony thereafter began to express its independence more openly. Even the intimacy of accord and understanding which had characterized the relationship between the Massachusetts and the English Puritans disappeared, and the Puritan leaders in England became "almost as hostile to the ruling oligarchy in Massachusetts as were King Charles and Archbishop Laud." [133] Ancient bonds were dissolved, and the force of English ways lessened as orthodoxy became more deeply entrenched and isolationism more pronounced. Dogmatic, self-confident, and completely convinced of the rightness of their mission, fiercely intolerant of opposition from within and without, the colony leaders were prepared to, and did, take every step necessary through the instruments of government and otherwise to guarantee the success of their enterprise. This was the Massachusetts commonwealth established under a "due forme of Goverment both ciuill and ecclesiasticall." [134]

V

The Instruments of Civil Government

I<small>N</small> 1630 the region embraced by the grant to the Massachusetts Bay Company was wild, uncultivated, and largely uninhabited. A pestilence which had broken out among the Indians twelve years before had come close to wiping out the native population, so that little trace remained of the "paradise" which that indefatigable adventurer Captain John Smith had described in 1615.[1] The few scattered trading stations which English settlers had established along the coast had been small and of slight importance, and even the valiant community of the Dorchester Adventurers on Cape Ann had been doomed to extinction in 1626. The only significant settlements still extant in 1630 were the recently established communities at Salem and Charlestown.

Physically, then as now, the coastal area of the region presented considerable variety. North of the rocky promontory of Cape Ann were the salt marshes and the sands of Ipswich; south were the harbors of Salem and Marblehead and the vast island-dotted bay into which the necks of Charlestown and Boston protruded. A fringe of low hills to the westward circled the so-called Boston basin, forming its quiet horizon and terminating at the ancient Great Blue Hill from which Massachusetts took its name.[2] Through the basin the Charles and the Mystic rivers—slow, meandering streams—wound towards the sea and ended in long tidal estuaries of the bay. At high tide they flooded the low-lying flats and marshes and at the ebb left them reeking of mud and wet grass.

Navigable for short distances only, these streams, which were the chief means of transportation, tended to restrict settlement to their borders or to the neighborhood of the sea. Nearby were good stands of pine, oak, ash, and other timber, interspersed with rocky hillsides, ponds, swamps, and boulder-strewn fields.[3]

So inhospitable was the appearance of the countryside as compared with England that an early settler at Cambridge grumbled that the colony was "builded vpon rocks, sands, & salte marshes." [4] The soil was indeed rocky and, in many places, barren, and what fertility it had was far from uniform. Yet the uneven fields soon brought forth good harvests of grains and other crops, the long seashores yielded a plentiful supply of mussels and clams, and the coastal waters abounded in lobster, bass, and cod. Sea and land fowl were easily come by, and even deer were plentiful.[5] Geographical features thus dictated an economy of subsistence agriculture, fishing, and hunting as the basis of life.

A gentlewoman writing near the middle of the seventeenth century observed that the "air of the country is sharp, the rocks many, the trees innumerable, the grass little, the winter cold, the summer hot, the gnats in summer biting, the wolves at midnight howling." [6] Then, as now, the climate was hard and the weather changeable. Long winters of bitter cold and penetrating dampness were followed by torrid summers with scarcely any spring between. Yet at all seasons, the snow, sleet, rain, or fog could quickly give way to the invigorating sun-laden air that blew in on the north and westerly winds. The country therefore had its fair aspects. If it was bleak and desolate in winter, the grass bent, the trees bare, the birds muted, the fields and marshes sagging under deep snow, in summer its starkness was veiled in green foliage, and it rejoiced in the songs of birds, the brilliance of blue water, and the wildflowers in the meadows.

Such, briefly, was the land and the climate of the region into which the Winthrop group had come. Originally, the leaders had contemplated building a single fortified town, but the prevalence of sickness, together with the shortage of food and water, compelled them to abandon that project, with the result that the colonists divided and grouped themselves into a number of compact settlements in the tidewater area about Boston Bay.[7] Charlestown,

already inhabited by a number of families which had recently removed from Salem, became the seat of the new colonial government but was shortly abandoned for that purpose in favor of
Boston. Charlestown and Boston were ill suited for farming,[8] but
they were selected for settlement because the necks upon which
they were situated were easy to defend and had commanding positions over Boston Harbor. Other sites were chosen chiefly for the
availability of fresh water and meadow,[9] and before winter five
others had been chosen: Dorchester and Roxbury, south of the
Boston neck; Watertown, a few miles up the Charles; Medford,
on the Mystic above Charlestown; Saugus (later Lynn) along the
coast toward Salem.[10]

Out of the first communities so established developed the town-
ship system, which became a prominent feature of the social and
governmental organization of the entire colonial period. Almost
immediately, indiscriminate settlement was prohibited as the Court
of Assistants undertook to regulate the conditions and institutions
of local government. At a meeting of that court in September,
1630, it was ordered that no one should settle within the limits of
the patent without the consent of a majority of the governor and
assistants;[11] thereafter, it was provided that the General Court
should have the exclusive authority to dispose of lands [12] and to
regulate the settlement of new plantations.[13] After 1636, most towns
began as "plantations," settled by permission of the General Court,
and were later raised to the status of self-governing communities
under the Court's authority.[14] Under the system thus inaugurated,
the body of proprietors in each town became grantees of the colony
land and acted as agents of the colony in the distribution thereof to
individual settlers.[15] It was a system which was markedly different
from those of the proprietary colonies to the south, where terri-
torial policies were dictated in the first instance by considerations
of profit.[16]

From the outset, therefore, the colonial government exercised
close supervision over all the settlements within its borders. Supervision was not limited merely to the allotment of lands. In the early
years constables were selected for the towns,[17] and the towns were
ordered to provide common weights and measures,[18] to supply
arms to the inhabitants,[19] and to record allotments of land.[20] By

1636, however, detailed regulation was no longer practicable, and in March of that year the General Court authorized the towns to dispose of their own lands, to choose their own officers, and to make such orders as were needed for regulating their affairs, provided that such orders were not repugnant to the laws and orders of the General Court.[21] Yet despite this grant of local self-government, the Court continued to exercise extensive control over the towns, individually and collectively, for purposes of safeguarding and promoting the welfare of the colony. The magistrates understood that the centrifugal forces set in motion by the dispersal and localization of social and economic life posed a potential threat to the solidarity of the colony and hence to its mission. Partly, at least, for this reason, the towns were consciously utilized as local units for taxation, for the organization and training of the militia, for the care of the poor, for the maintenance of highways, for supplying juries, and for the registration of births, deaths, and marriages. Particular acts regulated disputes concerning the planting of common fields [22] and ordered the towns to maintain fences [23] and to enforce educational requirements.[24] Thus, although numerous individual divergences might appear, the continual supervision of the towns by the magistrates and the General Court tended to bring about uniformity in the pattern as well as in the scheme of local government.

In their physical aspects, the first towns, as well as those which were subsequently established, reflected not only the economic necessities of settlement but English practices and institutions with which the colonists were familiar. Home lots sufficient for a house, outbuildings, and a garden were laid out on streets in close proximity to one another. The surrounding arable land was divided among the individual settlers in a manner to ensure equality of distribution: that is, each proprietor received not compact grants but several scattered allotments of a few acres each, according to the configuration and worth of the land.[25] The records of the allotments of land preserved in the Cambridge land records are typical of the arrangements made in all the early towns. Thus, Andrew Warner was alloted one house and about one rood for a back side and garden in Marsh Lane within the town; in the west end he was given about one acre; in Ox Marsh three acres and a half; in the

Old Field about twelve acres and a half; on the neck eighteen acres; in the Great Marsh about fifteen acres and a half.[26]

In this way, there was reproduced a system of common fields similar to that which the colonists had known in England—a system under which the fields were owned in severalty but cultivated in common.[27] On the outskirts was the common land of the town, used initially for pasture and wood, but available for future distribution to individuals by the proprietors. Common herding of cattle was also a prominent feature of the town's agricultural life and was a consequence both of English manorial tradition and of the system of common fields.[28] Cattle, sheep, goats, and swine had been brought over from England, and they were put into town herds under the charge of a herdsman employed and paid for by the town.[29] These as well as other aspects of town life make it clear that the colonists sought to reconstruct the community life which they had known in England insofar as consonant with local conditions and with the objectives of their migration.

The first towns were cohesive social and political units which were further cemented by the circumstance of their having been settled by groups which had either migrated as, or soon joined together as, religious congregations.[30] With a common determination to walk in the faith of the gospel, they naturally wished to exclude elements which were incongruous with that central purpose. For example, when Dedham was settled, the townsmen covenanted "to keepe of from vs all such, as ar contrarye minded. And receaue onely such vnto vs as be such as may be probably of one harte."[31] However, although the towns were settled primarily as congregations and functioned both as religious and as political units, they were also associations for economic purposes. This feature of the Massachusetts towns has attracted the attention of but few historians, yet from many standpoints the town was a common economic venture, almost a partnership.[32] Although grants were made to individual proprietors, the management of the common fields and common herds required cooperation and extensive regulation. The town records are replete with detailed provisions governing the maintenance of fences,[33] the building and care of highways,[34] the gathering of firewood,[35] and the ringing of swine.[36] These orders continually emphasized in daily life the economic as

well as the social ties of the community, and they helped further
to promote cohesiveness within each town, already knit together
both by religious beliefs and by the common background and traditions of those within it. The carrying out of town regulations required supervision by a horde of town officials, such as fence viewers, haywards, hog ringers, surveyors of highways, with the result
that a substantial number of the inhabitants were involved in the
management of town affairs. Hence, the community in its political
aspect coincided with the community in its social and economic
aspects.

Local solidarity was further enhanced by the system of land allotment. Since each community had the responsibility of making allotments of land to individuals, each town had a direct interest in
admitting or excluding new members who would participate in the
community organization.[37] For this reason, numerous town orders
restrained the alienation of land and forbade strangers to settle
within the town limits. In Watertown, for example, it was ordered
that no man should sell to any "forrainer" his lot on the "Towne
plott," "It being our reall intent to sitt down there close togither." [38]
In Boston it was ordered that no further allotments of land were to
be made to newcomers unless they were likely to be received into
the congregation; it was also ordered that no one should sell his
house or allotment to any newcomer "but with the consent and
allowance of those that are appointed Allotters." [39] The Boston
records reveal that any sale made in contravention of the order was
declared void, and the grantors fined from one to six pounds.[40]
There are recurrent references to the question of admitting new
inhabitants,[41] and to orders prohibiting the entertainment of strangers [42] and requiring unauthorized persons to depart.[43] Such orders
were motivated both by a desire to retain intact the social and religious solidarity of the group and by a concern lest newcomers
become a charge upon the town.[44]

Many of these provisions were supplemented by colony orders
which reflected the same underlying policies. As already stated,
the Court of Assistants had declared in 1630 that no one should be
permitted to settle in the colony without the permission of the
magistrates.[45] In 1637, when the so-called Antinomian controversy
was at its height,[46] the General Court enacted that no town should

entertain any stranger for a period longer than three weeks or allow him any lot or habitation without permission of some member of the council[47] or of two other magistrates.[48] Such provisions were dictated by the government's recognition of the need to promote uniformity of attitude and orthodoxy of belief.

By continually nurturing community sentiment, the colony government was able more effectively to utilize the towns as units of local administration and to keep alive the memory of the English parish and manor as self-contained, group-minded communities, the focus of social life as well as agencies for self-government.[49] The group was thus the characteristic feature of social, political, and economic life. The lone frontiersman who later typified the settlement of the West was practically unknown in the early Bay Colony. Indeed, the law required that men as well as women should not live alone but should be members of some household or family.[50]

The magistrates' supervision of the affairs of the towns was facilitated by the judicial organization of the colony already discussed.[51] Sitting on all the courts of first instance, particularly the County Courts, they had an opportunity to observe at firsthand the kind of problems which affected the welfare of the colony as a whole. Their judicial functions enabled them not only to mold the life of the communities through court orders and through the imposition of fines and sentences but to perceive what remedial legislation might be required in the General Court. In addition, since the magistrates resided in the more important towns, they were in a position to make their personal influence felt through the contacts of everyday living as well as in the town meetings in which they were regular participants.[52]

By 1642 official recognition appears to have been accorded to twenty-one communities, and by 1647 the number had increased to thirty-three,[53] most of which were situated along or near the coast not far from Boston.[54] Each community regulated its affairs in the first instance through the town meeting. Since the individual proprietors were regarded as integral parts of the community, each was expected to bear his share of the common responsibilities. Attendance at town meeting was therefore generally compulsory.[55] The earliest meetings appear to have been informal, called as the occasion required. Their chief business was the allotment of lands to individuals, the admission of new settlers and the enactment of orders and bylaws for the regulation of community affairs. As the population increased, their procedures and functions became institutionalized, and the town meeting, where all inhabitants were free to speak if not to vote, became a vehicle for distilling public opinion. Since the towns elected the deputies to the General Court, they inevitably became centers of debate on the great controversial issues that affected the entire colony—the Hutchinson affair, the Child Remonstrance and the issue of the negative vote.

The historian of Deerfield has summarized the scope of the towns' activities and responsibilities as follows:

"The Town" acted on all matters pertaining to the welfare of the community: Divided the land, built fortifications, meetinghouses, schoolhouses, ferry boats, and pounds; hired the minister and schoolmaster; chose military officers; laid out highways and graveyards; levied rates, prescribed the "specie" in which it should be paid, and fixed its price; fixed the price of grain betwixt man and man, and the price of labor; looked carefully after the common field, the fences and the stock; fixed the time for opening and closing the meadows; regulated the building of mills, and settled the toll for grinding and sawing; . . . enforced attendance on divine worship and its own meetings.[56]

At the outset, those attending the town meeting consisted of the proprietors to whom allotments of land had been made. Many of these were church members and had been admitted as freemen of the colony; others who were not freemen also took part in town government, but the extent to which they and later arrivals participated is not wholly clear. An act of the General Court in 1635 provided that "none but freemen shall have any vote in any towne, in any action of aucthoritie." [57] However, the records disclose that nonfreemen served on *ad hoc* town committees and even as town officers after that date,[58] and it may be assumed that they were also permitted to vote on certain types of matters.[59] As time went on and the number of nonfreemen increased, it was thought necessary to modify the 1635 order, and in 1647 it was provided that nonfreemen who were over twenty-four and who had taken the resident's oath of fidelity to the colony might vote in town meeting for town officers and on questions of roads, schools, and lands.[60] At about the same time, since it had become apparent that many church members had failed to become freemen in order to escape service in town affairs, it was enacted that such persons might be required to serve on juries and as town officers.[61] Other townsmen, who are described merely as inhabitants and cottagers, were men without shadows who apparently took little part in local government except insofar as they may have contributed to the weight of public opinion. Yet they, in common with every inhabitant of the colony, freeman or nonfreeman, were expressly accorded the right to attend any session of any court or town meeting and "either by speech or writing, to move any lawfull, seasonable, or material question; or to present any necessarie motion, complaint, petition, bill or information wherof that Meeting hath proper cognisance." [62] Thus, although the power of official action was substantially confined to freemen, one of the basic constitutional guarantees of modern democratic governments was assured to everyone who resided in the colony.

In most towns, routine and regular business was delegated to "selectmen," [63] and the centralization of authority in their hands served further to promote a sense of unity within each community. The selectmen were the most important of the town officials, and their powers were broad. The records of some towns set forth those powers in considerable detail, whereas others merely describe them in general terms, subject to specified limitations.[64] Meeting once a month or oftener, the selectmen usually supervised the local financial administration,[65] sold or allotted town lands,[66] appointed minor town officials [67] and took care of a host of administrative duties [68] on behalf of both the town and colony governments.[69] These duties were more extensive in a large town like Boston than in smaller communities. There, for example, the selectmen are found granting permission for the building of wharves [70] and other structures,[71] for mowing of meadow,[72] for sinking of wells.[73] They ordered the repair of fences [74] and regulated the location of cellar doors,[75] and they issued licenses to brewers [76] and "victualling houses." [77] The records also reveal the selectmen active in the exercise of quasi-judicial functions—imposing fines,[78] issuing injunctions,[79] settling claims to land,[80] and abating nuisances.[81] They also heard and determined small causes when a magistrate or commissioners were disqualified to sit.[82] These illustrations underscore the importance of the town in areas which we would today call public or municipal law, and at the same time they demonstrate the extent to which private substantive law was secreted in the interstices of nonjudicial activities.

Numerous other officials supplemented the work of the selectmen in managing the affairs of the town and resolving problems which arose out of conditions of close living. Of these lesser officials the most important was the constable, whose duties included the execution of punishments ordered by the magistrates, together with a variety of police functions and numerous administrative duties.[83] So onerous had the constable's duties become by the 1650's that the listing of them required twenty-six clauses,[84] and it became necessary to compel men to accept office by substantial fines.[85]

Among other town officers were generally a town clerk or recorder,[86] a pound keeper,[87] a common drover or herdsman,[88] fence viewers[89] and hog reeves.[90] Boston had a drummer,[91] a water bailiff,[92] and a bellman.[93] As the century progressed, still other officials, such as tithingmen and overseers of the poor, were added.[94] Yet the list does not stop here. Superintending most aspects of commercial activity was a host of minor officials—packers, sealers of weights and measures, sealers of leather, cullers of fish, cullers of lumber, surveyors of wheat and flour.[95]

Students of English history will recognize in the foregoing list of functionaries the names and titles of those who took part in and supervised the work of local government in the English towns, manors, and parishes of the period.[96] The similarity was not merely one of nomenclature, for the town officers of Massachusetts Bay performed on behalf of their communities substantially the same duties as their English counterparts, and the town oligarchy paralleled the oligarchy of the English parish. The fact that the Massachusetts towns, in regulating their own affairs, drew upon their antecedent experience in the parish vestries and manorial courts again emphasizes the extent to which English institutions and customary modes of action were carried into the New World. The same point is further brought out by the uses to which the town officers were put on behalf of the colony government. In England, in the sixteenth and seventeenth centuries, local officials, locally appointed, were made to carry out policies formulated by the central government. The English had never employed anything comparable to the French bureaucratic system of *intendants* for the supervision of local government. Instead, they had built upon and developed the deeply-rooted tradition of what has been termed self-government at the king's command.[97] Under Elizabeth the duties of the justices of the peace had been enlarged to carry out through local units, primarily the parish, extensive functions of local government—the apprehension of vagabonds, the upkeep of bridges and highways, the care of the poor, wage and price regulation. This the justices accomplished through numerous parish officials—notably constables, bridgewardens, surveyors of highways, and overseers of the poor—who were made responsible to them.[98]

Just as in England the crown habitually depended on the manor and the parish to carry out its orders on a nation-wide basis,[99] so in Massachusetts the colony government turned to the towns as analogous units of local administration to carry out their orders on a colony-wide basis. Indeed, there is a remarkable similarity not only between the records of the Massachusetts County Courts and those of the quarter sessions of the English justices of the peace [100] but between the type of orders which the General Court directed to the towns and those which the Privy Council directed to the English local units of the period.[101]

The Massachusetts town, like the English parish and the English borough, was primarily a unit of obligation by means of which the services required by the community as a whole could be exacted, generally without compensation.[102] This conclusion is illustrated not only by the examples above adduced, but also by the fact that, as in England, the local community was the primary unit of taxation and defense. With respect to taxation, however, the colony system drew less on English practice in levying the national subsidies than on those of the county and the parish in levying rates and of the trading companies in exacting assessments from its members. Osgood has observed that the "levy of direct taxes . . . was a remarkable extension of the right of trading corporations in England to levy assessments on their stockholders." [103] Strict observance of this right would have limited levies to those who were freemen, but in Massachusetts, contrary also to English governmental practice, all inhabitants were made liable.[104] Nevertheless, as in England, each locality was the primary unit of tax liability.[105] The system of defense was likewise based largely on the English principle of universal military obligation, and men procured for service were organized into local trained bands imitative of those in London and the counties.[106]

In order adequately to delineate the pattern of Massachusetts society and the structure of its government, it is important to emphasize the degree to which nearly every aspect of town life was minutely regulated by public officials, far beyond what might be supposed to have been the needs of local government. In England, regulation of agricultural and manufacturing practices was characteristic of the policy of mediaeval manors, towns, and guilds and had survived into the seventeenth century.[107] Moreover, supervision of countless details of local life was a marked feature of local government in that age, which fined communities for defective bridges and highways and punished men for that elastic offense known as the common nuisance. So numerous were the activities dealt with by English local courts that it can fairly be said that "it is difficult to find any kind of personal conduct, whether intrinsically innocent or plainly criminal," which might not find its way into jury presentments.[108] In Massachusetts, however, such regulation and supervision was carried to the point where official intrusion completely permeated the fabric of local society. Wages and prices were fixed,[109] exports limited or prohibited,[110] impressment for farm labor authorized.[111] In order to encourage good habits and the profitable use of "precious tyme," lying and idleness were punished [112] and sumptuary legislation enacted to regulate food, drink, clothing, and amusements.[113] Not only did the colony government prescribe the conditions under which wine and liquor might be sold or consumed [114] and tobacco smoked [115] but it fixed the price of meals "to prevent extravagance in diet" [116] and banned the consumption of venison and cakes except under specified circumstances.[117] The wearing of silks, laces, and furs was the subject of several enactments,[118] and games of dice, cards, and shuffleboard were proscribed.[119] Manufacturing and commercial undertakings of every kind were extensively regulated,[120] as the law undertook to fix wharfage charges, interest rates, and the toll that millers could charge for grinding corn.[121] Strangers were discouraged or denied permission to settle.[122] Education was made compulsory, and the selectmen of the towns ordered to catechize the children of the colony to make sure that they had learned to read.[123]

Many of these practices, as already indicated, had their counterparts in the local English law and in the paternalistic regulatory statutes of the Tudors and the first Stuarts. Price regulation was an ingrained feature of governmental policy at the end of the sixteenth century.[124] Alehouses and innkeepers, tippling, the smoking of tobacco, and excesses in dress were subjected to regulation by statutes of James I,[125] and frequently for the same reasons as in Massachusetts.[126] Profane swearing,[127] nonattendance at church,[128] unlawful games [129] and Sunday sports [130] were punishable by justices of the peace or in the Star Chamber. Precedents for the colonial hostility to strangers can be found in town ordinances and the jury presentments of the manorial courts.[131] However, Massachusetts went much further in undertaking to supervise personal conduct than did England.[132] The greater degree and comprehensiveness of this sort of regulation, both at the local and at the colony levels, may have resulted in part from the inspiration of Calvin and from practices at Geneva, where, in the sixteenth century, blasphemy, profane oaths, excessive drinking, and even the entertainment of strangers were proscribed.[133] But it resulted principally from conceptions derived from Puritan doctrine, which prescribed strictness of living and upright conduct as essential for salvation. If doctrine was to be translated into action, and if the community was to function as a unit to carry out God's purposes, society must be regimented to a far greater degree than that to which its members had been accustomed in England. To a substantial extent, the churches could be counted on to inspire and direct the conduct of its members, yet those agencies of social control were not always successful in guiding the actions of wayward, mortal men, and in any event needed the firm authority of the civil government to fall back on. More importantly, the greater part of the colonists were not church members, and they were no longer subject to the disciplinary action of the English ecclesiastical courts, which had jurisdiction over numerous types of moral offenses.[134] The disruptive tendencies which that element was capable of setting loose were a constant source of concern to the civil government. Hence, the legislature undertook to proscribe, and the courts to punish, activities which to the modern eye are matters pertaining entirely to private conduct.

The extensive regulation and supervision to which the Massachusetts communities were subjected provides convincing evidence of their belief that it was possible to shape their social and economic lives by controls which were in part self-imposed and in part thrust upon them by the colony government. Not only the colony leaders but the freemen generally had complete confidence in their ability to change and adjust the conditions of their community life by deliberately eliminating what they felt to be bad and establishing what they looked upon as good.[135] The activities of the towns in this respect represent another aspect of the Puritan determination to make over society in the image of the ideal which they had conceived. Underlying uniformities in social behavior tend to make such action more feasible in small, self-contained communities where there are common traditions and a strong sense of common purpose than in large and more amorphous political units. The success of similar efforts in ancient Athens, and more particularly in the Greek colonies of southern Italy,[136] illustrates the wisdom of the observation of a distinguished political scientist that because in Massachusetts the possibilities of common action were so patent, community action "took naturally and inevitably the form of political action."[137] When the end of law is viewed as the orderly arrangement of the whole community, so that every aspect of community life comes within its scope, and when the individual is viewed only as a member of that community, few departments of his life are left free from the control of law in the interest of the whole group.

The cohesiveness of group life within the towns owed much to the organization of the family, which was the basic social unit in the colony. The greater number of those who emigrated to Massachusetts Bay had come as members of a family group, which comprehended servants and apprentices as well as parents, children, and close relatives. The natural force of the family bonds was strengthened by the mediaeval conception of the holy family—the stern but just father, the suffering and compassionate mother, and the obedient child. That conception, however, was infused with Puritan ideals and made to strengthen the group life of the community, so that the relations between husband and wife, parent and child, master and servant were viewed as far more important than they had been in England. Indeed, those relationships were described as the very ligaments by which society was held together—"the root whence church and Commonwealth Cometh." [138]

From the outset, therefore, the colony leaders promoted family life and were paternalistically solicitous of its welfare. Early laws sought to bring everyone under the control of family government. Thus, in 1629, the officers of the company instructed Governor Endecott from London to divide the servants belonging to the company into artificial families, so that they might live together rather than separately. [139] In 1638 the General Court ordered every town to "dispose of all single persons & inmates within their towne to servise, or otherwise." [140] The economic needs of family groups were taken into account in making the first allotments of land, [141] and the courts were given power, in the administration of decedents' estates, to vary the shares allocable to distributees [142] in order to hold the family together and to safeguard the interests of minor children. [143]

Numerous orders and laws regulated the relationships among the members of the family group. Of principal importance were those relating to husband and wife. From the outset, it seems to have been assumed that sexual misconduct by or with married persons was likely to occur when the opportunity presented itself, [144] and efforts were therefore made to prevent such occurrences in a variety of ways. In October, 1631, adultery was made punishable by death, [145] and, although there were few convictions under that act, [146] those suspected of adultery, or of dissolute carriage with married women, were promptly punished. [147] Jury presentments were frequently made of married persons living apart from their spouses, [148] and court orders, [149] as well as a statute of 1647, [150] enjoined such persons to resume their conjugal relationships except upon the showing of just cause. Other aspects of the relationship between husband and wife were also a subject of attention. The wife was admonished to submit to her husband's instructions and commands, [151] and the courts did not hesitate to inquire into domestic discord and to enjoin its termination. [152] However, when corrective action appeared useless or impossible, a marriage could be terminated by divorce proceedings in the Court of Assistants.[153] Desertion,[154] and later cruelty and adultery by the female spouse, were typical grounds for granting a divorce.[155]

Children and their relationships with their parents were objects of special solicitude in Massachusetts. Pursuant to biblical precept, and also in recognition of the dangers which could result from the impairment of parental authority, the colony laws provided that a rebellious son should be put to death and that a child who cursed or struck a parent should be similarly punished.[156] Neither law appears ever to have been invoked, but there are several cases before 1650 of whippings inflicted upon sons who disobeyed or struck a parent.[157] The importance attached to the family is further illustrated by the fact that the courts often remitted children to the family unit for correction or punishment, as in the case of two boys who were found to have been accessories to a theft and were ordered whipped "by the Governor of the Familie wher they had offended." [158] Parental approval of the marriage of a daughter was considered of sufficient moment to warrant legislation imposing penalties on any who might seek "to draw away the affections of any maid . . . under pretence of marriage before he hath obtained libertie and allowance from her Parents or Governours (or in absence of such) of the neerest Magistrate." [159] Parents were under an express duty to support their children,[160] and also to instruct them in "some honest lawful calling, labour, or imployment." [161] They were also under a duty to see that in due course their children were suitably married.[162] Willful or unreasonable denial of a timely marriage, or unnatural severity toward children, gave the latter the right to legal redress in the courts.[163]

Since servants and apprentices were considered members of the family unit, they too were within its government. Broadly speaking, the term "servant" connoted anyone who did work for another. Thus, the class included voluntary servants—hired, apprenticed, or indentured—and involuntary servants—slaves, captives of war, and those condemned to servitude by the courts. The Massachusetts apprenticeship system, in imitation of that prevailing in England under the Statute of Artificers and the Poor Law of 1601,[164] imposed upon masters responsibility for the moral and bodily welfare of their servants. Generally, those responsibilities were set forth in indentures which were enforceable in the courts,[165] but the mutual obligations of masters and servants were also expressly set forth in the colony laws.[166] By a law of 1642, masters were also required to see to it that their apprentices learned to read, and the selectmen of the towns were charged with superintending compliance.[167] Masters had the right, indeed a duty, to admonish and correct their servants, and those whose crimes or delinquencies brought them before the courts were, as in the case of children, often remitted to their masters for punishment.[168] However, a servant who was cruelly treated or who suffered bodily injury at the hands of his master might seek redress in the courts.[169] Yet in Massachusetts, as in New England generally, "servitude" was much more than a means by which one class exacted work from another. "It was also a school, where vocational training was combined with discipline in good manners and guidance in religion. . . ."[170] To that end, wealthy and even aristocratic parents frequently placed their children as servants to the families of friends and even of strangers.[171]

The family was thus a small but important agency of social control in the colony. Its jurisdiction was both strengthened and supplemented not only by the civil government but by the churches, which continually emphasized the duties and responsibilities of the members of the family group to one another and to the community.[172] The colony leaders would certainly have understood the wisdom of Napoleon's instructions to his lawyers engaged in drafting the Civil Code: "Make the family responsible to its head, and the head to me, and I will keep order in France."[173] In Massachusetts Bay the stability of the social system was fostered in several ways through the family, which was deliberately employed as a quasi-official agency to effectuate specific governmental policies, such as literacy, the suppression of doctrinal divergences, and the maintenance of good order in the community. However, the courts were always at hand to assist the heads of families who were unable or unwilling to carry out their appointed functions, and the magistrates regularly employed fines, whippings, admonitions, or recognizances for good behavior in dealing with the unruly servant, the cruel husband or master, and the scolding wife.[174] The aid of the courts could also be invoked to help children and servants aggrieved by undue severity on the part of family government. The availability of judicial remedies in such situations was but another instance of the policy of the colony leaders to act as the final arbiters of the law and institutions in the commonwealth.

Government supervision of family life, and the utilization of the family unit as an agency of social control may appear, and have sometimes been represented to be, consequences of Puritan beliefs. Undoubtedly, those beliefs, together with the assumptions upon which the colony government was based, accounted in large measure for much in the form and function of family life in Massachusetts. However, in this respect, as in the case of other institutions and practices, the colonists drew upon and modified attitudes and usages with which they had been familiar in England. The apprenticeship system, as is attested by the colony laws and by the few indentures that have survived, was based fundamentally upon that obtaining in England,[175] and the procedure for dealing with disputes between master and servant was not greatly at variance with contemporary English practice.[176] Moreover, judicial supervision of family relationships was common in both the civil and the ecclesiastical courts of the time. For example, English justices of the peace employed the recognizance for good behavior as a means of punishing or preventing sexual misconduct on the part of man or wife. At a quarter sessions in Nottinghamshire in 1610, Richard Walker complained that Peter Rod "being a married man had unbecomingly kept company with the wife of the said Richard," despite Peter's having entered sureties "that he would not further keep company with the wife of the aforesaid Richard." [177] Cecilia Bower, in the same county, was charged with incontinence and entered a recognizance that she would henceforth be "of modest and honest behaviour" and would not keep company with Richard Hancock.[178] Deserting husbands were not only ordered to receive back their wives and to support and "live quietly" with them,[179] but required to put up sureties lest their families become a public charge.[180] On the ecclesiastical side, the Archdeacon's Court regularly punished married persons living apart, and sompnours spied upon and reported the *amours* of the parish in order to bring offenders to trial.[181] Numerous cases are recorded in which the Church courts ordered men to resume their conjugal duties [182] and sentenced them openly to acknowledge lewdness, cruelty, and refusal of cohabitation.[183]

The strong sense of solidarity bred in the towns by the various factors detailed in this chapter goes far to explain the willingness of the colonists to subject themselves to detailed regulation of personal behavior in the interest of the community. As in early Greece, law was viewed, to a substantial extent, as a restraint upon individual action in order to promote a wider goal, that is, the interest of the whole group to which the law applied.[184] The maintenance of good order in the community was thought to give individuals a wider freedom. It was an attitude that had much in common with the Delphic teaching, repeatedly expressed in Greek literature, that to obey the law is to be free.[185]

The control exercised by the magistrates and by the clergy over the local units of settlement was not only consistent with, but strongly supplemented by, the centralization of the colony government in accordance with the purposes for which the enterprise had been undertaken. Massachusetts Bay was no mere federation of towns. As in mediaeval England, men were drilled and regimented into communities in order that the state might be strong.[186] The task of the leaders was immensely facilitated both by widespread acceptance of the premises upon which society was organized and by the fact that close supervision of daily affairs by government authority was precisely what the colonists had been accustomed to in England. The introduction and adaptation of familiar institutions and practices was as wise as it was politic, for little violence was done to inherited sentiments upon which the strength, and often the survival, of a society must depend. Thus the varied threads of tradition and design were woven together to fashion the strong web of the new commonwealth.

Communities of Visible Saints

No ACCOUNT of local government in the Bay Colony would be complete without reference to the role of the churches in the affairs of the commonwealth. Not only did religious beliefs and doctrines permeate the daily lives of the colonists and stimulate their awareness of the mission to be fulfilled, but religion was the primary basis of public and private morality. Moreover, the solidarity of town life which resulted from common political and economic interests was continually supplemented and strengthened both by the church organization and, more especially, by the work of the ministers and other officers of the churches.

Each town was prompt to organize its own church as soon as possible after settlement. The earliest churches consisted sometimes of only a handful, sometimes of larger groups which had migrated and then settled together. Initially, the "gathering" of a church was a spontaneous affair within each town,[1] and those who joined would sign a covenant "to walke in all our wayes according to the Rule of the Gospell, & in all sincere Conformity to his holy Ordinances, & in mutuall love, & respect each to other, so neere as God shall give us grace."[2] It was the covenant that transformed a body of believers into a church. The election of the minister and church officers followed, and, in due course, the meetinghouse, as it was invariably called, was constructed.[3] This was built near the center of town, a plain and rectangular structure, lacking the spire that is today a part of the New England sky; it served a dual function, as the place for Sunday worship and lectures and for town meetings.

Before long, the gathering of churches was subjected to the authority of the colony leaders. An order in 1636 provided that no new church might be established without notifying the magistrates and elders and receiving their approbation.[4] The purpose of the order was to promote orthodoxy and uniformity within the churches, and thus to ensure that they entirely subserved the essential mission of the colony. Thereafter, the magistrates supervised the gathering of churches,[5] but the election of the ministers and church officers was left to the individual congregations.[6]

Each church was in the primary charge of a pastor and a teacher. These were known as the "teaching elders"—the one to exhort to right living, the other to explain and inculcate doctrine. Frequently, in smaller towns, these functions were combined in one person. In addition, there were the "ruling elders," solid and influential men of unimpeachable orthodoxy, chosen from the laymen of the congregation, who were thoroughly familiar with religious doctrine and entirely capable of expounding it.[7] Their duties involved the examination and admission of new candidates for church membership, the summoning of the congregation, the admonition of those who gave signs of falling from grace, the excommunication of the unfit, and the supervision of all details of church business.[8]

Admission to church membership was an affair of great earnestness and followed a solemn pattern of procedure in order to ensure the fitness of all in the congregation.[9] Both men and women were eligible, but "sainthood" was a prerequisite, and this the candidate had to establish before the elders by a review of his whole life, a description of his conversion, and his subsequent experience in the ways of grace. If the elders were satisfied by the examination, the candidate would be called before the congregation, there publicly to make a confession of sins and a profession of faith.[10] Then, if accepted by the congregation, he would agree to the various heads of the church covenant and would promise to forsake his former corruptions and to give himself up to the Lord Jesus as his only prophet, king, and lawgiver.

The standards for admission to a church took no account of wealth or social status, for their purpose was to bring about that fellowship of "visible saints" which had been a primary object of the migration. All who could lead the kind of life enjoined by the strict precepts of the Puritan ethic contributed to the fulfilling of God's commission to Massachusetts. Servants, even Negroes, who could satisfy the congregation of their godly conversation among men were as welcome as the most prominent persons in the colony.[11]

The church covenants to which the members subscribed vividly illustrate that religion was not only a guide to conduct and a source of solemn personal joy but a basis for mutual privilege and obligation within the group. Thus, the covenant of the Dorchester church recites:

And lastly wee do hereby Covenant & promise to further to our utmost power, the best spirituall good of each other . . . by mutuall Instruction, reprehension, exhortacion, consolacion, and spirituall watchfulnes over one another for good. . . .[12]

To social and institutional forms within the towns these covenants lent a special solidarity, the more so since members of congregations were enjoined not to remove or depart without consent from the church that they had joined.[13] The principle that the churches were independent of one another likewise encouraged cohesiveness within the towns, for every member was expected to attend only his own church and might not even partake of the sacraments elsewhere without letters of recommendation from his own church.[14]

In principle, each congregation was self-governing in the sense that its members had come together in voluntary association and elected the minister and the elders. However, the latter wielded, within the ambit of their jurisdiction, wide powers which were enhanced by their ability and by their social standing in their respective communities. All business was prepared and brought up by them, and the congregations were expected to, and generally did, entirely support their recommendations. Puritan belief in the necessity of submission to authority further strengthened their position, so that there developed an ecclesiastical oligarchy which was in many ways comparable to the oligarchy of magistrates. Despite the principle of the independence of the churches, the elders frequently conferred together on their own motion, or at the request of the magistrates,[15] in order to help promote that uniformity of doctrine which was essential to the preservation of the commonwealth. At an early date, meetings of the elders were arranged to discuss the common problems of the churches, and in time these meetings became regularized as church synods. "It belongeth unto synods," declared the Cambridge Platform, ". . . to debate and determine controversies of faith . . . to bear witness against mal-administration and corruption in doctrine or manners in any particular church; and to give directions for the reformation thereof."[16] However, although every effort was made to eliminate doctrinal divergences, the concept of church independence was preserved by insisting that the synods had no power to exercise church censures by way of discipline,[17] and the Code of 1648 expressly provided that the churches were not to impose authority upon one another.[18]

To the magistrates the churches were a vital part of the scheme of government, and indispensable instruments for molding the pattern of daily life in the colony. Not only did they go to great lengths to promote doctrinal uniformity,[19] but they continually promoted the welfare of the churches by supervising their establishment and by orders such as those assessing all town inhabitants for the salary and lodgings of the minister.[20] In addition, it was ordered that no house in any town should be built more than half a mile from the meetinghouse,[21] and church attendance was made compulsory for all inhabitants, whether church members or not.[22]

The role of the churches in the life of the colonists is particularly revealed in contemporary sermons, which emphasized the ways of godliness by encouraging meditation, cautioning against idleness, condemning fraud and injustice, warning against bad company and drunkenness, enjoining frugality, and urging mutual love and peace among Christians.[23] Individual sermons were frequently directed toward some current problem or issue in the colony or in particular towns. For example, Thomas Shepard pleaded for stricter observance of town bylaws,[24] Hugh Peter urged the support of economic programs,[25] and John Cotton preached on the ethics of trade and business practice.[26] Each year, special election sermons exhorted reverence for the symbols of government by commending the fit character of civil leaders.[27]

On the elders devolved the responsibility of supervising the conduct of church members, and hence, with respect to the offenses within their jurisdiction, they were a particularly effective agency of law enforcement. Misdemeanors which were viewed either as offenses against morals or against ecclesiastical discipline were principal subjects of accusation, confession, and punishment. Chief among them were drinking, lying, swearing, theft, adultery and fornication, on the one hand, and the expression or advocacy of heretical doctrines on the other.

Most of these offenses were independently punishable by the civil authorities as well, so that wrongdoers who were church members could normally expect to be twice visited with penalties for the same offense.[28] Thus, it will be recalled that after Anne Hutchinson had been sentenced and banished by the General Court she was then tried by the Boston Church and excommunicated.[29] Another example is afforded by the case of William Webb's wife, who was several times rebuked in court and by officials of the market, and finally excommunicated, because she customarily "nimed off bitts from each loaf" of bread to diminish their weight.[30] Despite occasional differences between the civil and the church authorities,[31] the two jurisdictions cooperated closely with each other and well supplemented each other's work. Some offenses the magistrates believed could be better punished in the first instance by the churches. Thus, the County Courts sometimes sentenced a miscreant to confess his sin before his congregation.[32] Again, Winthrop describes sending for the elders to discuss their dealing with excesses in dress and costliness of apparel.[33] Only when it appeared that the churches had failed to take adequate corrective action "at hoame" did the General Court enact a law proscribing a variety of ornaments and styles in dress.[34] Other offenses, although essentially of an ecclesiastical nature, the churches called upon the civil arm to aid in punishing: idolatry, blasphemy, heresy, and the venting of corrupt and pernicious opinions the Cambridge Platform expressly declared were to be restrained and punished by the magistrates.[35]

Thus, the church communities were not only active agencies of law enforcement within the colony but also sources of positive law in the sense that law consists of the rules and standards whereby men are expected to order their conduct. This fact is one of the most notable features of the colonial legal system. However, to men accustomed to the jurisdiction of the English ecclesiastical courts it was hardly an innovation to confer upon the Massachusetts churches extensive powers over a wide variety of crimes and offenses. In contemporary England, notwithstanding the secularization of ecclesiastical affairs that the Reformation had brought about, those courts still exercised disciplinary authority over the religious life and moral conduct of most of the population.[36] The Archdeacon's Court regularly punished not only contempt of the clergy and Sabbath breaking,[37] but drunkenness,[38] incontinence,[39] adultery,[40] disorderly carriage,[41] idleness,[42] lying,[43] swearing and blasphemy.[44] The churchwardens of every parish were bound by oath to inquire at all times into the delinquencies of parishioners and to report them to the archdeacon, with the result that whatever offense "escaped through the sluices controlled by constable and justice was captured in the finer mesh of the archdeacon's net."[45] Despite the colonists' antipathy to much that concerned the Established Church, they substantially reproduced this dualism of authority that they had known in England.

The jurisdiction of the Massachusetts churches, however, was much broader than that of the ecclesiastical courts. Their procedure also was vastly different in that in New England the whole congregation acted both as judges and jurors of the accused. Their weapons were limited, and their powers did not for most purposes extend to nonmembers, who constituted the bulk of the population.[46] Yet they were not confined to regulating only offenses against religion and morals in the accepted modern sense, but supervised family life, personal conduct of all kinds, and even business relationships. In 1635, for example, a member of the First Church of Boston was cast out of the church for "scandalous oppression of his wives children in selling away their inheritance from them." [47] Another parishioner was excommunicated for cruel correction of servants,[48] and another "for extortion, deceipt, and lying, in and about Iron Worke which he made for one Mr. Jacob." [49] The wife of Martin Stebbins "was so vyolent in her passion, that she offered vyolence to her husband, which being divulged, was of such infamy, that she was cast out of o[ur] Church." [50] Robert Keayne, the prominent merchant involved in the case of the missing sow,[51] was censured by the Boston church for making excessive profits on the sale of goods and forced tearfully to "acknowledge and bewail his covetous and corrupt heart." [52] After this latter episode, in order to prevent such practices for the future, John Cotton undertook to draw up for the colonists a code of business ethics and fair trade practices.[53] It is important to note that the rules laid down by Cotton were based upon mediaeval conceptions of the "just price" still current in contemporary England.[54]

In carrying out their duty of supervising personal conduct, the elders were aided initially by the members of the congregation, who exercised mutual inspection, or "holy watching," over one another's lives, and reported delinquencies that came to their attention. By his covenant vows, each of the faithful bound himself to watch over his neighbor's soul as his own, in order to promote the spiritual and moral welfare of his fellow members,[55] as well as to keep untainted the household of God by preventing "scandalous persons" from defiling holy things.[56] John Cotton had preached to the Winthrop group as they left England, "goe forth, every man that goeth, with a publicke spirit, looking not on your owne things onely, but also on the things of others." [57] Holy watching therefore emphasized the welfare of the group and thus fostered solidarity within the community of the church. At the same time, the performance of this duty was of great assistance to the colony government in that much crime came to light through the vigilance of church members who distilled the *fama publica* of the vicinage. The civil courts accordingly welcomed testimony from this source for the prosecution of crimes that came within their jurisdiction.[58]

English experience likewise prompted, at least in part, the practice of holy watching, although it had also been among Calvin's recommendations for promoting Christian living in Geneva. The records of the city of Norwich reveal that adult males were under a duty to disclose and bring to punishment every breach of the laws and customs of the community, and contemporary legal manuals amply attest that this obligation was not confined to East Anglia but was enforced in many parts of England.[59] The practice appears to have been a survival from the days when local communities were made responsible, and subject to punishment, for the misdeeds of their members.[60]

The procedure which the Massachusetts churches employed in dealing with the numerous types of offenses of which they took

cognizance demonstrates that a primary concern was with repentance and the reform of the individual involved, for salvation
was the end of mortal life.[61] The severity of the punishment—rebuke,
admonition, or excommunication—depended on the seriousness of
the offense and the attitude of the offender; but no sin was unpar-
donable, and one whose contrition was complete could again be
restored to the privileges of church membership. Thus, Temperance
Sweet, admonished for having given entertainment to disorderly
company and "ministering unto them wine and strong waters even
unto drunkenness," was released from the admonition upon open
acknowledgment of her sin.[62] Every effort was made, and the
greatest patience exercised, to discover the personal reasons for the
commission of the offense and to bring the culprit to see the error
of his or her ways before sentence was passed. Each case was therefore treated individually, and the participation of the whole congregation in the trial helped to prevent the process from becoming
self-righteous or arbitrary.[63] "In dealing with an offender," states
the Cambridge Platform, "great care is to be taken that we be
neither over strict or rigorous, nor too indulgent or remiss: our
proceeding herein ought to be with a spirit of meekness, consider-
ing ourselves, lest we also be tempted. . . ."[64] This leniency on the
part of the churches is illustrated by the case of Anne Hibbon, who,
openly and upon insufficient grounds, charged certain carpenters
with extortion and combining to fix prices. The matter was laid
before the elders who, after due investigation, admonished her for
her uncharitable jealousies and causeless suspicions. Neither the
admonition nor subsequent patient effort to bring her to reason had
any effect; she resisted all overtures, defied the church, and persisted in her groundless accusations, with the result that finally, after
the proceedings had dragged on for six months, she was cast out of
the church.[65]

Even the sentence of excommunication was neither final nor
irrevocable, and true repentance would normally result in the offender's regaining membership.[66] The church records disclose several cases of persons excommunicated more than once and as many
times restored.[67] This process of reform was aided by the colony
laws which prescribed that any person who had been excommunicated must endeavor to restore himself within six months or

be presented to the Court of Assistants "& there proceeded with by fine, imprisonment, banishment, or further." [68] Yet, in Massachusetts, as explained earlier, excommunication did not entail the serious civic disabilities which accompanied it in contemporary England.[69] Not even the right to hold office was lost by excommunication from one of the Massachusetts churches.[70]

Underlying the idea of church punishment was the importance not only of right living but of upholding the Puritan conception of a church. The sin of one was the sin of all, and the infection of that sin so tainted the whole that it ceased to be a church if it continued to harbor within itself any member who was unworthy.[71] The Cambridge Platform declared:

The censures of the church are appointed by Christ for the preventing, removing, and healing of offences in the church; for the reclaiming and gaining of offending brethren, for the deterring of others from the like offences; for purging out the leaven which may infect the whole lump; for vindicating the honor of Christ, and of his church, and the holy profession of the gospel; and for preventing of the wrath of God, that may justly fall upon the church, if they should suffer his covenant, and the seals thereof, to be profaned by notorious and obstinate offenders.[72]

The Puritan conception of the church as a group of professed believers, held together by their covenant to walk in the ways of godliness, was one of the deepest and most persistent influences on the life and institutions of the colony. It was to seek such a fellowship that the enterprise had been undertaken, and from that purpose had sprung the conception of civil government which limited political power to the proven elect and concentrated authority in a small group of leaders to whom full obedience was owed. By the 1640's, the greater proportion of the colonists were probably outside the churches; but, as Thomas Weld wrote, "If the Saints be thin sowen, who can helpe it?" [73] It was the "fault of the people, not of the rule, nor of the way," [74] By the end of the 1640's, the Massachusetts churches had achieved, on the ecclesiastical side, a counterpart of the "due form" of civil government. They had, as Professor Miller so aptly says, "solved one half of the old Puritan dilemma, by showing how a discipline gathered out of the Word could subserve the political ideals of civil supremacy and national unity." [75]

VII

The Sorts and Conditions of Men

THE institutions of government established in the Massachusetts Bay Colony effectively illustrate the extent to which the generation of those that settled the colony between 1630 and 1650 were heirs to the political traditions of the England from which they had removed. Born, and for the most part matured, in the age of Elizabeth or of the first James, all had been reared in a climate that nurtured a strong and centralized monarchy, and all were accustomed to the supervised autonomy prevailing in the towns, parishes, and manors in which they had lived. Most were acclimated to the localism of rural life, with its immemorial customs and ancient farming practices upon which Tudor and Stuart legislation only slightly impinged. At the same time they were also heirs to English social and intellectual traditions, and these included not only attitudes which had come down to them from the Middle Ages but new outlooks generated by the Protestant Reformation and by the economic and other adjustments which had taken place in the reign of Elizabeth. In nearly every respect the colonists' attitudes, manners, prejudices, and superstitions reflected their English heritage and differed little from those of their contemporaries in the social classes or localities from which they had sprung.

So ingrained were English traditions in the colonists' thinking that countless features of English social life were duplicated in early Massachusetts. The East Anglian type of house, with its second-story overhang and its leaded casement windows, rose along the village streets;[1] English cattle, sheep, and pigs grazed on the commons and meadows;[2] English grains—wheat, barley, oats, and rye—grew in fields cultivated by English implements; and gardens were planted with familiar English vegetables—peas, beans, carrots, cabbages, parsnips, and turnips.[3] English fruit trees—the apple, the cherry and the plum—thrived in their orchards.[4] Tastes in food, principally a stout diet of meat, fish, bread, and pottage, remained the same, and beer was the staple drink.[5] Like Englishmen of their day, the colonists wore bright-colored clothes, and their furnishings and household utensils were imported from England or copied from English models.[6] Even the social distinctions and class consciousness obtaining in contemporary England tended to persevere in the colony. The fact that there were continuing and regular contacts with old England, through letters and the arrival of new immigrants, helped during the first ten years not only to keep alive but to strengthen ancient memories, traditions, and associations. Only in their religious and intellectual interests, which reflected Puritan beliefs and ideals, were the colonists notably different from the majority of contemporary Englishmen.

No one who gives thoughtful attention to contemporary sources can fail to appreciate that the colonists were not a drab, forbidding, or gloomy people, but were human beings, alive and moving always in a colorful scene reminiscent of English village life. Children had their dolls, toys, and games; and if the diversions and laughter of their elders were tempered by a sense of the urgency of their mission and of the importance of not wasting "precious tyme," many allowed themselves the luxury of rich clothes, elaborate furnishings, and fine silver, and enjoyed—in moderation—the pleasures of good food and wine. Court records, as well as contemporary accounts, amply attest to the zest of the humbler classes for contention, gossip, and the fellowship of the tavern; and the low cost of colonial justice afforded them ample freedom to indulge their litigious instincts. Upper-class Puritans tended to be serious and sober-minded. Death or disaster might strike at any time by the will of God, and personal losses were endured with resignation and without self-pity. Yet even the Puritans were of this world and could yearn for and rejoice in the pleasures of secular love and in the loving, if grave, companionship of marriage. Moreover, the soft beauty of the native countryside was not lost upon such people as John Winthrop, who took time to record that the offshore breeze near Mount Desert carried "a sweet air" and "a smell . . . like the smell of a garden"; and Anne Bradstreet, daughter of Thomas Dudley, who described in lyric verse the "mixed hue" of native autumn leaves and "stones and trees insensible of time." [7]

The strength of tradition in all phases of early Massachusetts life was such that no appreciative understanding of the colony's political structure, or of its laws and institutions, is possible without some reference to contemporary English society. It is true, of course, that many practices and patterns of English life suffered a "sea-change" in the course of transplantation because of new conditions prevailing in the colony. For example, the wattle and daub of the East Anglian house were found insufficient to withstand the rigors of a New England winter without the protection of wooden clapboards; likewise, the thatch of their roofs was supplanted by shingles because of the greater danger of fire. Obviously, religious beliefs also affected the extent to which English ways were carried over to the colony. Tastes in art and literature conformed to and were molded by Puritan principles, and sermons became the absorbing intellectual interest. In addition, insofar as most of the colonists had an interest in improving their situations as compared with England, there was a conscious desire to reform or alter what they had known at home. Nevertheless, and notwithstanding these necessary qualifications, the first generation, at least, remained basically English in their outlooks, habits, and understandings.

The social structure of England in the early years of Charles I differed little from what it had been in Elizabeth's reign. Vigorous and enduring, the outlooks and usages of the Elizabethan age had carried over into the two reigns that followed. Even during the first forty years of the seventeenth century, as Trevelyan says, "No industrial, agricultural or social change of importance took place. . . ." [8] Men continued to live by farming, sheep raising, cloth-making, shipbuilding, commerce, and fishing, as well as by the innumerable crafts and trades that were to be found in every city, borough, town, and village. Except for a very gradual increase in the level of prices, and for occasional economic dislocations in particular areas, conditions remained relatively settled and gave little hint of the seeds of revolution germinating beneath the soil. Class divisions continued to be recognized and accepted, and were in fact accentuated by the increasing importance of money, which had become one of the most important of social determinants. Broadly speaking, society was divided into four classes: first, the nobility and the gentry, made up of landed proprietors who did not live by manual labor,[9] and from whom were recruited most government officials; second, the merchants, engaged in commerce and manufacturing;[10] third, the yeoman class, "Land hungry and land loving," [11] described by a contemporary as "farmers to gentlemen . . . or at the leastwise artificiers, and with grazing, frequenting of markets, and keeping of servants . . . do come to great wealth, . . . and often setting their sons to the schools, to the universities and to the Inns of the Court;" [12] fourth, the artisans and wage earners of town and country, freed from the taint of mediaeval villeinage, mostly poor but generally independent and self-reliant.[13]

These class divisions were neither hereditary nor fixed, and there was, to use Pareto's phrase, a marked "circulation of the elite." [14] Despite a tendency toward stratification which resulted from the still current idea that people were born into particular stations in life, wealth, and to some extent education, had become important determinants of social status, and those of one class were constantly moving into another. People of different classes intermingled freely, and there was little of the snobbery that was later to characterize the gentry of Jane Austen's day. Much of this fluidity is attributable to the importance attached to wealth, but it also resulted from the fact that town and country were not so clearly separate as they are today. When Milton writes of the populous city "Where Houses thick and Sewers annoy the Aire," [15] it should be remembered that even the largest cities were clustered about with gardens and orchards. The country was always close by, and the country was the home of most Englishmen. Then, too, contacts between the towns and rural areas were continuous. Well-to-do merchants often lived upon country estates without losing their city affiliations, and younger sons of the gentry were regularly apprenticed to merchants or guild members in the towns.[16]

The pattern of English class distinctions survived the migration to New England and persisted, though with diminishing influence, throughout the seventeenth century. From the outset, their importance was continually emphasized by the magistrates and the clergy and justified on the basis of religious ideals. Differences in wealth or in social position were looked upon not only as ordained by God but as reasonable in themselves because they accorded with inherited attitudes. Equally important was the leaders' conviction that the existence of class distinctions made for good order within the community by differentiating the superior and governing class from those of inferior status.[17] The persistence of English class distinctions was also significant because they provided the matrix for certain psychological attitudes and ideas which unquestionably influenced both the structure of colonial society and the development of the law. Most of the original colonists appear to have been of the yeomen and artisan class, men who were bred to a belief in hard work, and in not wasting "precious tyme," to the end that God's bounty might be improved and wealth acquired. Many of these had come from areas which had felt the impact of the enclosure movements and were consequently anxious to have land of their own assured to them. Nearly all believed in the innate inequality of man, fostered by class distinctions, and upon that premise the structure of the colony government had been reared. Both the Body of Liberties and the preamble to the Code of 1648 expressly refer to the liberties, immunities, and privileges "due to everie man in his place, & proportion." [18]

Of the settlers who came with the Winthrop Fleet, it has been estimated that perhaps a tenth were of a social rank above yeomen, and among these the nobility was hardly represented.[19] Nearly one-fifth appear to have been apprentices and indentured servants who had bound themselves out for a term of years in return for their ocean passage; the remainder, as stated, were small farmers, tradesmen, skilled and unskilled laborers.[20] Generalizations about those who came later are likely to be misleading in the absence of detailed biographical information. For the most part, however, they, too, appear to have been mainly of middle- and lower-class rank—yeomen, tenantry, and domestic servants, with only a small percentage from the gentry.[21] Many of the colonists were nevertheless persons of wealth and substance. For example, Captain Keayne, whose involvement in the lawsuit over the missing sow brought to a head the issue of the negative vote, brought with him £2000 or £3000 "in good estate." [22] Elaborate documents of sale, leases, powers of attorney, and the like have survived to demonstrate how extensive were the property and commercial interests of many of the colonists as early as the late 1630's.[23]

Although English class distinctions were not forgotten,[24] they were soon modified as society began to regroup itself into new classes in response to local conditions. Within a short period after settlement, it is possible to identify among the settlers in Massachusetts five fairly distinct groups, each characterized by common traditions or by adherence to particular ways of life.[25] From the standpoint of the colony's law and legal development, these classes were chiefly significant because of the privileges, exemptions, and disabilities which attached to membership therein. Important though religious orthodoxy was in the colony, it was not of itself a determinant for membership in any social class: as in England, wealth, family connections, and education were chiefly what determined social status. Nevertheless, orthodoxy did prescribe that many of the outward and visible signs of social distinction might be enjoyed only by the elect, as is evidenced by President Dunster's compulsory resignation from Harvard because of his views on infant baptism.[26] The descent to Avernus was easy.

Of the five social classes identifiable in Massachusetts Bay, the most important was an "upper" class composed of men of wealth and education, united to a substantial extent by the ties of marriage, blood or friendship, and above all by a dedicated belief in the undertaking upon which the colony had embarked. Nearly all of these were recruited from the English gentry and merchant classes. Most of the magistrates belonged to this group, and, because of the importance of education as a social determinant in the colony, so did the clergy and elders. Few of the colony's laws were expressly enacted for the benefit of this upper class, and most of the privileges and exemptions which the law accorded its members were granted by virtue of their offices, or positions, rather than because of their social status.[27] A notable exception is the provision in the Body of Liberties that no "true gentleman, nor any man equall to a gentleman be punished with whipping, unles his crime be very shamefull, and his course of life vitious and profligate." [28]

The second, or "middle" class, was the backbone of the social and economic structure and was made up of artisans, tradesmen, shopkeepers, and also of independent farmers and proprietors. Hence, because it cut across many occupational lines, it was more inclusive than the English middle class of the period. This wider inclusiveness is explained by the fact that everyone, farmers as well as village artisans, lived in compact town communities which made for a social solidarity that was fostered by closeness of daily living and weekly worship.

A free "lower" class was a feature of early Massachusetts society, but in the first decade of the Bay Colony's existence it was not a large group. It consisted of common and unskilled laborers, poor and, for the most part, owning no house or land but living with their employers or in a neighboring cottage. The "have-not" character of this class made it identifiable as a separate group rather than adhesive to the middle class with which its members lived in close contact.[29] Their low standard of living tended to promote both criminality and civic irresponsibility, particularly among those who were not members of the churches, with the result that the impact of the laws against idleness, loitering, and drunkenness were especially felt by this group. At the same time, the law attempted to alleviate their condition by provisions for the maintenance and employment of the poor and their families "for the ease of the Countrie." [30]

The fourth, or "servant," class was composed of bonded and indentured servants who had sold their personal freedom for a period of time, either to pay the costs of ocean transportation or to pay off other debts to creditors in the colony;[31] it also included apprentices who had been bound out to learn a trade. Since the bondage of those in this group was not indeterminate, and since all could look forward to eventual freedom, generally to membership in the middle or lower class, the grouping is in a sense artificial, particularly since in their backgrounds and attitudes they differed greatly among themselves. Nevertheless, social mobility during the period of bondage was next to impossible; and this fact, together with other restrictions which the law or the terms of their indentures and agreements laid upon them, gave them an outlook and a position which make them separately identifiable as a group. Moreover, special class legislation imposed particular disabilities and penalties upon servants, who were not allowed to trade without their masters' consent and were forbidden taverns and similar diversions.[32] Whipping, rather than restitution, was the punishment imposed upon them for theft.[33] At the same time, the law accorded them certain rights already referred to, such as food, shelter, and clothing, and it also protected them against undue harshness of treatment at the hands of their masters.[34] Despite such provisions for their welfare, their status and the degree of control exercised over them tended to encourage irresponsibility and criminality, and they, too, were the objects of criminal statutes and of the laws against idleness.[35] The early records provide ample testimony not only of the negligence and heedlessness of servants,[36] but of their running away, stealing, and committing other crimes.[37] However, the class of servants began to shrink after 1640 as the terms of their initial bondage expired and the cessation of immigration prevented others from taking their place.[38]

Clearly demarcated from the servant class was the fifth and lowest class consisting of "slaves" for whom bondage was nearly always permanent. The class was numerically insignificant—a few Negroes, a few Indian captives of the Pequot War, and a few sentenced to slavery for crime.[39] In 1676 it was estimated that there were only two hundred in all of New England.[40] Most of them were household servants and farm hands, and, like bonded servants, they appear to have been prone to criminality.[41]

These classes, although separately identifiable, were not rigid. Early Massachusetts society was hardly the caste society that Brooks Adams has described:[42] on the contrary, as in contemporary England, there was a marked degree of elasticity within, and mobility between, all classes except the lowest.[43] The conditions of settlement offered numerous opportunities for initiative and action, and ability or capacity for leadership received prompt recognition. To such recognition class distinctions were no deterrent. Men who began in the free lower class, or in the servant class, could, with diligence and hard work, move up into the middle and even the upper class, and their choice of occupation was relatively free. Wealth, however, remained the primary factor in the determination of social status. The existence of undeveloped land provided an opportunity to accumulate surplus through the sale of agricultural and forest products, and the small trade which flourished on the rising tide of immigrants during the 1630's also provided men with means for improving their situations. Moreover, the apprenticeship system, together with the educational facilities of the grammar schools and of Harvard College, also provided avenues whereby the eager and the gifted might become men of substance or rise to positions of prominence in civil or religious affairs. Birth and blood, aided by the laws governing the descent and distribution of property, were likewise determinants of social status, and intermarriage with the leading families therefore furnished still another means of social ascent. Unquestionably, this elasticity and mobility were among the factors which tended somewhat to modify the oligarchical nature of the colony organization.

The existence of class distinctions helps to explain the inequalities which characterized early Massachusetts society and which have been discussed in describing its political features. Those distinctions, like so much else in seventeenth century life, owed their origin to mediaeval ideas which taught that every individual was born into a particular class through the providence of God, that each had his appointed function to perform in his proper place, and that each must accept his status and not attempt, by imitation or otherwise, to escape it.[44] These lingering ideas were not only generally accepted but, as already stated, were in fact fostered by the colony leaders with a view to reinforcing class sentiments. Winthrop began his discourse on Christian charity by stating that by divine providence "in all times some must be rich some poore, some highe and eminent in power and dignitie; others meane and in subieccion;" [45] and he emphasized that the existence of inequality was reasonable in itself and led, through a distribution of duties, to the general improvement of society.[46] The churches also insisted that none of their members "live inordinately, out of rank and place. . . ." [47] To such ideas may be traced not only the form of the colony government but specific class legislation, such as the laws with respect to servants and apprentices,[48] and those proscribing extravagance in clothing and dress, which were intended, at least in part, to prevent the lower classes from aping their social betters.[49]

Certain leveling factors tended to minimize, but by no means obliterate, class distinctions, which tend to be overlooked or to become less important in an environment where all have to work, regardless of social status. Endecott apparently took his turn at the saw pit, and Winthrop himself is said to have put his hand "to any ordinarye labour with his servants." [50] Common participation in the tasks of local government and of defense unquestionably had a leveling tendency, as did the town meeting, the system of land distribution, and education in common schools. The churches, too, tended somewhat to diminish the importance of social classes inasmuch as admission to a congregation depended not upon status or wealth but upon proving oneself to be of fit character. Moreover, all inhabitants, regardless of status, stood equal before the law,[51] and even nonfreemen were expressly accorded the right to attend public meetings and "to move any lawfull, seasonable, or material question." [52] None of these practices, however, was inconsistent with the existence of social classes, and no one believed in the so-called equality of man. Such equality as existed in the colony was an equality of the elect; it transcended, but did not displace, class distinctions.

Significant as were social distinctions in Massachusetts Bay, those resulting from the insistence on religious orthodoxy had a far more fundamental influence on the development of the laws and institutions of government in the course of the first twenty years. Political rights depended not upon wealth or inherited position but upon whether a man had been admitted as a freeman, and this in turn depended upon whether by reason of his personal conduct and beliefs he was acknowledged to be a "visible saint" through membership in one of the churches.[53] Hence, in describing the sorts and conditions of men, it is essential to distinguish between the freemen, who participated in the work of government, and the nonfreemen, who constituted a majority of the population but who had few political rights except in the towns in which they lived.[54]

Among the freemen three groups are distinguishable: the magistrates, the ministers and elders of the churches, and the remaining freemen who, by 1640, appear to have numbered about thirteen hundred.[55] The dominating influence of the first two of these groups in the life of the colony has been repeatedly emphasized. The third group made affirmative and even significant contributions in the routine work of government,[56] but one of their most important functions in the political affairs of the colony was as a group check upon the magistrates through annual elections and through the opposition of their deputies to the latters' legislative programs and policies. Many of the deputies were men of substance, merchants and large landowners. Most of them served for successive terms, and several by 1650 were veteran legislators with extensive experience on important committees of the General Court.[57] The influence of such men, individually and as a group, inevitably made itself felt in the development of the colony's laws and institutions. However, the majority of the freemen led obscure lives and played a subordinate role in the life of the colony. Yet their sentiments and attitudes are not to be discounted, for the strength of Massachusetts institutions ultimately depended upon those who accepted them and lived within their framework. In constructing the law and institutions of the commonwealth, the colony leaders did little violence to inherited traditions, and for that reason they had the general support of the freemen in their work. For instance, nearly all the freemen had had some experience with self-government in England, and their familiarity with legislation restrictive of economic and personal freedom made feasible similar legislation in the colony. On the other hand, they had learned to cherish the economic independence which had resulted from the break-up of the manorial system and the decay of feudalism, and were intent that neither should be reestablished. Those who had come from East Anglia brought with them memories of tenantry dispossessed to make room for sheep raising. Such sentiments were undoubtedly influential in the enactment of laws assuring certainty of title to land [58] and proscribing the incidents of feudalism,[59] if they did not in fact provide the initiative therefor.

It is nevertheless plain that direction of the colony's civil affairs came primarily from the magistrates. It was they who, as leaders in the enactment of orders in the General Court, and as judges in the courts where those orders were applied and developed, were the most important of the defined groups in colony life. In their own eyes they were a ruling class set apart by divine law as governors of the people.[60] Their experience and intellectual attainments, together with their practical capacities, undoubtedly account in large measure for the deference they were paid by the colonists who had been accustomed to revering the local gentry in old England. Moreover, most of the magistrates had been born or trained to the responsibilities of leadership and had had substantial administrative or business experience. Several had served in positions which gave them firsthand knowledge both of local customs and of the common law of the central courts of justice in England. Needless to say, that experience left a marked impression on the law of the colony.

Unquestionably, the leading figure among the magistrates, and the one who chiefly inspired the development of law and government, was John Winthrop.[61] His early life particularly qualified him for the tasks and problems which confronted him in New England. Born in 1588, the year of the Armada, he was the grandson of a self-made businessman who had acquired the lordship of the Manor of Groton, in Suffolk, forty-odd years before.[62] After less than two years at Trinity College, Cambridge, Winthrop returned to Groton and, in due course, was appointed a justice of the peace and became engaged in the administrative and criminal work of the petty and quarter sessions.[63] In his twenties, he was admitted to Gray's Inn;[64] in his late thirties he was appointed attorney in the Court of Wards and Liveries.[65] Although that office was not one which gave him the experience of what might be termed general practice, since his duties involved the law of guardians, wards, and estates, it afforded him an opportunity for legal draftsmanship and necessarily involved him in other aspects of English law.[66] That he had some such general knowledge of law is apparent not only from the fact of his admission to Gray's Inn and from parliamentary bills which he drafted but from specific references to English law in the course of his writings.[67] Well and widely read, Winthrop was able to express clearly and with force theological as well as political ideas, with the result that much in the scheme of colonial government, as well as recommendations for particular legislation, was the consequence of his individual effort. A devoted public servant, he was temperate among many who were extremists, "not sparing, but always as the burning torch spending his health and wealth for the good of others." [68]

The backgrounds of several of Winthrop's associates who served as assistants and officers of the colony should again be emphasized. Thomas Dudley and Simon Bradstreet had served in turn in the responsible position of steward of the estates of the Earl of Lincoln, and Dudley, though self-educated, is said to have "learned much skill in the law." [69] Richard Bellingham, who served on one of the committees that worked on the Code of 1648, had received a legal education, had been a member of parliament, and had held the important legal office of recorder of Boston in Lincolnshire. [70] John Winthrop, Jr., had been admitted a barrister of the Inner Temple, and William Pynchon had served as a justice of the peace in England. [71] John Humfry was a member of Lincoln's Inn and had reputedly been an attorney in the Court of Wards; in addition, he had had substantial business experience in London as treasurer of the old Dorchester Adventurers which had planted the early colony on Cape Ann. [72]

Of the ministers and elders, both as a group and as individuals, some account has already been given. [73] All had an important influence on the law of the colony insofar as the discipline of the churches regulated the conduct of their members; [74] but, in addition, five of them—John Cotton, John Norton, Hugh Peter, Thomas Shepard, and Nathaniel Ward, who were the most distinguished ministers in Massachusetts—served on one or more of the committees that drafted the provisions of the Code of 1648. [75] Of these five, the most influential were Cotton and Ward. Although Cotton had no legal training, he framed in 1636 a proposed code which Winthrop referred to as "Moses his judicials." [76] He also served on the committee that drafted the Body of Liberties in 1641, and the enactment of several provisions therein undoubtedly owed much to his suggestions. [77] Ward's contribution was more substantial. Before his entry into the ministry, he had studied law, [78] and by his own statement he had "read almost all the Common Law of *England*, and some Statutes." [79] It was he who was primarily responsible for the Body of Liberties, and he was an active member of the committees which produced the final draft of the 1648 Code. [80]

Important as the English heritage was in determining the patterns of life and thought in Massachusetts Bay, the conditions of settlement had an equally significant influence upon the life of the colony. Although religion was a dynamic force pervading the organization and conduct of church and civil affairs, and although men could sit in rapt attention listening to the sermons of Cotton and Shepard in a meetinghouse chilled by piercing winter winds, it could hardly provide the substance by which they lived. Like their contemporaries in old England, the men of early Massachusetts made their livings from the land and from the sea, through trade, business, and manufacturing. As stated earlier, those who settled in the first towns sought to re-create the community life with which they had been familiar in the towns and parishes from which they had come. Initially, the Massachusetts towns were primarily agricultural or fishing communities, with such trades and crafts as were necessary to such a life—those of the smith, the miller, the wheelwright, the carpenter. Later towns began in the same way, but in both the original and the later settlements the increase of population was accompanied by specialization. During the first years, with immigrants arriving at the rate of about a thousand a year, the first problem was subsistence and shelter. As the towns grew and multiplied, however, opportunities for industrial and commercial activity appeared. Thus, men who were trained in England as artisans or craftsmen began life in the Bay Colony as farmers but often resumed their trades at a later time; others, arriving after the period of first settlement, would at once take up their accustomed occupations.

In the 1630's the economy of the Bay Colony was essentially one of subsistence agriculture. Fishing also provided needed food and, in addition, furnished a basis for trade, as did trapping, especially of the beaver.[81] A few ships were built for fishing[82] and some coastwise commerce developed as occasional vessels came into Boston Harbor.[83] Although highways and causeways were constructed, ferries put into operation,[84] and weekly markets or fairs instituted at Boston, Salem, Watertown, and Dorchester,[85] trade was for the most part local and in needed commodities purchased by exchange or sale of surplus agricultural commodities and livestock.[86]

A significant stimulus to commerce and manufacturing was provided by the economic depression which befell the colony in 1639 as a result of the drift toward civil war in England. Immigration came virtually to a halt as the success of the parliamentary cause seemed more assured and men decided to stay at home and take up arms should the need arise. The onset of war in 1642, together with the colony's growing reputation for intolerance, not only discouraged new settlers but even caused many of the colonists to return to England or to settle elsewhere.[87] These developments had a profound effect on the economy of the colony.[88] Those above the subsistence level of farming who had made money by the sale of surplus cattle, lumber, or crops to newcomers, and those who had sold their labor, suddenly found they had no market.[89] The value of domestic commodities fell sharply: the price of a cow, for example, dropped from £20 to £5 within the space of months.[90] Money suddenly became short, and foreign commodities virtually unobtainable.[91] With the appearance and rapid growth of a debtor class, and an attendant increase in crime,[92] it became vital to encourage industry and the manufacture of exportable commodities.

The urgency of the situation was apprehended by the practical-minded leaders of the colony, who understood that if Massachusetts was to go on in the ways of godliness and stand as a permanent example to the world, prompt and efficacious steps had to be taken. To stimulate and regulate trade and commerce through governmental action was entirely consistent with contemporary English economic ideas and practices, which regulated prices, wages, trade, manufacturing, and the quality of goods on a national scale.[93] Indeed, from the very beginning the colony government had undertaken to fix wages and prices and to prescribe the conditions under which men might enter particular trades and callings.[94] Accordingly, to meet the emergency, special laws were enacted to provide tax exemptions and other benefits for those engaging in the fishing and mining industries [95] and to permit the payment of local debts in corn, fish, and similar staples.[96] The planting of hemp and flax was encouraged,[97] and clothmaking,[98] mining,[99] manufacturing,[100] and sheep raising [101] were stimulated. In 1640 earlier orders prohibiting the export of pipestaves, plank, and other wrought timber were repealed.[102] In 1641 a special mission headed by Hugh Peter and Thomas Weld was sent to England to obtain extensions of credit and "for ease in Customs and Excise." [103] Ships were needed for foreign trade, and these soon began to splash down the ways.[104] At the same time, and to ensure the success of that trade, a series of laws provided for the inspection and approval of various types of exportable commodities.[105]

Efforts to find foreign markets met with quick success.[106] Within less than a decade, the vessels of Boston and Salem were trading not only in the middle American colonies but in Holland, in the Canaries, and in Spain.[107] Men bred to the land, or to trades and crafts, forsook the plow and the shop for the rising star of ocean commerce. The rapid increase in commercial activities also provided a stimulus to local trades and crafts and, in addition, brought into existence a substantial merchant class.[108] These developments led to the enlargement of the body of law dealing with commerce and maritime law as suits arose over wages, demurrage, charter parties, and the like.[109] So important had commercial law become by 1650 that the General Court ordered that Malynes' *Lex Mercatoria* be studied and such laws extracted as were applicable to Massachusetts needs.[110]

Within ten years the colony's economy changed to one in which diversity of occupation, abundance, and even luxury had begun to appear. Edward Johnson, writing in the early 1650's, states that "this poor Wilderness hath not onely equalized England in food, but goes beyond it in some places." [111] Cotton and sugar came in from the Barbados; butts of wine from the Canaries; fruits, oil, and soap from Spain; to say nothing of manufactured articles, carpeting, silks, and pewter from England.[112] Although many of these commodities were reexported, the bulk of them was consumed or used in the colony.[113] The wealth and the tastes for luxury which this trade engendered were such as to become a source of concern to the colony government.[114] The entire basis of the Massachusetts economy had altered, and with that change were born new ideals which shook, and eventually undermined, the religious foundations of the colonial government. The immediate effect of the change was, paradoxically, to strengthen the political structure formed during the first twenty years, for the religious minority which controlled the government found it necessary to consolidate and entrench their position. For several decades the original character of that structure was to endure in semi-isolation, glacialized in the efforts of the government to assure permanence for the ideals of its early leaders. In time it crumbled as the religious aspects of life necessarily gave way before the relentless march of commerce.

The economic development of Massachusetts in the 1640's unquestionably improved the material conditions of daily life far beyond what any of the immigrants could have dreamed in 1630. During this time other influences were also shaping the form of colonial society and the character of its citizens. No survey of the sorts and conditions of men in early Massachusetts would be adequate without some reference to their intellectual life, which exercised a pervasive effect on all aspects of the colony's development. Puritanism provided a stimulus to intellectual activity which was not lessened by the demands that the new environment and the problems of government made upon them. The intellectual level among the colonists generally was high to begin with. Many were university graduates,[115] and they were determined that learning should be made to vitalize and strengthen the institutions they had established. Education was essential in order to know and do the will of God and to defeat "that ould deluder, Satan." [116] Every church must have its minister who could properly interpret the Scriptures, and the congregation must be sufficiently educated to be able to understand his exposition. Moreover, good citizenship prescribed that all should know the capital laws, and it was expressly enacted that children should be taught to read for that purpose.[117] Yet in their emphasis on education the colony leaders had an even broader purpose, for they hoped to preserve the European civilization and culture they had known and to counteract the necessarily materialistic and leveling influence of the frontier.

These purposes, which were at once religious, intellectual, and social, were promoted through the setting up of a printing press, through the establishment of a public school system and, most notably, through the founding of Harvard College.[118] The printing press was operating in Cambridge by 1639, the earliest in North America outside Mexico, and it began immediately to publish Puritan sermons and tracts and, in due course, the colony's laws, works of history, biography, and poetry.[119] The Massachusetts public school law was enacted in 1647, the earliest general education legislation of modern times.[120] Although several towns had established elementary schools as early as 1640,[121] this act made education a general public responsibility by requiring that every town of fifty or more householders should have a school, which was public in the sense that it was open to all who were qualified and that no one was excluded because of lack of funds from obtaining an education for which he was fitted.[122] The colonists' greatest achievement in education, however, was the founding of Harvard College—"first flower of their wilderness"—in 1636. Reflecting the course of studies of the University of Cambridge on which it was modeled, the Harvard undergraduate course demonstrates that its founders had a far broader objective than the training of ministers; namely, "to advance *Learning* and perpetuate it to Posterity." [123] In assuming at once the power to grant degrees, the college took what has been described as "a bold step, . . . the first declaration of independence, in that it declared and settled for the colonies the principle of freedom of education from control by Church and State in the mother country." [124]

These attitudes provide yet another indication of the way in which the colonists drew upon their cultural heritage in fashioning the new civilization of Massachusetts Bay. However, unlike the English social and institutional heritage in which all the colonists shared to a greater or less extent, the intellectual heritage—despite the pervasiveness of its influence in the colony—belonged primarily to those among them who were Puritans.[125] To them, in varying degrees and according to their education and capacities, the philosophical aspects of religious and church doctrine were overriding interests, which are amply revealed in contemporary sermons and in their libraries, chiefly filled with books on theology and ecclesiastical polity. Yet their libraries also contained books on natural science, literature, and history, which emphasizes that they shared with contemporary Englishmen, Puritan and non-Puritan alike, much of the legacy of the humanism of the Renaissance.[126] In this respect, however, they were eclectic and took "what seemed to them to consort with their philosophical and religious standards and to be best adapted for their special purposes." [127] Thus, they read the classics less for pleasure than for the lessons and examples which they afforded. Nathaniel Ward, for example, in his election sermon in 1641, propounded moral and political principles grounded upon those of Greek and Roman government,[128] and Winthrop frequently referred to the experience of antiquity in deciding important public questions.[129]

Except for its special concern with Puritan developments of

Reformation doctrines and the philosophical aspects of Christianity, the New England mind in the first half of the seventeenth century differed little from the English mind of the same period.[130] Credulous and superstitious, even the colony leaders attributed to the hand of providence the sickening of cattle, the detection of a criminal, and successes against their enemies. Those who are tempted to be scornful of attitudes which explained the drowning of a child by the fact that its father had done work on the Lord's day [131] should remember that, even to educated men in England, Marlowe's death in a tavern brawl was proof of God's judgment on the impious.[132]

It must again be emphasized, however, that the English heritage was continually molded by the convictions of the colony leaders that that heritage must be purified so that Massachusetts could stand before the world as an example of godliness and of Christ's way. Responding to those convictions and to the forces unleashed by the new environment, institutional forms and religious doctrines came quickly to maturity, hardened and crystallized. By 1649 John Winthrop could die in peace, knowing that his "due form of government" had become a reality. Autocratic and authoritarian, Massachusetts by mid-century had become the dominant social, economic, and intellectual influence in New England. The colonists had achieved, for the time being, all the goals for which the enterprise had been undertaken twenty years before.

VIII

The Path of the Law

FROM the description of the instruments of government and of the main currents of political and religious thought in early Massachusetts, there have emerged in outline some of the principal features of the colony's legal system. Because of the attention accorded institutional developments, the system has necessarily been viewed primarily in its public law aspect, that is, from the standpoint of arrangements for securing and adjusting interests involved in political and social life as contrasted with those involved immediately in individual life. At the same time, because of the premises upon which the colony was organized, there have also been adumbrated, although in outline less sharp, many features of private law, that is, the rules governing the relationships of individuals toward each other in the communities to which they belonged. Since the welfare of the commonwealth and the accomplishment of the colony's mission were thought to depend upon adherence to Christ's way, the discipline of the churches and the orders emanating from the various agencies of government had as a principal aim the shaping and regulation of the conduct of the citizens. The result was that few aspects of individual life were left free of governmental interference or control. In a sense, therefore, the modern dichotomy of public and private law is artificial, and perhaps even misleading, because in the colony the two were in many respects so intermingled as often to be incapable of differentiation. Nevertheless, the distinction is useful for purposes of emphasizing the extent to which interests that would today be termed private were then subordinated to those of the public generally.

Any attempt to describe the development of the legal system of a civilization whose assumptions about the ends and purposes of government, and about the relations of individuals to one another and to the state, were so different from those to which we are accustomed must be accompanied by a warning as to the danger of reading back into an earlier time the ideas and values of a later day. It is not easy to think the thoughts of men who have been dead three centuries, or to appreciate that many of the conceptions and much of the subject matter of modern law were entirely unknown, or were in their infancy, in the seventeenth century. In England at that time, for example, the law of agency, of sales, and of business corporations were at very early stages of development, whereas public-utility law was obviously hardly recognized.[1] On the other hand, although the English law of trusts was well advanced, economic conditions in the colony were such that there was little need to resort to the trust device in the early period. Too much, therefore, must not be expected of the colonial system which, compared with our own, was relatively simple and which, in addition, was developed upon premises that require thought and reflection to comprehend. Nevertheless, the colonists wrestled with, and found their own answers to, troublesome questions which for centuries have vexed the Western mind and conscience—questions as to the proper balance between law and liberty, between authority and the individual. At the same time, the Bay Colony had to deal with numerous types of interest conflicts that are common to all politically organized societies—conflicts that arise because men steal, quarrel, break their promises, injure, and kill. Much, therefore, of the substantive law of the colony can be described in terms of the familiar modern categories of crime, contract and tort.

One of the most striking general characteristics of the path of the law in early Massachusetts is the autonomous course that it followed during the first decades of the colony's history. Notwithstanding their substantial reliance upon traditional legal ideas, the colony leaders felt free, within limitations which were either self-imposed or which developed out of community sentiment, to adopt legal rules which to their minds would best effectuate the purposes for which the colony had been founded. From the outset, they not only refused to permit appeals to England from the colony courts but paid scant heed to the prohibition in the charter against establishing laws contrary to those of England.[2] Much of this independence of attitude was a consequence of the Separatist principles upon which the colony had been founded and also of the conviction of the magistrates and clergy that they were instruments for carrying out a divinely inspired mission.[3] However, the open assertion of independence from English ways was possible chiefly because of the absence of interference in the colony's affairs on the part of the English government. The *quo warranto* proceedings of 1634 had proved abortive,[4] and the increasing preoccupation of the crown thereafter with domestic affairs left the colony almost entirely free to pursue its own course. Hence, the growth of the law was not only continuous and unhampered by external influences, but its development could more readily respond to the molding force of legislation. In 1646 the attempts of Dr. Child and his fellow remonstrants to appeal to parliament from their sentences in the General Court were frustrated;[5] and when the Court's position was supported by the Commissioners for Foreign Plantations in England, the colonists could feel assured that the accomplishments of the preceding years were to remain undisturbed.[6]

A second striking characteristic of the early path of the law was its responsiveness to conditions within the colony. At an early date Winthrop emphasized the government's concern that laws should take account of the nature and disposition of the people, together with "the condition of the country and other circumstances," and that "such laws would be fittest for us, which should arise pro re nata upon occasions."[7] In large part, that concern resulted from the magistrates' determination to control the course of colony affairs and to decide themselves, as the occasion arose, on the solution required. At the same time, as practical and experienced men, they were astute both to recognize the pressures engendered by community sentiment and also to perceive the emergence of new problems in time to take corrective action. Conditions arising out of the initial scarcity of labor and commodities, for example, brought forth orders regulating prices and wages,[8] and other types of shortages produced orders prohibiting certain exports.[9] The scarcity of money resulted in orders making corn and beaver legal tender [10] and providing that bullets should pass as farthings for obligations under twelvepence.[11] The substitution of divisible inheritance of real property for the English rule of primogeniture was undoubtedly attributable in part to a recognition of the needs of younger children,[12] while the same concern is reflected in the varying sizes of allotments which the courts made to widows from their husbands' estates.[13] Legislation of the General Court was likewise responsive to local conditions and problems. Thus, the growth of the fur trade and of commerce with the Indians required special legislation,[14] and the rapid increase in population was responsible for the elaboration of the machinery of justice and for the more precise definition of the jurisdiction of the courts.[15] The importance of labor was undoubtedly a chief reason for ordering that laborers might be pressed into service [16] and for prescribing, when feasible, penalties other than imprisonment. Long confinements would have depleted the labor force, would have been costly to the government, and would also have rendered many families destitute.[17] As the "due form of government" grew toward completion, attention turned to such social needs as the promotion of literacy, education, and the care of the poor.[18]

Necessarily, specific events also had an impact upon the law. The challenge to orthodoxy presented by the Antinomian controversy resulted in stringent laws against strangers, heretics, and those unsympathetic to the colony aims.[19] When three men were convicted of sexual misconduct with John Humfry's infant daughters, the Court immediately formulated a definition of rape of a minor child.[20] The depression of the 1640's led, first, to enactments designed to stimulate manufacturing and commerce [21] and, in due course, to the development of maritime law.[22]

These few among many examples demonstrate not only that the law was not static, but that experimentation, expediency, and social and economic pressures continually influenced its growth. However much the colony leaders relied on the Bible as providing the fundamental constitution by which men's conduct was to be governed, they recognized that the precepts of Scripture could not, and indeed should not, provide a complete guide for the adjustment of the varied interests which continually pressed for recognition and accommodation. Winthrop, for instance, observed that the Bible furnished examples of divine prescriptions of where future genera- tions "should dwell, what quantityes of land they should till: what places they should tende vnto: what diet they should use, what Clothes they should weare etc;" and he went on to say, in a tone which left no doubt that he assumed the concurrence of his audi- ence in his conclusion, that "no man will take these as warrant for vs to laye suche iniunctions vpon those which come after us, be- cause they are to have the same interest, and freedome in their estates and persons that we have in ours." [23] Again, although on a different tack, Winthrop pointed to the absence of scripturally prescribed penalties for many crimes as evidence that the Lord, who had laid down precise penalties for many offenses, "could have doone the like in others, if he had so pleased," and therefore clearly intended that magistrates, as God's regents on earth, should exercise their "guifts," as the situation might require, in dealing with the offenses for which the Bible prescribed no penalty.[24]

Neither the autonomous development of the law, nor its respon- siveness to local conditions, affords justification for an assertion that the seventeenth century in Massachusetts was "a period of rude, un- technical popular law." [25] On the contrary, the court orders and legislation of the first twenty years demonstrate that the legal sys- tem, in the context within which it functioned, was both developed and sophisticated. It will be recalled that, as early as 1630, the assistants conferred upon certain of their members the powers of English justices of the peace, thereby deliberately incorporating into the colony's legal system a wide area of procedural and administra- tive precedents.[26] At the same session certain technical English forms of judicial process were prescribed in connection with the institution of legal actions: the summons and the writs of *capias* and *distringas* for attachment and distraint.[27] Subsequently, detailed rules were set forth with respect to notice, costs, fees, and appeals,[28] and specific provision was made for the impecunious in proceedings *in forma pauperis*.[29] Juries were empaneled from the outset,[30] and, in due course, their province defined.[31] In addition, standard English terms were used for civil actions: debt, replevin, trespass, and case.[32] The intricate common-law distinctions and technicalities which characterized those forms of action in England were not observed, and certainly not understood by most of the colonists, but it is pertinent to point out that on the criminal side well over a hundred separate kinds of offenses were demarcated and made punishable before 1650.[33] Further evidence of the developed character of the law is found in surviving collections of elaborate and technical documents, many of them in Latin, whereby powers of attorney were conferred, contracts entered into, assignments made, and land conveyed.[34]

The notion that the colonists' ideas of law were the primitive ones of ancient Israel or of a rude frontier is belied by their own statements, particularly in Winthrop's writings and in the Epistle prefaced to the Code of 1648.[35] These statements make it plain that the end of law was viewed not merely as the avoidance of the wrath of a vengeful Jehovah but as the advancement of righteousness and Christ's way "according to the rules of his most holy word." [36] If the simple injunctions of the Old Testament were relied upon in prescribing penalties for certain types of criminal offenses, the New Testament and critical exegesis thereof were sources of highly sophisticated ideas about the ethical content of the rules that regulated the relationship of men to one another and to the state.[37] This feature of early Massachusetts law is especially noteworthy, since it again illustrates the importance which the Puritans attached to upright conduct, and thus emphasizes the close connection that then existed between law and morals.[38]

Reflection about the philosophical aspects of law was not by any means wholly the consequence of Puritan reliance upon the Scriptures and the writings of the theologians. In contemporary thinking about law and politics, both in the sixteenth century works of St. Germain and Fortescue, and later even in Coke, the idea of an immutable, God-given "natural law," underlying the positive laws of man, found frequent expression as part of the intellectual heritage of the Middle Ages.[39] References to natural law obtrude in colonial sermons, in the Epistle to the 1648 Code, and in the writings of Winthrop, particularly in his treatise on arbitrary government.[40] The currency of these natural-law ideas, together with the colonists' application of the sophisticated Puritan theology to the problems of law, ensured that the development of the colony law would be an intellectual and philosophical rather than merely an expedient, or empiric, process.

Much of the colony law in the first decade was developed primarily through orders and decisions of the magistrates in the Court of Assistants. This was so not only with respect to the completion of the institutional arrangements, which was a principal concern of the government during the first six or seven years, but with respect to substantive and procedural rules for delimiting and adjusting public and private interests—crime, tort, inheritance, conveyancing, licensing, and domestic relations. In the exercise of their powers in the courts, the magistrates' discretion played a large part, particularly, as repeatedly emphasized, in the imposition of penalties. A substantial segment of the substantive and procedural law was thus the result of the judicial process. After the enlargement of the General Court in 1634, the deputies insisted upon taking an active part in the formulation of legal rules, and thereafter legislative enactments in which they participated became a progressively more important source of law. Although the difference between the judicial and legislative aspects of lawmaking was hardly perceived in any modern sense, the character of the deputies' activities, particularly from the standpoint of their insistence that the colony laws be reduced to writing, justifies describing them in legislative, rather than in judicial, terms. Accordingly, a further characteristic of the path of the law was the transition from a period in which law was primarily judge-made to one in which it was made increasingly through the legislative process. The publication of the 1648 Code ended this second, or legislative, phase of the colony's legal history. The period that followed became chiefly concerned with the enforcement and application of the Code in the courts, with the result that there was a return to the development of law primarily through the operation of the judicial process, but now upon a relatively stable corpus of statutory written law.

The movement for written laws was one of the most important developments of the second, or legislative, period. The significance of the movement is fourfold. In the first place, the progressive reduction of the colony laws to writing imposed a curb on the power of the magistrates by displacing to a substantial degree the process of judicial lawmaking. In the second place, the movement involved a conscientious revision of the colony laws into coherent and comprehensive form, with the result that much of the vacillation and experimentation which had characterized the early years was eliminated, and a hard core of fixed rules substituted as the heart of the legal system. Thirdly, culminating as it did in the Code of 1648, the movement produced the first modern code of the Western world, antedating by twenty years the project of Colbert in France and by even more those of Austria and Prussia in the eighteenth century.[41] Finally, the Code became the fountainhead of Massachusetts law during most of the seventeenth century, and even thereafter, and its provisions were widely copied by other colonies, or used by them as models in framing their own laws. Through such intercolonial borrowing, its influence spread into other parts of New England, beyond to New York and even to Delaware and Pennsylvania.[42]

If the origins of the movement for written laws are traceable in part to the inclusion of deputies in the General Court, and to their insistence on participating in the lawmaking process, its principal momentum came from the controversy between the magistrates and the freemen over the question of discretionary justice.[43] From the beginning, the magistrates resisted the freemen's progressively stronger pressures for the administration of justice through fixed rules rather than through the application of discretion which might vary from case to case. Winthrop expressed the fear that to publish a code of laws would draw the crown's attention to colonial divergences from English law and hence could result in the revocation of the charter.[44] More importantly, he and the other leaders believed, as already stated, that the law should develop *pro re nata*, in response to particular situations as they arose, and that it should be declared by magistrates who were "Gods vpon earthe." [45] Although Winthrop emphasized the importance of legal growth through custom, and although he justified the propriety of that process on the ground that it was the way in which English law had developed, his thinking went well beyond both the concept of folk law and the English analogy. From the context in which Winthrop used the word "custom," it seems clear that he was thinking in terms of the mediaeval usage, well known from Bracton, which contrasted unwritten custom with written law.[46] Certainly he did not intend custom in the sociological sense of standardized responses to given situations which establish "relatively fixed points around which the conduct and interests of different individuals can shape themselves." [47] Such a view would have precluded the magistrates' idea that law should be developed by the adjudication of successive cases on their individual facts by judges who were guided by divinely-given insight and were untrammeled by precedent. The magistrates, as a group, were even less proponents of democracy in lawmaking than in politics, and they would have been unalterably opposed to the idea that the "people" should be allowed to develop rules for resolving their interest conflicts either by recourse to popular folk law or to fixed rules which they had declared or framed.

As Winthrop and most of the other magistrates envisaged law, it was a primary means whereby God's mission was to be accomplished.[48] Hence, it was far more than a customary *lex non scripta:* it was an adaptable and liberating, rather than a merely preservative, agency. Custom, in the sociological sense referred to, works effectively in a static, and hence characteristically in a primitive, society. The complex, varied, and changing interests of a society evolving toward maturity do not lend themselves to resolution by stereotyped customary formulas. Such a society requires the flexibility inherent in formal law determined and dispensed by a governmental agency. Moreover, to an extent that suggests that the need for adaptability in a legal system bears a direct relation to the rate of social and economic change, the persons charged with administering the system typically seek, and generally obtain, greater discretion in times of rapid change. Clearly, the society of Massachusetts in its first twenty years was neither primitive nor static. Rather, as has been repeatedly emphasized, the colonists substantially reproduced a developed social and economic structure which, in response to new conditions and new aspirations, acquired a volatility that required all the talents of the colony rulers to control.

This phase of the development of Massachusetts law in the first decade is paralleled in certain respects by the course of English law in the Tudor era. Faced with the problem of adjusting the concepts of the feudal world to the exigencies of a rapidly evolving, increasingly individualistic society, the new dynasty had noticeably cracked, if it had not broken, the cake of centuries of custom crystallized in many doctrines of the common law. Led by Chancery and the Star Chamber, English law, in the name of substantial justice, had emphasized the flexibility and adaptive potential of judicial and executive discretion, more needed, perhaps, than at any time since the thirteenth century. This had been accomplished at the expense of the relative certainty and immutability of many traditional rights guaranteed by ancient law.[49] The colonial leaders' insistence on the formulation of law through magisterial authority, with minimal precedential limitations, was thus by no means a novel departure in terms of relatively recent English experience to which several of them were hardly strangers. Their attitude, and particularly Winthrop's, appears to have resulted in large part from an instinctive feeling for the efficient development of law and the administration of justice in a highly volatile society. That this attitude found support in biblical authority, and that it was reinforced by Puritan beliefs in obedience to God's duly constituted authority and by a remarkable practical success in its application, further served to convince the magistrates of the rightness of their views, and to promote popular acquiescence sufficient, at least in the colony's early years, to ensure its continued application.

The danger of permitting an authoritative organ to settle interest conflicts is, of course, the danger that it will be arbitrary. Hence, the insistence throughout Western history that, in the settlement of controversies, the adjudicative organ shall act according to rules. When those rules are publicly known, they create confidence that the organ will act impartially, that is, that it will arrive at the same kind of decision reached in a previous conflict of the same character. The late John Dickinson has pointed out that as a community develops, "the chief problem connected with its governmental organization is how to secure that flexibility of direction which authoritative control is capable of supplying, while at the same time retaining the advantage of government through known rules."[50] This was precisely the problem confronting the magistrates in the mid-1630's. They needed the power to depart from precedent and to make new rules consonant with the purposes of the colonial enterprise and the changing needs of the developing community; yet they were under the heavy pressure of community sentiment to codify, and hence to stereotype, those rules at a time when flexibility seemed to them most urgently required.

The idea of a known and fixed law limiting the power of civil rulers runs back in English history beyond Runnymede, and owes much to Germanic conceptions about the immutability of immemorial usages which had crystallized about particular ways of life in particular places and had no assignable beginning. In this conception, law was viewed as something permanent which, though it might require promulgation and definition, could be found and declared, but not made.[51] Ideas about "fundamental law" underlay the concessions which the barons wrested from King John in 1215 and which were embodied in Magna Carta. With the passing of time, that famous treaty had come to be regarded as a palladium of constitutional liberties, establishing rights for English subjects which the crown was powerless to change. Beliefs in the stability of law were also fostered by the procedural guarantees which the common-law courts had evolved with respect to notice and hearing and open public trials and which these men had come to cherish as a birthright.[52] Uniformity as well as stability in the law had also been promoted by ancient writs backed by the king's command, with the result that substance as well as currency had been given to the idea of a rule of law which, when challenged, became a political creed. Early in the seventeenth century, the challenge had come from Stuart kings whose prerogative courts and commissions claimed not to be bound by the accepted procedures of the common law. Particularly vivid in men's minds were the battles that Coke, and later the parliamentarians, had fought to maintain the "knowne certaintie" of the law against the summary and discretionary justice of Chancery and the Star Chamber.[53] Fixed customary rules were also a feature of the law of the local communities from which the colonists had come; many had been reduced to writing, and the sense of security fostered by these customs, and by the liberties granted and assured by the charters of the crown, was deeply ingrained.[54] Typically, moreover, Puritans attached great importance to the written word as evidenced both by literal use of the Bible as authority and by early demands for explicit church canons which would leave no doubt as to what the law was.[55]

These sentiments first found expression in the colony in 1634, when the freemen asked to inspect the charter, which they looked upon as the basic written guarantee of their liberties, and again in the next year, when they began to agitate for written laws. In 1635 Winthrop wrote that the deputies were fearful of the dangers that could result from the "want of positive laws" and that consequently it was agreed to have prepared "a body of grounds of laws, in resemblance to a Magna Charta, which, being allowed by some of the ministers, and the general court, should be received for fundamental laws." [56] It seems clear from ensuing discussions that the freemen did not believe that the magistrates could be counted upon to decide fairly and to impose equitable penalties, in accordance with inherited ideas of justice and fair play, unless the rules which were to guide their decisions were public property. The movement for written laws therefore resulted both from the importance the colonists attached to stable and written laws and from their distrust of discretionary justice.[57] Their demands are in many ways reminiscent of those which resulted in the codification of the laws of the early Greek city-states and in the guarantees of the Twelve Tables at Rome. Once those laws were codified and made public, "a festering grievance was removed." [58] Indeed, as Sir Henry Maine has observed, among the chief advantages of all early codes "was the protection which they afforded against the frauds of the privileged oligarchy." [59]

Despite the resistance of the magistrates, the General Court, beginning in 1635, appointed a succession of committees to prepare a draft of "fundamentals." The first committee consisted only of magistrates—Governor John Haynes, Deputy-Governor Bellingham, Winthrop, and Dudley—and it apparently accomplished nothing.[60] A second committee was constituted in May, 1636, and to it were named the four former members, together with the new governor, Sir Henry Vane, and three members of the clergy—John Cotton, Hugh Peter, and Thomas Shepard. The committee was requested to "make a draught of lawes agreeable to the word of God, which may be the Fundamentalls of this commonwealth, & to present the same to the nexte Generall Court." [61] The first concrete step in the direction of preparing a written code appears to have been taken by one member of that committee, John Cotton, who, in October of 1636, "did . . . present a model of Moses his judicials, compiled in an exact method, which were taken into further consideration till the next general court." [62]

Cotton's draft was never enacted into law,[63] and probably for that reason its importance has been generally ignored.[64] Nevertheless, there are several reasons why it deserves to be remembered. To begin with, it was the first constructive effort to carry out the mandate of the General Court and to produce a written body of laws which would serve as a constitution for the colony. Second, its heavy reliance upon Scripture provides an important illustration of the strong religious influence which infused Puritan thinking about law and the administration of justice. This attitude was not confined to the Massachusetts leaders but appeared also in England, particularly in the Interregnum, when Fifth Monarchists urged the abolition of the common law and the enactment of a simple code based upon the law of Moses.[65] Third, it became the basis of the early laws enacted at New Haven and Southampton, and thus had an enduring influence outside Massachusetts.[66] Finally, and most importantly, a number of provisions relating to crime and civil liberties found their way through the Body of Liberties of 1641 and the Code of 1648 into the permanent laws of the colony.[67]

The proposed Cotton code is a document of ten chapters, covering several printed pages, which set forth the powers and duties of the colony officers and of the freemen, provisions relating to taxation, military affairs, inheritance, trade and commerce, crime, wrongdoing, and the administration of justice.[68] Specific sections guarantee protection from arbitrary imprisonment [69] and enunciate standards of judicial process by requiring two witnesses for conviction in civil or criminal causes.[70] The criminal provisions and penalties are harsh and severe. Pursuant to literal texts of the Old Testament, the death penalty was prescribed for blasphemy, idolatry, witchcraft, false worship, sabbath breaking, murder, adultery, incest, sodomy, bestiality, man stealing, false witness, reviling the magistrates, cursing or smiting of parents.[71] That penalty was also prescribed, but without Scriptural authority, for willful perjury and treason.[72] Other provisions, such as those relating to town government,[73] the regulation of prices and wages,[74] inheritance,[75] restrictions on the alienation of land,[76] and the probate of wills,[77] reflect in some measure current practices in the colony.[78] Of particular interest among these latter sections are those prescribing fair-trade practices, which Cotton was later to enunciate in greater detail after the conviction of Captain Keayne for oppressive business practices.[79] The draft provided for the appointment of judges in each town to set "reasonable rates" on all commodities and to limit the wages of workers.[80] In drafting these provisions, Cotton appears to have been less preoccupied with the economic issues that concerned the Assistants than with ethical standards stemming from the mediaeval conception of the "just price," elsewhere defined as a due price, answerable to what others offer without fraud.[81]

Although there is a biblical basis or justification for most of the criminal and for several noncriminal provisions, the evidence clearly controverts the statement of James Truslow Adams that the Cotton draft "was based entirely upon Bible texts." [82] It is hardly remarkable that Cotton, who was a minister and a spiritual leader of extraordinary personal and professional ascendancy, convinced as were the other leaders of the rule of God's word, should turn to the Bible for precedent and justification for his code. Indeed, the General Court had instructed the committee of which he was a member to frame a draft "agreeable to the word of God." [83] What is remarkable is that Cotton, who had no legal training and who was not an officer of the colony, should have had as complete a grasp as he did of the fundamentals of its government, of the laws already in existence, and of the need in certain directions for guarantees of due process and civil rights.

It is possible only to speculate as to why the Cotton draft was not accepted by the General Court. Undoubtedly, many of its capital provisions were thought too severe.[84] Probably, in the light of the draft later accepted as the basis of the Body of Liberties, the Court determined that it was not sufficiently comprehensive, and that, notwithstanding their mandate to the committee, something more in the nature of a bill of rights was required. However, from the standpoint of making the freemen aware of the kind of code they did want, the Cotton draft served a further and very important function.

Aside from Cotton's individual effort, the second committee appears to have accomplished nothing. In March, 1638, the General Court appointed a third committee consisting of Winthrop, Dudley, and Bellingham, together with representatives of the churches and two prominent freemen, William Spencer and William Hathorne.[85] After noting the continuing lack of written laws which "have put the Court into many doubts & much trouble in perticuler cases," the court proceeded to direct that the freemen of every town should "collect the heads of such necessary & fundamentall lawes as may bee sutable to the times & places whear God by his providence hath cast vs" and to deliver "the heads of such lawes" to the new committee by early June.[86] The committee was instructed to survey this material and to make an abridgement thereof, adding to it or removing from it what seemed best, and to report back to the Court at its autumn session.

The records do not make clear to what extent the foregoing order was carried out, but the evidence indicates that the work progressed slowly.[87] In any event, prior to the November, 1639, meeting of the Court, another draft or "model" had been prepared by Nathaniel Ward, who was a member of the third committee, of 1639, and was presented to the Court at that session.[88] According to Winthrop, the Cotton draft was again submitted for consideration at that time.[89] The Court then ordered that a fourth committee, consisting of four magistrates—Winthrop, Dudley, Bellingham, and Israel Stoughton—together with two or more deputies from Boston, Charlestown, or Roxbury should "pervse all those modells, which have bene, or shalbee further presented to this Court, or themselues . . . & shall drawe them vp into one body." [90] The laws so framed were to be sent out "to the severall townes, that the elders of the churches & freemen may consider of them against the Generall Court." [91]

The actions of the General Court in 1638 and 1639 suggest that the deputies had decided that only by appointing some of their own number to sit on a law committee, and by providing for the participation of the freemen generally, would the task of reducing the laws to writing be accomplished. There can be little doubt that the magistrates had deliberately impeded the preparation of a code. However, to suggest that "Never were the demands of a free people eluded by their public servants with more of the wisdom or of the contortions of the serpent" [92] is not only an exaggeration but fails entirely to take into account the practical and political considerations that motivated the magistrates. Moreover, to refer to "free people" and their "public servants" is completely to misconceive the nature of the colony government and to view it entirely through modern eyes.

Apparently, Ward's "model" was approved by the fourth committee and sent out to the towns for the elders and freemen to criticize.[93] To what extent it was there amended is not known, but it is interesting to note in passing that Ward was not a little annoyed at the submission of "Court busines to the common consideration of the freemen." [94] Nevertheless, the submission of the draft to the freemen at large provided them with an opportunity to suggest the inclusion of local customs which they had known in England and, more importantly, to articulate their opposition to certain features of English law which they regarded as outworn. Whether or not they availed themselves of this opportunity cannot be known, but, in any event, the Body of Liberties reflected in its final form the high importance which they attached to constitutional guarantees and liberties.

The next official entry relating to the preparation of the Code is in May, 1640, when the General Court voted that the elders of the churches and other freemen should, by the autumn meeting of the Court, "endevour to ripen their thoughts & counsells" about the "breviate of lawes . . . formerly sent fourth." [95] Then, in June, 1641, Bellingham, as the new governor, was appointed "to peruse all the laws, & take notice what may bee fit to bee repealed, what to bee certified, & what to stand," and report to the next General Court.[96] The result of this perusal and of the deliberations of the Court at its autumn session was apparently the adoption of Ward's draft, revised into the collection of laws known as the Body of Liberties. According to Winthrop, the Court then revised and amended the draft "and established 100 laws, which were called the *Body of Liberties*. They had been composed by Mr. Nathaniel Ward . . . formerly a student and practiser in the course of the common law." [97] In Winthrop's own hand is a written attestation on the original record that "the bodye of laues formerly sent forth amonge the Freemen, etc., was voted to stand in force, etc." [98] The enacting clause referred to the Body of Liberties as containing the "rites, freedomes, Immunities, Authorities and priveledges, both Civill and Ecclesiastical [which] are expressed onely under the name and title of Liberties, and not in the exact form of Laws or Statutes, yet we do with one consent fullie Authorise, and earnestly intreate all that are and shall be in Authoritie to consider them as laws." [99]

The Body of Liberties was less a code of existing laws than it was a compilation of constitutional provisions. Its one hundred sections were, for the most part, framed in no logical order, and the majority of them dealt in a broad and general manner with such matters as the institutions of colony and town government and the relations between them, the relations between church and state, and judicial safeguards and procedures. Viewed as a whole, it resembles a bill of rights of the type which was later to become a familiar feature of American state and federal constitutions. That characteristic, underscoring an early concern for civil rights, is obviously of fundamental importance in the development of Massachusetts law, for it reflects the Englishman's traditional concern for due process of law and for safeguarding personal liberty from the arbitrary action of governmental authority. In ringing words, the first provision proclaims:

No mans life shall be taken away, no mans honour or good name shall be stayned, no mans person shall be arested, restrayned, banished, dismembred, nor any wayes punished, no man shall be deprived of his wife or children, no mans goods or estaite shall be taken away from him, nor any way indammaged under coulor of law or Countenance of Authoritie, unlesse it be by vertue or equitie of some expresse law of the Country waranting the same, established by a generall Court and sufficiently published. . . .[100]

Other provisions guaranteed equal justice under law to every person within the jurisdiction, "whether Inhabitant or forreiner," and assured freedom from arbitrary arrest and imprisonment, cruel punishments, impressment and torture.[101] Bond slavery, villeinage, and captivity were forbidden except as to captives taken in "just warres," "such strangers as willingly selle themselves or are solde to us," and those "who shall be Judged thereto by Authoritie." [102]

In several respects the Body of Liberties went well beyond protecting the traditional rights of Englishmen, as the colonists knew them. For instance, it announced the rights of freedom of speech and assembly [103] and the right of every person to remove freely from the colony except insofar as specifically denied;[104] it prohibited cruel and barbarous punishments, as well as torture to extract confessions,[105] and it provided for the number of witnesses required for conviction of a capital crime.[106] It also made provision for bail, ensured that men should not be twice sentenced by the civil courts for the same offense, and announced a limited privilege against self-crimination.[107]

Several of the Liberties attempted to improve upon English law. For example, the vestiges of feudalism, although largely a dead letter in England, still evoked unpleasant memories of the preceding century. Hence, the incidents of feudalism—wardship, marriage, relief, heriots, and primer seizins—were proscribed and lands declared free from fines and licenses upon alienation and from escheats and forfeitures.[108] Monopolies, which had been a great public issue under Elizabeth and James I, and which had been granted in the colony on a limited basis,[109] were specifically proscribed.[110] Imprisonment for debt, a standard English remedy available to creditors, was outlawed to the extent that "the law can finde competent meanes of satisfaction otherwise from his [i.e., the debtor's] estaite." [111] A further illustration of dissatisfaction with English law is provided by the simplification of judicial procedure, which assured that the conduct of law suits should not be impeded or arrested by the technicalities of pleading or by mistakes.[112]

Although what may be termed the constitutional guarantees of the Body of Liberties were among the most significant of its provisions, from the standpoint both of the colonists and of modern interest in the development of civil rights, it did codify existing law in numerous respects. Judicial procedure is dealt with in terms of appearance, arrest, attachment, bail, distress, evidence, jury trials, pleading, and witnesses.[113] Other provisions relate to capacity, the trespass of cattle, domestic relations, intestacy, masters and servants, strangers, wills, and wrecks.[114]

Among the most important of the public law provisions were those relating to capital crimes.[115] Nearly all of these were drawn from, and were annotated to, the Mosaic code of the Old Testament, and many undoubtedly had their origin in John Cotton's proposed draft of 1636. Except for the capital laws, biblical influence does not obtrude, save in the explicit provision that no laws, customs, or proscriptions should be established contrary to the law of God.[116]

The Body of Liberties marked a notable step not only in the direction of reducing the colony laws to writing but, more importantly, toward the development of a commonwealth of laws and not of men. Almost all of its provisions, most of them in more extended form, were ultimately reenacted in the Code of 1648 and became part of the permanent law of the colony.[117] Despite the colonists' efforts in 1646 to demonstrate the extent to which the Body of Liberties conformed to English common law,[118] its provisions were clearly at variance therefrom in many respects and, as indicated, represented notable improvements thereon from the colonists' standpoint. Yet, despite the scope of the compilation, it failed to satisfy the deputies, either in terms of finality or of comprehensiveness. Even at the time of its approval, the General Court expressly provided that the provisions should be "Audably read and deliberately weighed" at every General Court for the next three years.[119] Since the Body of Liberties, although reduced to writing, appears not to have been printed, this order was also presumably issued to afford the kind of publicity which the colonists felt necessary for giving law a binding effect.[120] However, in 1642, it was ordered that the provisions relating to capital offenses, as amended, should be separately printed.[121] The fact that those laws were printed in London, and that several were substantially at variance with English law,[122] suggests that the reason for not printing the Body of Liberties was the wish further to revise them rather than to keep their contents unknown to the English government.

Among the chief causes for dissatisfaction with the Body of Liberties was that it did not resolve the problem of the magistrates' discretion, for which the general provisions of that compilation still provided wide scope. Indeed, it was after its publication that the controversy over arbitrary penalties reached its high pitch,[123] and it seems clear that that controversy provided further momentum for a complete reduction to writing of the colony laws. Moreover, many orders and acts in force in the colony had not been included in the Body of Liberties, and others had been stated only in general terms. Not only did the freemen want a code that was complete and comprehensive; they also wanted specific rules, applicable to specific situations. This attitude was later expressed in the Epistle to the 1648 Code, which stated:

Nor is it sufficient to have principles or fundamentalls, but these are to be drawn out into so many of their deductions as the time and the condition of that people may have use of. And it is very unsafe & injurious to the body of the people to put them to learn their duty and libertie from generall rules. . . .[124]

Once again, therefore, committees were appointed to proceed with the preparation of a comprehensive compilation of the colony laws. In 1643 the "former committee" of magistrates and deputies was named to "examine & perfect" the laws.[125] In March, 1644, three magistrates—Winthrop, Dudley, and Hibbens—were expressly asked to review the Body of Liberties prior to the next General Court in order to determine what should be repealed and what allowed to stand. At the same time, the magistrates residing at Ipswich were appointed a committee for the same purpose, and Bellingham was directed to "finish that which was formerly committed to him"—presumably an abridgment of all the laws in force in the colony—and "to present the same to the next Court." [126] In the following year three county committees, consisting of magistrates, members of the clergy and freemen, totaling eighteen persons, were appointed to draw up a body of laws.[127]

The composition of these three county committees is instructive from several standpoints. In the first place, they included at least three men who had had legal training—Winthrop, Bellingham, and Ward—and it was, of course, the latter who had prepared the draft on which the Body of Liberties was based. The committees also included the three leading ministers of the colony—Cotton, Shepard, and Norton. Prominent among the other members were: Nathaniel Duncan, who had frequently served as a deputy and was auditor general of the colony; Captain Edward Johnson, deputy, sometime clerk of writs at Woburn, and subsequently author of *Wonder-Working Providence;* Richard Mather, elder of the church of Dorchester, who prepared the draft of the Cambridge Platform of Church Discipline; George Cooke, speaker of the house of deputies and prominent in committees dealing with military affairs; Bozoon Allen, who had been the storm center of the Hingham militia affair; and William Hathorne, of Salem, a principal agitator in most of the controversies with the magistrates, but a man who had had considerable judicial experience as an associate of Endecott on the Essex County Court.[128]

In the autumn of 1645, the committees were requested to meet and report on what they had done.[129] In May, 1646, the General Court accepted their labors and requested a new committee of five, consisting of two magistrates (Bellingham and Symonds), Nathaniel Ward, Edward Johnson, and Nathaniel Duncan, each of whom had served on a county committee, to cause the returns to be transcribed so that each committee could see what the others had done. To that end, they were to meet together, on or before August 10th, at Salem or Ipswich, and to peruse the labors of the county committees, together with "the abreviation of the lawes in force, which Mr. Bellingham tooke greate store of paines, & to good purpose." [130] Return was to be made at the next session of the Court, at which time the Court expected to establish "so many of them as shalbe thought most fit for a body of lawes amongst us." [131] In November, 1646, yet another committee was appointed to "peruse, examine, compare, transcribe, correct, & compose in good order all the liberties, lawes, & orders extant with us, & further to peruse & perfect all such others as are drawne up," and to suggest what should be added, and how the whole should be transcribed.[132] The Court then went on to emphasize the basis of the whole codification movement by stating that the purpose of this enlarged compilation was to have it available for "ready recourse . . . upon all occasions, whereby we may manifest our utter disaffection to arbitrary goverment." [133]

Six months went by, during which the committee apparently failed to accomplish what had been expected of it, and in May, 1647, still another committee consisting of three magistrates—Winthrop, Bellingham, and William Hibbens—together with Nathaniel Duncan and Joseph Hills, was appointed to complete the work.[134] The work of Hills, who was then speaker of the house of deputies, is particularly deserving of comment. So much credit has customarily been given to the roles of Bellingham and Ward in drafting the Code [135] that the part taken by others—even Winthrop—has been lost sight of or ignored. The official records tell us little of how the committees did their work, but a petition for compensation, which Hills later presented to the Court, provides evidence of the thoroughness of their labors and particularly of the extent to which they drew upon English sources. According to Hills' petition, the entire Code was reviewed from the standpoint of English statutory law. He states that as a member of a county committee he had perused "all the Stat. Laws of Engl. in Pulton att Large out of which J took all such as J conceiued sutable to the condition of this commonwealth which with such others as in my observation Experiences & Serious Studies J thought needful." [136]

Meanwhile, the General Court was active in a direction upon which comment does not seem to have been made in existing accounts of the codification movement. In 1646 and 1647 a number of detailed laws, incorporating former laws as well as much new material, were enacted by the Court. The dates appended to the provisions in the Code in themselves provide evidence of the extent of the work done in those years, but comparison of enactments in the Court's records reveals that many of them were not only very similar but frequently identical to provisions in the Code as it appeared in final form.[137] Indeed, most of the legislation of those two years was carried forward without substantial change.

That this outburst of unprecedented legislative activity was the result of recommendations of the law committees can only be determined by inference, but the evidence is impressive.[138] First in the Court records for November, 1646, appears a group of statutes dealing with religious matters—laws concerning blasphemy, Indian "paw-waws," heretics and seducers, contempt of the Word and of ministers, absence from worship, disturbing church service, vain swearing, instruction of the Indians in Christianity, cursing or smiting of parents, and incorrigible sons. After them comes a group of laws relating to crimes not involving religion. These laws, in the order of their appearance on the record, dealt with arson, fires set through inadvertence, embezzlement by servants, gaming, and theft. Thereafter, under the heading of "Prudentiall Lawes," appear statutes dealing with the disposition of idle persons, regulating the making of tile earth, requiring artificers to work in the fields at harvest if needed, establishing assizes of bread and of wood.[139] Finally, under "Juditiall Proceedings," are laws dealing with forgery, vexatious suits, prison keepers, penalties for nonappearance, hue and cry, and charges for transporting prisoners.

The grouping of these statutes can scarcely have been fortuitous, for there is no single piece of legislation that does not fall within one of the four groups. It seems likely, though not susceptible of definite proof, that the fourfold classification reflects the constitution of the drafting committees. If so, the laws dealing with religion may have been essentially the work of the ministers, those pertaining to ordinary civil crimes and to judicial proceedings the work of the magistrates, and those relating to town government and the like the work of the deputies on the committees. It is not improbable that thereafter the select committee, as directed, had presented draft legislation which it deemed "most fit for a body of lawes amongst us" to the General Court, and that the Court then enacted all or part of them with the understanding that they would form part of the proposed Code.

At the General Court of November, 1647, it is also clear that the Court was enacting laws with the Code in mind. For example, under a heading "Military Affairs" in the Court records is a detailed statute treating the whole area of military matters;[140] this act, joined to an act of 1645,[141] appears without substantial change in the Code under the title "Militarie Affairs." [142] Significantly, in enacting this provision, the Court directed that "The constables watch . . . be refferred to title constables," [143] indicating that the Court then had before it a draft with titles corresponding in part at least to those which finally appear in the Code. [144] Four laws enacted at this session passed directly into the Code without having been entered in the court records.[145]

As the work of compilation drew toward completion, the Court, presumably for the advancement of its labors, ordered two copies each of six legal texts then in wide current use in England—*Coke on Littleton*, *Coke on Magna Carta*, Coke's *Reports*, the *New Terms of the Law*, the *Book of Entries*, and Dalton's *Country Justice*.[146] In the spring of 1648 the final amendments were added, and the manuscript was delivered to the printer in Cambridge.[147]

The importance of the Code cannot be too often restated. It incorporated, in revised and elaborated form, most of the provisions of the Body of Liberties,[148] together with the specific laws still in force which were enacted since the time of settlement, and it also included a substantial number of entirely new laws enacted in order to provide completeness. Bearing the title of *The Lawes and Liberties of Massachusetts*, it is one of the crowning achievements of the Bay Colony. Together with a few later amendments, it provided the basic statutory law of the colony throughout most of the seventeenth century. It is no accident that the project came to fruition and achieved its final synthesis in the same year that ecclesiastical discipline was codified in the Cambridge Platform of Church Discipline.[149] In their respective religious and civil spheres, the Cambridge Platform and *The Laws and Liberties* represented the culmination of an extraordinarily creative period during which the colonists applied conscious design to received tradition and produced a system of civil and ecclesiastical polity that was at once logical, coherent, comprehensive, intellectually and politically sophisticated, and, above all, eminently workable.

The Laws and Liberties was both a restatement of the law and a code of statutes for the future, by no means the result of scissors and paste. About one-quarter of its provisions can be traced to enactments or orders made prior to 1640, but these were thoroughly revised and expanded. About one-third date from the period 1646–1647 when the Code was being completed, and of these about one-half were entirely new. Altogether, it was a detailed and comprehensive statement of the orders and enactments in force in the jurisdiction. Not only was it an authoritative compilation of constitutional provisions and civil administration—justice, courts, trade, taxation, licensing, agriculture, education, military affairs, and the relations between church and state—but, as already explained, it also included much substantive law relating to such matters as crime, inheritance, and domestic relations. Its intended comprehensiveness is forcefully illustrated by the statement in the Epistle that "all generall laws not heer inserted nor mentioned to be still of force are to be accounted repealed." [150] Altogether, it is a "lawyerly piece of work." [151] Arranged in systematic fashion under alphabetical headings that begin with "Abilitie" and end with "Wrecks of the sea," it is reminiscent of contemporary English abridgements, such as those of Brooke and Fitzherbert in common use at that time, but to what extent such manuals were relied upon or used cannot be stated with certainty. The fact that it contained much English law and reflected numerous practices of the various English courts in itself suggests that English manuals and treatises were available to its compilers,[152] and it is significant that much of the work of preparation had been consigned to Winthrop, Bellingham, and Ward, three men of substantial legal experience.

Comprehensive though it was, the Code did not, and did not purport to, set forth every legal rule applied or to be applied in the courts. Thus, it did not attempt to define a contract, defamation, or trespass; neither did it set forth in any detail the remedies to which the injured party in such actions might be entitled. Again, the probate of wills is not mentioned, nor are the standards to be applied thereto. In this respect it was far less comprehensive in its civil and "private" aspects than in its criminal and "public" aspects. In other words, a substantial segment of what might loosely be termed the common law of the colony, that is, the nonstatutory law applied in the courts, was not included. Yet the Code did draw upon antecedent judicial experience and perpetuated in several areas the pattern of development in the courts. For example, the provision dealing with fornication prescribed that offenders be punished by "enjoyning to Marriage, or Fine, or corporall punishment, or all or any of these as the Judges in the courts of Assistants shall appoint most agreeable to the word of God." [153] These were precisely the penalties, singly or in combination, which the magistrates had imposed during the twelve-year period prior to the enactment in 1642 of the statutory provision upon which this section of the Code was based.[154] A further example is provided by the law of intestate succession, which was based upon the practice of partible inheritance followed by the courts since the early 1630's.[155]

Among the many striking features of the Code is the fact that it represents in many areas of the law a very clear break with traditional law. Here was no mere compilation of English common-law rules or of established local custom, no haphazard syncretization of popular equity and biblical precepts, no mechanical piling of new legislation upon old; it was a fresh and considered effort to establish new provisions and revise former ones which were suitable to the conditions of a new civilization and which would also provide starting points for future development in the community. For example, the provision for dividing intestate land among all children reflected a solicitude for the needs of younger children, and the law of creditors' rights took into account the inappropriateness in the colony of imprisonment for debt.[156] Although many traditional elements are present, both rules of the English common law and customs of the towns or districts from which the colonists came, these elements were consciously reworked into a carefully thought-out and integrated pattern, consistent with the ideals upon which the colony had been founded. When traditional rules were inconsistent with the general plan, or appeared archaic and obsolete, they were modified or ignored.

Comprehensive as the Code was intended to be, perfection did not, even to its framers, seem possible. The Epistle states:

. . . . For if it be no disparagement to the wisedome of that High Court of Parliament in England that in four hundred years they could not so compile their lawes, and regulate proceedings in Courts of justice &c: but that they had still new work to do of the same kinde almost every Parliament: there can be no just cause to blame a poor Colonie (being unfurnished of Lawyers and Statesmen) that in eighteen years hath produced no more, nor better rules for a good, and setled Government then this Book holds forth: nor have you (our Bretheren and Neighbours) any cause, whether you look back upon our Native Country, or take your observation by other States, & Common wealths in Europe) to complaine of such as you have imployed in this service; for the time which hath been spent in making lawes, and repealing and altering them so often, nor of the charge which the Country hath been put to for those occasions, the Civilian gives you a satisfactorie reason of such continuall alterations additions &c: Crescit in Orbe dolus.[157]

Far more clearly than the scattered entries in the court records, the Code as a whole reflects the problems, pressures, and conflicts which the colonists sought to resolve through legal rules. Thus, it defined civil responsibilities as well as civil liberties, and it crystallized the constitutional ideas and political thinking which had developed in the preceding eighteen years. The Epistle, for example, explicitly states that government and law had been made necessary by man's corruption, and it goes on to emphasize the importance of the welfare of the whole in words reminiscent of Winthrop's sermon on Christian charity delivered on the outward voyage:[158]

. . . obedience to them [*sc.* the laws] must be yeilded with respect to the common welfare, not to thy private advantage, and as thou yeildest obedience to the law for common good, but to thy disadvantage: so another must observe some other law for thy good, though to his own damage; thus must we be content to bear oneanothers burden and so fullfill the Law of Christ.[159]

This passage is also significant because it is illustrative of the strong ethical element that permeates much of the Code. Inevitably, legal rules reflect in some measure the picture of what men of a particular time regard as the ideal of relations among men. In this respect, many provisions of the Code are particularly striking in their recurrent emphasis upon the importance of right conduct and the need to extirpate sin in all its forms. Not only the capital laws (which even children were expected to read and understand), but those that punished drunkenness, gambling, idleness, lying, and unfair trade practices, bear witness to the deep Puritan conviction that mortal man could be enjoined or persuaded to order his conduct in accordance with exacting moral and ethical standards.[160]

One other passage in the Epistle deserves attention because it reflects certain views of the colonists as to the source and basis of law. The importance that the Puritans attached to logic and reason in the formulation of religious and political doctrines can hardly be overemphasized, and there is no clearer, nor more pointed, articulation of the colonists' reliance upon those processes in the framing of their laws than that contained in the concluding paragraph:

That distinction which is put between the Lawes of God and the lawes of men, becomes a snare to many as it is mis-applyed in the ordering of their obedience to civil Authoritie; for when the Authoritie is of God and that in way of an Ordinance . . . and when the administration of it is according to deductions, and rules gathered from the word of God, and the clear light of nature in civil nations, surely there is no humane law that tendeth to common good (according to those principles) but the same is mediately a law of God, and that in way of an Ordinance which all are to submit unto and that for conscience sake.[161]

So reminiscent are these words of many passages in Winthrop's tracts that one cannot help conjecturing that he may have been their author. Whether or not this is so, the passage reflects the Puritan view that the path of the law was one of logic as well as of experience.[162] At the same time, it reaffirms the belief in fundamental law—eternal though brief principles from which clear deductions can be drawn and positive laws framed. The law of nature and the law of God were consociated, and their lasting and unchanging qualities were assured by belief in the perfection and immutability of divine law and reason.[163] Positive law, that is, the law made by man, was believed to have to comport with a higher, divine law for its validity. This idea of higher law, although later secularized, was to become an enduring legacy of the colonial period.[164]

IX

A Rule to Walk By

"In all their administrations," wrote John Winthrop in defense of the constitutionality of the early Massachusetts government, "the Officers of this Bodye Politick have a Rule to walk by . . . which Rule is the *Worde of God.* . . ." [1] The basic content of that rule, in Puritan eyes, was to be found in the Bible, wherein God had provided an immutable constitution not only, as John Cotton said, "for the right ordering of a private mans soule to everlasting blessednes with himselfe, but also for the right ordering of a mans family, yea, of the commonwealth too, so farre as both of them are subordinate to spiritual ends. . . ." [2]

That the word of God provided the mainspring for the colony mission is hardly open to doubt. The reform and purification of church discipline and doctrine through a return to the principles of the primitive apostolic church was not only the deliberate and unswerving aim of the early Puritans in England but the primary purpose of the founding of the Bay Colony. To God's word as declared in Scripture the colonists consistently turned for guidance and justification, both in matters of church polity and in the framing and administration of their laws. The decisions of the courts were expected to conform to that Word, and an order of the General Court in 1636 had expressly so provided in situations for which no positive law had been established. [3] Moreover, the Epistle to the Code of 1648 proclaimed that it had been "no small priviledge, and advantage to us in New-England . . . to frame our civil Politie, and lawes according to the rules of [God's] most holy word," [4] and the capital laws therein contained were specifically annotated to chapter and verse of the Old Testament. Several of those provisions, as well as other enactments, incorporated literal biblical phraseology into the body of statutory law.[5]

The colonists' reliance upon biblical precedent and authority, apparent in the pronouncements of their leaders and in the fabric of the legal system, has led some scholars to conclude that the law of early Massachusetts was essentially biblical,[6] and even to characterize the colony as the "Bible Commonwealth." [7] Although such generalizations are not without foundation, their value is lessened by failure to examine them from the standpoint of the law as a whole and with reference both to the special conditions of settlement and to the social, political, and legal inheritance which the Puritans shared in common with other seventeenth century Englishmen.

At the outset, it should be observed that influential as the Bible was in the lives of the colonists, it also held a position of extraordinary importance for their English contemporaries. Recourse to, and reliance upon, the teachings of Scripture was by no means confined to the Puritans and was common throughout England in the sixteenth and seventeenth centuries. By the time of the settlement of Massachusetts, the Bible in English translation had been widely available for nearly a century.[8] Henry VIII had at one point sought to stem developing interest therein through a prohibition against its being read by servants and women; yet the impetus of the English Reformation so stimulated popular demand for free access to the Scriptures that by the 1530's Bible reading was actively encouraged by the Tudor government. In 1538 it was ordered that every parish in the country should purchase a copy of the Bible in English, to be set up in each church, "where the parishioners might most commodiously resort to the same and read it." [9] As the century wore on, the Bible, in cheap and readily available editions, had become the common property of all classes of English society. Children in school were taught to read from books studded with scriptural selections,[10] and by the beginning of the seventeenth century virtually every literate English household had its own copy.[11] The rich imagery of its texts quickened the imagination and left an indelible imprint upon English speech and letters, while its precepts and parables, no longer buried in the obscurities of the Latin tongue or meted out at the discretion of a priestly caste, became a powerful force not only in molding religious ideas but in shaping the everyday conduct of English people in all walks of life.

By the end of the sixteenth century, critical study of biblical texts and of Christian philosophy was an important feature of the curricula of the English universities, particularly at Cambridge, and theology and church polity had become leading intellectual interests of the day.[12] Ecclesiastics of all persuasions turned to the Bible in defense or in support of their views. Bishop Jewel, an apologist for the Elizabethan establishment, was convinced no less than his Puritan opponents that he had searched out of the Bible "one sure form of religion," returning thereby "unto the primitive church of the ancient fathers and apostles." [13] In the eagerness and intensity with which the Puritans studied the Bible, and in the conclusions they drew therefrom, the Puritans did, however, differ from their contemporaries. The renaissance of Hebrew studies which had accompanied the Reformation particularly affected them, since the ancient texts helped to provide a key to the word of God. Such men as John Cotton, Nathaniel Ward, and John Eliot read Hebrew as well as Latin, and its study was made a part of the required curriculum at Harvard College; but is should be observed that this interest is as much attributable to then current English standards of education as to the specific influence of Puritanism.[14]

Hardly less striking was the influence of the Bible upon English law and legal thinking. Belief in the Scriptures as a source of law was widespread among educated Englishmen, partly because of the persisting influence of mediaeval scholasticism and partly because of the tendency of Protestant theologians to equate natural law with Mosaic law.[15] English exiles who had lived at Geneva during the reign of Mary had seen at firsthand a legal system that owed much to biblical precepts,[16] and the influence of Calvinism in Scotland had resulted in the enactment of the eighteenth chapter of Leviticus as the positive law of the northern kingdom.[17] As part of the effort to prove the English Church's claim to apostolic succession, the sixteenth century had seen the publication and widespread praise of the early code of Alfred the Great, which incorporated the Decalogue and much of four chapters of Exodus as part of the laws of England.[18] Thomas Cromwell, Henry VIII's Chief Minister, had even ordered the reading of the Ten Commandments at the end of every Sabbath service.[19]

Among lawyers belief in the Bible as a source of law was given special cogency by the wide popularity of St. Germain's *Doctor and Student* and other texts which sought to demonstrate that the law of England was grounded upon the law of God.[20] As early as 1551, the king's attorney argued before the Exchequer Chamber that "the Christian Kings of this realm in former times have made their laws as neer to the laws of God as they could," and then proceeded to cite Deuteronomy as authority for the rule for which he was contending.[21] The argument merely reflected the tendency of the age, for reliance upon and reference to the Bible was habitual among English judges and legal writers during this period. Lord Chancellor Ellesmere, in the reign of James I, began an opinion with the words: "The law of God speaks for the plaintiff, Deut. XXVIII. 30." [22] In a manslaughter case in 1611, a justice of the King's Bench cited, in Latin, Christ's warning that he who lives by the sword shall perish by the sword.[23] Coke's report of Ratcliff's Case, decided in Queen's Bench in 1592, noted that the court's conclusion that inheritances may lineally descend, but not ascend, was reinforced by the argument "that in this Point as almost in all others the Common Law was grounded upon the Law of God . . . as it appeareth in the 27 Chap. of *Numbers*," the relevant text of which was summarized and quoted in the report.[24]

Justices of the peace, according to Lambarde, customarily addressed their charges to the jury under heads corresponding to the Ten Commandments [25]—a practice which was also followed in Massachusetts.[26] The exhortation to the jury outlined in Kitchin's standard manual for the conduct of courts leet begins: "Feare God and keepe his Commandements," and goes on to cite or quote the Old and the New Testament ten times in the course of a small printed page.[27] The peroration of the charge to the jury printed in Fitzherbert's manual for justices of the peace is explicit as to the application of God's laws to the affairs of man:

Saint *Iames* saith, *He that knoweth how to doe well, and doth it not, to him it is sinne.* And the *Gospell* saith, *He that knoweth his Masters will, and doth not perfome the same, shall be beaten with many stripes.* Which places of Scripture, although they chiefly pertain to the Transgressors of the Law Divine: yet sith Subiects are bounden in conscience to keepe the Lawes of their Princes and Countries, which are not against the Lawes of God, it is not impertinent to applie the said places of Scripture to the breakers of the same Lawes.[28]

Unquestionably, therefore, Englishmen of the sixteenth and seventeenth centuries were thoroughly conversant with the Bible and accustomed to looking upon it as authority. It is equally without question that the influence of the Bible upon conceptions of what the law ought to be was more pronounced and more inclined toward literalism among the English Puritans than among their non-Puritan countrymen. The former saw themselves as children of Israel, openly imitated Hebraic practices, and likened their persecutions to the misery of the Jews at the hands of Antiochus.[29] By the same token, they were convinced that much of the law that God had given to ancient Israel continued to bind the people whom He had chosen as His own in the England of Elizabeth and James. "So soon as God had set up Politicall Government among his people Israel," recites the Epistle to the Code of 1648, "hee gave them a body of lawes for judgement both in civil and criminal causes. These were breif and fundamental principles, yet withall so full and comprehensive as out of them clear deductions were to be drawne to all particular cases in future times." [30] Pursuant to this kind of thinking, Thomas Cartwright, in the time of Elizabeth, had urged the necessity of the death penalty for blasphemers and unruly children;[31] and Puritan reformers of the Interregnum were to employ the same reasoning in pressing for the literal enactment of the Mosaic code.[32]

None of the Massachusetts laws more clearly reflects biblical influence than do the provisions of the capital laws contained in the Code of 1648. Idolatry, witchcraft, blasphemy, bestiality, sodomy, adultery, rape, man stealing, treason, false witness with intent to take life, cursing or smiting of a parent, stubbornness or rebelliousness on the part of a son against his parents, and homicide committed with malice prepense, by guile or poisoning, or "suddenly in . . . anger or cruelty of passion"—all were punishable with death.[33] Each of these provisions, with the exception of that relating to rape, was annotated to some chapter and verse of the Pentateuch, and several exactly reproduced its language. No more striking proof of literal reliance upon the Bible in this area of the law can be found than in the law relating to rebellious sons,[34] which is here quoted in full, to the right of the text of Deuteronomy 21:18–21:

If a man have a stubborn and rebellious son, which will not obey the voice of his father, or the voice of his mother, and that, when they have chastened him, will not hearken unto them: Then shall his father and his mother lay hold on him, and bring him out unto the elders of his city, and unto the gate of his place; And they shall say unto the elders of his city, This our son is stubborn and rebellious, he will not obey our voice; he is a glutton, and a drunkard. And all the men of his city shall stone him with stones, that he die . . .

If a man have a stubborn or REBELLIOUS SON, of sufficient years & understanding (*viz*) sixteen years of age, which will not obey the voice of his Father, or the voice of his Mother, and that when they have chastened him will not harken unto them: then shal his Father & Mother being his natural parents, lay hold on him, & bring him to the Magistrates assembled in Court & testifie unto them, that their Son is stubborn & rebellious & will not obey their voice and chastisement, but lives in sundry notorious crimes, such a son shal be put to death.

Other capital laws contain clauses, phrases, or words taken directly from the Old Testament. Thus, the witchcraft provision defined a witch as one that "hath or consulteth with a familiar spirit" [35] in terms of Leviticus 20:27 and Deuteronomy 18:11, which speak respectively of one "that hath a familiar spirit" and of "a consulter with familiar spirits." Again, it is prescribed in Leviticus 20:15 and 16 that "if a man lie with a beast, he shall surely be put to death: and ye shall slay the beast," and a similar punishment was provided "if a woman approach unto any beast, and lie down thereto"; by comparison, the bestiality law of Massachusetts states that "If any man or woman shall LYE WITH ANY BEAST, or bruit creature, by carnall copulation; they shall surely be put to death:

and the beast shall be slain, & buried, and not eaten." [36] In the same chapter of Leviticus, 20:13, it is stated that "If a man also lie with mankind, as he lieth with a woman, both of them have committed an abomination"; the colony law against sodomy prescribes that "If any man LYETH WITH MAN-KINDE as he lieth with a woman, both of them have committed abomination . . ." [37] In Exodus 21:16 it is declared that "he that stealeth a man, and selleth him, or if he be found in his hand, he shall surely be put to death"; in Massachusetts law, "If any man STEALETH A MAN, or Man-kinde, he shall surely be put to death." [38] Finally, the colonial provision that "If any child, or children . . . shall CURSE, or SMITE their natural FATHER, or MOTHER; he or they shall be put to death:" [39] is paralleled by Exodus 21:15 and 17, to the effect that "he that smiteth his father, or his mother . . . And he that curseth his father, or his mother, shall surely be put to death."

At the same time, even those capital laws which are unequivocally based upon the Bible contain evidence of substantial non-Scriptural influences. The sodomy law, for example, is qualified by an exception in favor of one who was "forced (or be under fourteen years of age in which case he shall be severely punished)." [40] This exception demonstrates that in the course of revising an earlier law, first enacted in the Body of Liberties, the colonists not only took account of the element of intent but introduced the recognized English legal presumption that a boy under fourteen years of age was deemed to be legally incapable of committing sodomy. [41] Significantly, legal presumptions based upon age are also apparent in the colony law against cursing or smiting of parents and in that dealing with stubborn and rebellious sons. Those laws, which were originally enacted by the General Court in November, 1646, were made applicable, respectively, to "any child, or children, above sixteen years old, and of sufficient understanding," [42] and to a son "of sufficient years & understanding (*viz*) sixteen years of age." [43] In the former law a second qualification of Scripture was introduced for cases in which "it can be sufficiently testified that the Parents have been very unchristianly negligent in the education of such children; or so provoked them by extream, and cruel correction; that they have been forced therunto to preserve themselves from death or maiming." [44] This qualification appears to represent, as the absolute biblical injunction does not, an effort to accommodate the community's interest in ensuring the observance of God's command that parents be honored with the Puritan view that parents should provide their children with a proper moral and religious education, and should use moderation in correcting them.

Like the sodomy statute, the blasphemy statute was amended in important respects between its original enactment in 1641 [45] and its incorporation into the Code in 1648.[46] The 1648 version is quoted in full, with the additions italicized in order to demonstrate the extent to which the draftsmen consciously applied considered policy to its revision:

If any person *within this Jurisdiction whether Christian or Pagan shall wittingly and willingly presume to* BLASPHEME the *holy* Name of God, Father, Son or Holy-Ghost, with direct, expresse, presumptuous, or high-handed blasphemy, *either by wilfull or obstinate denying the true God, or his Creation, or Government of the world:* or shall curse God in like manner, *or reproach the holy Religion of God as if it were but a politick device to keep ignorant men in awe; or shal utter any other kinde of Blasphemy of the like nature & degree they* shall be put to death.

The first of the three amendments specifically extends the reach of the capital law to the Indians, pursuant to biblical authority afterward cited that "as well the stranger, as he that is born in the land, when he blasphemeth the name of the Lord, shall be put to death." [47] The second, as well as the first amendment, introduces the fundamental Puritan idea of the offender's moral responsibility for a criminal act, based upon his knowing and deliberate choice. Equally important is the third addition, which requires that the offenders be "wilfull or obstinate," and emphasizes the Puritan belief, apparent in other aspects of the colony's criminal law, that persistent criminal conduct, in the face of clear warning and exhortation, was more deserving of punishment than the single commission of a wrongful act.[48] The remainder of the additions specify the kinds of utterances which are to be punished as blasphemous and are not greatly at variance with the common-law definition of blasphemy that appears in Blackstone at the end of the eighteenth century.[49]

Curiously, the language of the colony's homicide provisions, which were enacted originally in 1641 and reenacted without change in the 1648 codification, contains few biblical terms. "Wilfull murder," "manslaughter," and "premeditated malice" were common-law terms, as were "mere casualty against will" and "mans necessary and just defence." [50] The substance of at least one of these provisions, however, was not English but biblical. Homicide committed "suddenly in . . . ANGER, or CRUELTY of passion," was a mandatory capital crime pursuant to Numbers 35:20,[51] whereas under English law homicide under such circumstances was manslaughter and a clergyable offense.[52] Whether the murder statute, which appears on its face to make self-defense and lack of intention complete defenses, was based upon biblical authority is not entirely clear, but under English law homicide *se defendendo* and *per infortunium* were nevertheless crimes, although not felonies.[53]

The colonial prescription of the death penalty for adultery reflected not only biblical influence but the Puritan view that the family was the cornerstone of church and commonwealth. Hence, any threat to the sanctity and integrity of the family unit deserved the most serious punishment of which God's law approved.[54] Three generations of Puritan pamphleteers in England had advocated that adultery be punished by death instead of by the small fines and penances which the Archdeacon's Court normally imposed,[55] and even Winthrop, for all his leniency in many directions, regarded as absurd the notion that "we may passe by Murders, Adulteryes, Idolatryes, etc: without Capitall punishments. . . ." [56] Hence, the colonial law provided that "If any person committ ADULTERIE with a married, or espoused wife; the Adulterer & Adulteresse shal surely be put to death." [57] Here, again, the Bible provided the substantive formulation of, and the penalty for, the crime. In accordance with Mosaic law, Massachusetts defined adultery in terms of the matrimonial status of the woman, ignoring that of the man; whereas under English ecclesiastical law adultery was committed whenever either participant in the illicit act was married.[58] A second departure from the English definition of adultery was the extension of the crime to include intercourse with a woman espoused but not yet married.[59] This extension was clearly based upon the prescription of Deuteronomy 22:23 and 24, cited as authority both in the Cotton draft of laws and in the Body of Liberties,[60] to the effect, "If a damsel that is a virgin be betrothed unto an husband, and a man find her in the city, and lie with her; Then ye shall bring them both out unto the gate of that city, and ye shall stone them with stones that they die . . ."

The Massachusetts rape statute is the only one of the capital laws for which scriptural authority is not cited, and the reason for the omission appears to be that by the laws of Moses the offense was punishable not by death but by payment of damages and by an injunction to marry the victim.[61] At common law, rape was defined as consensual or forcible copulation with a female under ten and nonconsensual intercourse with a female over ten; the offense was a felony and punishable by death.[62] By the 1640's, the increase of sexual crime had become a source of grave concern to the Massachusetts authorities, and Winthrop had argued that "by the equity of the law against sodomy" intercourse with a child should be punished with death, "for it is against nature as well as sodomy. . . ."[63] When the shocking case of John Humfry's daughters came to light and it was discovered that between the ages of seven and nine the elder had had sexual relations with three servants of her father, "so as she was grown capable of man's fellowship, and took pleasure in it," the colony was in an uproar.[64] By English law, the men would have been hanged, and many in the General Court strongly urged the death penalty. Ultimately, after consultation with all the elders of Massachusetts, Plymouth, Connecticut, and New Haven, the court concluded that because the crime was not expressly capital by the word of God or by any express law of the colony the principal offender should be fined and have his nostrils slit and seared and should be required to wear a noose of rope around his neck.[65] The other two men were also fined and ordered to be severely whipped.[66] However, on the same day that sentence was passed, the General Court enacted its first addition to the capital laws of the Body of Liberties in the form of statutes prescribing mandatory death penalties for sexual intercourse, consensual or otherwise, with a child under ten and for forcible intercourse with a woman "married or contracted," and a discretionary death penalty for rape of any single woman above the age of ten.[67]

These enactments afford striking illustrations of the interplay of cultural forces in the shaping of the colony law. The inference is clear that the General Court, shocked and inflamed by the Humfry case, formulated a definition of rape that bore a close similarity to the common-law crime but justified it on the basis of scriptural authority for the punishment of sodomy.[68] From this standpoint, the subsequent history of the rape statutes is instructive. In the revision of the capital laws that preceded the codification of 1648, the two provisions imposing the mandatory death penalty were dropped from the capital laws, leaving only the law which related to forcible intercourse with a maid or single woman above the age of ten years and which decreed "death, or . . . some other greivous punishment according to circumstances as the Judges, or General court shal determin." [69] It seems probable that the scruples about a "warrant" from the word of God that had saved the lives of the defendants in the Humfry case had sufficiently revived so that the General Court was unwilling to retain a mandatory death penalty which had no specific biblical authority.

The provisions of the Massachusetts capital laws have been discussed in some detail because they illustrate not only the colonists' extensive reliance upon Scripture but also their unwillingness to follow its precepts when contrary to their own ethical and moral conceptions. Despite their dependence upon the word of God and the close connection that they saw between sin and crime, they were demonstrably reluctant to prescribe death for every offense that the Bible ordered so punished. Had they regarded the Bible's pronouncements as dogmatic injunctions, literally to be followed under all circumstances, the criminal laws should have embraced at least as many capital offenses as John Cotton included in his draft code.[70] In fact, the laws of Massachusetts prescribed relatively mild punishments for a number of such offenses, and the colonists' position seems to have been that no divine warrant was needed for the infliction of penalties that were *less* severe than those prescribed in the Bible. They were even more reluctant to extend the death penalty to offenses which were not expressly capital by the word of God, as the Humfry case illustrates. The General Court's decision in that case was entirely consistent with Puritan thinking on capital punishment. The author of the *Examen Legum Angliae*, who proposed reforms in the laws of England on the basis of biblical authority, stated it as "a Rule without Exception, given by the

Learned, That no humane law can justly take away the life of a man for any offence, without a general or particular warrant from God's word; because mans life is onely at God's disposing." [71]

In the criminal law, therefore, the authority of the Bible appears to have been sought less as a dogmatic rule to be blindly followed than as a justification, or "warrant" as the colonists termed it, for the infliction of death upon a fellow man. Within the limits and for the reasons suggested, they apparently felt free to determine what offenses should be so punished. Hence, the scriptural annotations to the capital laws provided the justification, although not necessarily the reason, for their choice. In this connection it is worth observing that before 1650 there were but few convictions under any of the capital laws and, under some of them, none.[72] This suggests that to a substantial extent, at least, those laws were believed, like the Decalogue, to fulfill a hortatory or *in terrorem* function, which is further emphasized by the order of the General Court that children be taught to read so that they would know the capital laws.[73]

Among the reasons for the paucity of convictions under the capital laws was the insistence of the courts upon clear and palpable proof of the commission of crime. That insistence resulted partly from general Puritan reluctance to take human life and partly from the precept of Deuteronomy 17:6 that "At the mouth of two witnesses, or three witnesses, shall he that is worthy of death be put to death; but at the mouth of one witness he shall not be put to death." The colony law specifically prescribed that "no man shall be put to death without the testimonie of two or three *witnesses*, or that which is equivalent therunto." [74] Although in the seventeenth century the two-witness rule was customarily followed in the English ecclesiastical courts and in the Star Chamber,[75] the common-law courts were moving away from the requirement of a fixed number of witnesses except in cases of treason and perjury.[76] That tendency, together with the colonists' discussion and use of the rule, emphasizes its biblical basis.[77] Not only were they sufficiently concerned about its scope to refer the problem to the elders of the churches,[78] but they were prepared to, and apparently did, extend it, in accordance with the provision in John Cotton's draft code, to civil as well as criminal cases.[79] Nevertheless, the adoption of the two-witness rule probably owed something to the colonists' English experience, and it is not without significance that Sir John Fortescue's fifteenth century treatise in praise of the laws of England referred to the law of God as forbidding proof by fewer than two witnesses.[80]

The capital laws are by no means the only part of the colonial criminal law that reflect biblical influence. The limitation on whipping sentences to forty stripes,[81] in contrast with the English formula "until his body be bloody," [82] was apparently based upon Deuteronomy 25:2 and 3. Similarly, the fornication statute, which empowered the magistrates to enjoin the parties to marriage,[83] was clearly agreeable to the Word as set forth in Exodus 22:16, as contrasted with the then current practice of English justices of the peace, who were primarily concerned with the economic problem of fixing responsibility for support of a bastard child upon its reputed father.[84] The Massachusetts law, however, had a further purpose in prescribing the marriage of the guilty parties, and that was the moral issue connected with the colonists' belief in the sanctity of the family unit and their conception of its role in community life. Here, again, in the adoption of the biblical rule, can be seen their insistence upon conforming their laws to the patterns of right living that had been developed in the colony.

Another striking departure from English law which apparently owed much to biblical authority was the colonists' adoption of multiple restitution and involuntary servitude for theft. At common law, the theft of a shilling, like other felonies, was punishable by hanging, and theft of a lesser amount by whipping.[85] Under a number of English statutes, restitution—single, double, or treble— was a common penalty imposed by justices of the peace for a variety of specified property crimes.[86] The Bible, however, prescribed multiple restitution as the penalty of the thief in most cases, or "if he have nothing, then he shall be sold for his theft." [87]

From the beginning, the colonial magistrates regularly followed the biblical patterns, imposing double restitution when the offender was capable thereof,[88] and requiring thieves unable to make restitution otherwise to satisfy the court's sentence by a term of service.[89] The exaction of these penalties was without specific statutory authority until 1646.[90] Prior thereto, the colonial treatment of theft furnishes an example of the shaping of law by magisterial discretion in the way favored by Winthrop. When restitution was feasible, it was usually the only punishment imposed,[91] but the courts did not hesitate to combine it with one or more of a variety of other penalties, ranging through whipping,[92] the stocks,[93] a fine to the court,[94] and degradation from the rank of gentleman.[95] Servants, and others incapable of making restitution in money or in kind, were generally whipped,[96] but theft by a servant from his own master appears to have been punished almost invariably by restitution, which was sometimes exacted in the form of an extension of the servant's term of service.[97] Significantly, when the colonists enacted the theft act of 1646,[98] they not only displaced the magistrates' discretionary power to vary penalties to which they had so long been opposed but adopted the English statutory penalty of treble restitution with which they had been familiar in rural England.[99] Thus, while the early use of restitution as a penalty for theft can be attributed with reasonable assurance to biblical influence, its later statutory prescription is reflective of English ways. The colonial practice in this area again vividly illustrates the interplay of the two cultural forces.

The foregoing account of the role of the Bible in shaping the criminal law of the colony demonstrates that its influence was important but not always controlling. When we turn from the criminal to the civil law of the colony, however, the apparent influence of the Bible is much less clear. Aside from the double portion allowed to the eldest son in cases of intestacy,[100] and the prohibitions against bond slavery and usury,[101] few provisions in the civil law can be attributed to scriptural influences. In one respect, however—namely, in the law of master and servant—those influences are unmistakable.

As already stated, a master was not only privileged, but under a duty, to correct his servant, and the servant might resort to the courts for protection against unjust or excessive correction.[102] One of the provisions of the Body of Liberties, retained without substantial change in the Code of 1648,[103] provided:

If any servants shall flee from the Tiranny and crueltie of their masters to the howse of any freeman of the same Towne, they shall be there protected and susteyned till due order be taken for their relife. Provided due notice thereof be speedily given to their maisters from whom they fled. And the next Assistant or Constable where the partie flying is harboured.

The provision had a sound biblical precedent in Deuteronomy 23:15 and 16:

Thou shalt not deliver unto his master the servant which is escaped from his master unto thee; He shall dwell with thee, even among you, in that place which he shall choose in one of thy gates, where it liketh him best: thou shalt not oppress him.

Characteristically, however, the Massachusetts law expanded the biblical rule by limiting the permissible grounds for self-help to "Tiranny and crueltie," and by ensuring the observance of due process of law through the requirement that proper notice be given to the servant's master and to an officer of the court. The effect of the colonial act was thus to give the oppressed servant an effective means of invoking the jurisdiction of the court to correct abuses, while also protecting the master's contractual rights.

A further provision of the colony laws which had explicit scriptural authority, decreed:

If any man smite out the eye or tooth of his man-servant, or maid servant, or otherwise mayme or much disfigure him, unlesse it be by meere casualtie, he shall let them goe free from his service. And shall have such further recompense as the Court shall allow him.[104]

A corresponding passage in Exodus 21:26–27 states that

. . . if a man smite the eye of his servant, or the eye of his maid, that it perish; he shall let him go free for his eye's sake. And if he smite out his manservant's tooth, or his maidservant's tooth; he shall let him go free for his tooth's sake.

Again the colonists expanded the scriptural formula. Restating verbatim the eye-and-tooth provisions, the Massachusetts law nevertheless used them as the basis for framing a general rule that servants should be freed in any case of maiming or "much" disfigurement, and added the important qualification that the master's act must be deliberate.

Still another of the "Liberties of Servants" enacted in 1641 and incorporated into the Code [105] declared:

> Servants that have served deligentlie and faithfully to the benefitt of their maisters seaven years, shall not be sent away emptie. And if any have been unfaithfull, negligent or unprofitable in their service, notwithstanding the good usage of their maisters, they shall not be dismissed till they have made satisfaction according to the Judgement of Authoritie.

Deuteronomy 15:12–14, had said that servants were to be freed upon completion of seven years' service:

> . . . in the seventh year thou shalt let him go free from thee. And when thou sendest him out free from thee, thou shalt not let him go away empty: Thou shalt furnish him liberally out of thy flock, and out of thy floor, and out of thy winepress: of that wherewith the Lord thy God hath blessed thee thou shalt give unto him.

Once more, and characteristically, the Massachusetts law incorporated inferences drawn from the bare text of Scripture. Only the good and faithful servant was entitled to a provision upon departing his master's service; more importantly, the negligent, unfaithful, or unprofitable servant was deemed obligated to make satisfaction for his shortcomings.

For all the biblical flavor of the colonial master-servant legislation, the Massachusetts courts' procedures for resolving disputes in this area did not greatly differ from contemporary English practices under the Statute of Labourers. In such cases, a single justice of the peace was empowered to "take such order and direction between the said master and his apprentice, as the equity of the cause shall require." [106] Appeal was allowed by either party to the next sessions of the peace, where four justices were empowered to put an end to the indentures between master and apprentice, or "if the default shall be found to be in the apprentice, then the said justices . . . shall cause such due correction and punishment to be ministered unto him, as by their wisdom and discretions shall be thought meet." [107] The Massachusetts rule, which permitted the mistreated servant to flee to the protection of a neighbor, who was thereupon obliged to notify the judicial authorities and the servant's master, had no statutory counterpart in England, but the disposition of such cases by the courts followed much the same pattern on both sides of the ocean. At Salem in 1645, Daniel Rumble, who confessed to striking Henry Hall in the head with a hand hammer, was fined and admonished for "Crueltie in Correcting" his servant.[108] By comparison, in Worcestershire in 1637 a man was presented at the sessions of the peace "for immoderately beating and misusing Owen Brown his apprentice." [109] In 1640 the Court of Assistants, finding that Samuel Hefford had "bene much misused by his master Jonathan Wade," freed him from Wade's service and put him out to another master for the remainder of his time.[110] Similarly, an order of a Somerset quarter sessions in 1630 declared:

Whereas it hath appeared unto this Court that William Culverhouse of Greinton, Blacksmith, hath misused and beaten ffrancis Sheppard *als.* Townsend his apprentice to the great hurt of the said apprentice we doe therefore for preventinge of further mischeife which may happen absolutely free, acquit and discharge the said ffrancis Sheppard the apprentice from his apprenticehood. . . .[111]

Thus, both the English and the Massachusetts systems enforced obedience, respect, and industry on the part of the servant, as well as rough standards of fair and humane treatment on the part of the master. The criteria applied in the colony undoubtedly owed as much to English precedent as to the Bible's texts. At the same time, the substantive similarity that each system bore to biblical precept suggests that Elizabethan legislators, like those of Massachusetts, were also influenced, though to a lesser degree, by the biblical inheritance in which they both shared.

At this point, it must be emphasized that the influence of the Bible apparent upon the face of the 1648 Code was only one, and by no means the most important, of its many manifestations in the colony's law. The spirit of the Bible, in the form of ethical rules and attitudes, no less than its detailed injunctions, was reflected in every phase of colony life; "the matter of the scripture," said Winthrop, "be always a Rule to vs, yet not the phrase." [112] That spirit, expounded in public preaching, and applied through brotherly admonition and communal vigilance, underlay the entire formal structure of the law and ensured its substantial acceptance. English Puritanism, from its earliest days, had been marked by a striking insistence upon its ethical elements. Elizabethan Puritans, accepting Calvin's teaching that every man was predestined to sainthood or damnation and hence utterly powerless to save himself by righteous conduct, nevertheless ordered their lives in accordance with strict moral principles.[113] The same concern over right conduct was likewise characteristic of the Puritans of Massachusetts, whose covenant theology, positing that man's free compliance with the moral law was required by the terms of his covenant with God as the consideration for the gift of grace, ensured that the role of moral obedience in Puritan society had sound theological footing.[114] God had provided, in the moral laws of the Scriptures and in the judicial laws appendant thereto, a rule whereby mankind, with the aid of right reason, could fulfill his covenant by walking in God's way. Puritan theology thus invoked the Bible directly as a guide to human behavior, but reliance upon it was as much a symptom of the longstanding Puritan absorption with moral conduct as it was a cause thereof. The pervasiveness of its influence within the community served to furnish both workable rules for the informal adjustment of neighborhood disputes, and simple standards of righteousness as guides for communal vigilance against sinful conduct.

Biblical influence also made itself felt in the law of the colony through the concept of a fundamental, divinely inspired natural law, which the colony leaders shared with educated Europeans generally. Familiar conceptions of natural and positive law were intimately related in their thinking to specifically Puritan ideas with respect to the threefold division of Mosaic law into its "moral," "judicial," and "ceremonial" aspects.[115] They believed that God's law was either natural or positive. The former embraced those precepts for the guidance of human behavior which could be immediately apprehended, or logically arrived at, by human reason; it was regarded as something instilled in the soul of man by God himself, and hence immutable. Commonly, natural law was equated with the law of reason.[116] "There is nothing in them," wrote William Ames of the Ten Commandments, "but what may be well enjoined from clear reason. . . ."[117]

God's positive law, on the other hand, was that law which was added to the natural law by some special revelation of God. It could be received, but not be arrived at, by reason. Moreover, unlike the natural law, it was not immutable, but "mutable and various according to God's good pleasure." [118] Specifically, God's positive law might, and did, vary between the Old Testament and the New; much of the positive law given to the Jews by God—the so-called "judicial" and "ceremonial" laws—was abrogated by the New Testament dispensation. All of the "ceremonial" laws—the dietary injunctions, the intricate Levitical rules as to worship and the like— were so abrogated because they were viewed as pertaining only to the Israel of the Old Testament. Many of the judicial laws of Moses, on the other hand, so commended themselves to reason that they clearly partook of the eternally binding nature of God's natural, moral law itself, and these laws were not abrogated, but remained in force because, "when the special intrinsical and proper reason of the law is moral, then it always follows that the law itself must needs be moral." [119] This aspect of the law of God—divine injunctions to the children of Israel, proved by their evident reasonableness to be meant to bind no less than the moral law of the Decalogue —was the principal source and justification of the biblical literalism that is evident in the colonial law of Massachusetts. As the Epistle to the Code recites, "These were breif and fundamental principles, yet withall so full and comprehensive as out of them clear deductions were to be drawne to all particular cases in future times." [120]

Finally, aside from the law of God in its natural and positive aspects, there were human laws, enacted by men for their various societies. In the Augustinian view accepted by Christians generally, man's perception of the moral law instilled in him by God was clouded by original sin. Human laws were particular applications of the natural, moral law (insofar as fallen man's reason was capable of perceiving it) to the varying needs of human states. The corruption of man's nature assured that no human law could ever perfectly reflect the moral law; but, to the extent that such human laws did reflect the moral law, they were as binding as natural law itself.

Puritan reconciliation of traditional natural-law ideas with the notion of the threefold nature of the Mosaic law was susceptible to varying emphases. John Cotton, for instance, consistently took the position that most, if not all, of the "judicial" laws of Moses reflected the moral law, and hence were as eternally binding as the Decalogue itself.[121] His emphasis upon obedient acceptance of explicit divine precepts is reflected in the literalism of his proposed code of laws. John Winthrop, on the other hand, emphasized those aspects of the orthodox theory which asserted the dependence of all civil laws upon natural law, and implied that a test of the law of nature was its agreement with the needs of the society to which it is applied.[122] Cotton, with small faith in the ability of man's corrupted reason to frame a just law, stated, "The more any Law smells of man the more unprofitable." [123] Winthrop did not quarrel with the idea that law-making was a divine function or that man's role was solely one of interpretation and application; but to that end, God had given "power and gifts to men to interprett his Lawes: and this belonges principally to the highest Authoritye: in a Common Wealth, and subordinately to other magistrates and Judges accordinge to their severall places." [124]

These ideas of Winthrop's were very similar to those expressed by common-law judges and lawyers who, since the Middle Ages, had affirmed that law was eternal and immutable, and hence could only be found by man but not made.[125] Despite their apparent consignment of a purely ministerial function to the human legislator, the practical effect of these beliefs was enormously to enhance the prestige of human laws. As expressed in the concluding words of the Epistle to the 1648 Code:

. . . when the Authoritie is of God and that in way of an Ordinance *Rom. 13.1* and when the administration of it is according to deductions, and rules gathered from the word of God, and the clear light of nature in civil nations, surely there is no humane law that tendeth to common good (according to those principles) but the same is mediately a law of God, and that in way of an Ordinance which all are to submit unto and that for conscience sake. *Rom. 13. 5.*[126]

One consequence of this type of thinking was to free the framers of the Massachusetts legal system from the necessity of literal adherence to scriptural precepts, by virtue of an idea which was itself biblically inspired and theologically orthodox; it echoes the think-

ing of John Calvin, who believed that all nations had liberty to enact the particular laws that they deemed expedient, and that such
enactments, to the extent that they followed "the perpetual rule of
love," were valid, "however they may differ from the Jewish law
or from each other." [127]

Winthrop, arguing in a recognizably Thomistic vein, but citing
Scripture for support, maintained that "law" and "penalty" were
totally different concepts; the former was eternal and binding, the
latter temporary, and belonging to the magistrates' discretion.[128]
John Cotton, on the other hand, believed that the judicial laws of
the Pentateuch, in which God had further elaborated upon the
moral laws of the Ten Commandments and had prescribed penalties
for their breach, were of a force in civil society equal to that of
the laws of the Decalogue.[129] Neither man, if pressed, would have
denied the validity of the other's view, so that the difference between them emerges as one of emphasis upon two widely held Puritan
beliefs. Winthrop's conception of the office of a magistrate in a
godly society, of which his ideas about "law" and "penalty" were
but one manifestation, was at least as important in the shaping of
the colony law as Cotton's relative literalism. Winthrop's view,
however, implied a place for human reason in the shaping of law
that was notably larger than that ordinarily assigned to it by men
such as Cotton, who reflected a more orthodox Puritan view.

At the same time, and somewhat paradoxically, the use of reason
was a crucial part of even the strictest Puritan literalism. If the
word of God furnished a perfect guide for man's righteous conduct in civil society, and for the laws required for its enforcement,
the fact remained that the Word was knowable only by the instrument of human reason. Not every pronouncement of the Bible was
binding upon all men in all places, and not every manifestation of
God's word was apparent in the Bible's literal text. Moreover, the
Puritans were not bound to apply the same standards in accepting
or rejecting the Bible's nontheological dictates as they applied to its
teachings on church polity, or upon divine grace and redemption.
In theology, the Bible as expounded by learned divines was the
supreme and unquestioned authority. Careful application to revelation was indispensable because the principles of divinity were not
deemed to be in man from nature: "None can learn it by the book

of nature, for there are some lessons in Religion which are not to be found in the book of Creation." [130] It was, however, characteristic of the Puritan mind that in the pursuit of politics, natural science, and every other human art dealing with God's creatures, as opposed to God's revelations, man must look to natural objects, using the Bible not as the fountainhead and authority which it was for theology, but as the confirmation or justification of rational conclusions drawn from natural premises. Even the "science" of ethics was not regarded by the Puritans as contained within the covers of the Bible, although its influence in this sphere was predominant for obvious reasons. Outside the field of divinity, revelation, in Professor Miller's words, only served "incidentally to substantiate and reinforce the patterns of ideas upon which the natural universe had been constructed." [131]

In law, too, aside from the Decalogue, the Bible was not so much binding precedent as enormously persuasive authority, and, like any persuasive force, the extent to which it swayed the lawmaker in a given instance was inversely proportional to the force of the exigencies of circumstance and the reasonableness of the arguments to whose thrust it was opposed. Because the colonists' use of specific biblical precepts in framing laws was selective, those parts of the Scripture that they rejected or ignored are no less significant for an understanding of the role of "revelation" in the law than the parts that they embodied in it. Even when they professed and appeared to be following God's word most literally, they were influenced by their English inheritance, intellectual as well as legal, and by pragmatic or expedient considerations growing out of the conditions of settlement. The same kind of eclecticism that was motivated, guided, and made coherent by the distinctive ethic that marked Puritan scholarship generally is clearly apparent in the shaping of Massachusetts law.[132] For all their reverence for the Scriptures, the colonists almost never enacted literal Bible texts as law before those texts had passed a rigorous logical justification.

The Bible in Massachusetts was an indispensable touchstone, but not the cornerstone, of Puritan legal thinking. Central as was its position in Puritan life and thought, it was only one influence among many in a rich cultural heritage which was quickened by the challenge of new problems in a new land.

X

After English Ways

DILETTANTE speculation at one time ascribed to the eighteenth century the beginnings of the reception of English law in this country. According to this notion, there prevailed in Massachusetts before then "a layman law, a popular, equitable system." [1] That this view is based upon mistaken assumptions should, by this point, have become entirely clear, for the extent to which the civilization of the Bay Colony was fashioned after English ways has been repeatedly emphasized. Countless patterns of life and thought reproduced the cultural heritage of England, and even the colonists' continual recourse to Scripture for guidance in the conduct of their affairs reflected traditions which had developed out of post-Reformation thought. In law, too, as has been substantially suggested, the colonists availed themselves of their antecedent heritage and drew extensively upon practices and procedures of the English judicial system.

To refer in generalities to the colonists' English heritage can give an impression of integration and uniformity that did not in fact exist. English life and culture in the seventeenth century presented no single pattern. Farming practices, architectural styles, town and rural government, even speech, often differed from county to county. The legal system was an unsystematized complex of old and new, and was even more diverse. [2] The ancient courts of the shire and the hundred were still held at their appointed times, and scores of courts leet and courts baron still functioned actively within the decaying manorial system. Every city and borough had its own courts for enforcing its own bylaws and long-established local customs. The ecclesiastical courts had survived the breach with Rome and still exercised jurisdiction not only over matters of church discipline but over morals, marital causes, and the distribution of decedents' estates. Special courts and franchises dealt with the disputes of miners, merchants, and members of the Universities. At the seat of the royal government were the Court of Chancery, the new prerogative courts, and the great courts of common law, which administered justice on a national scale. In due course, most of the local and special courts were to be displaced by those of the crown, but under the first Stuarts that time was still far off, and the pattern of English law, like that of so much else in that age, was one of great diversity.

In the seventeenth century the common law was essentially what it had been in the Middle Ages, that is, the law applied by the king's justices both at Westminster and on circuit. By the time of James I, the courts of common law included King's Bench, Common Pleas, Exchequer, and Exchequer Chamber. These were the central courts of justice, and the law they administered was a national law, common to all England, as contrasted with the special or customary law of particular localities. It was a law that had been secreted in the interstices of the forms of action—debt, replevin, trespass, and the like—devised by the royal chancery to remedy particular kinds of wrongs in particular ways. Suits involving the descent or recovery of land, breach of covenant, trespass, and personal wrongs were but a few of the numerous types of civil actions which came within their jurisdiction. To these central courts also belonged the correction of errors and default of justice in various local courts. Because they possessed this corrective jurisdiction and, more importantly, because they provided a form of justice that was both stable and uniform, backed by the power and prestige of the king's command, they had gradually superseded, but had by no means supplanted, local and seignorial justice.

Most of the administration of criminal justice had been committed initially to the hundreds of justices of the peace who sat locally, either singly or in petty and quarter sessions, throughout the kingdom. As appointees of the crown, they, too, administered king's law, and had jurisdiction over all crimes except treason.

Countless petty crimes and misdemeanors, such as card playing, drunkenness, incontinence, poaching and theft, came regularly before them for punishment. However, felonies and cases presenting special difficulty were usually reserved for the judges of the central courts, who periodically held the assizes on circuit. In addition to their criminal jurisdiction, the justices of the peace supervised the entire machinery of local government and performed a multitude of administrative tasks assigned to them by statute or by executive orders of the central government.

The Stuart age knew other central courts, some of quite recent origin, whose procedures and jurisdictions were very different from those of the courts of common law. The oldest was the Court of Chancery, which, in the name of equity and good conscience, enforced many types of bargains and agreements not cognizable at common law. Here, fraud and forgery might be relieved against, and the rigidities of the common law mitigated, its deficiencies supplied. The essence of its procedure was that it was summary; the essence of its justice was its adaptability. In striking contrast to the common-law courts, Chancery employed no jury, and evidence was received in the form of written affidavits or depositions. By the seventeenth century, its proceedings had become subject to long delays, and its justice was criticized as too discretionary, measured, as John Selden said, by the length of the chancellor's foot. It had come, moreover, to be associated with the instruments of the royal prerogative, and its jurisdiction was one of the chief causes of the controversy which flared up between Lord Chancellor Bacon and Sir Edward Coke.

Twin sister to Chancery was the Court of Star Chamber, born of that reserve of residual justice that remained always with the crown.[3] Like Chancery, the Star Chamber employed no jury and relied for acquittal or conviction upon sworn depositions. It was not a lawless court; indeed, the two chief justices customarily attended its sessions. It could and did strike rapidly and summarily against the rich and the powerful, whose position might otherwise have protected them, and against rioters, conspirators, and perjured jurors; it could and did afford protection to countless copyhold tenants faced with eviction from their lands by the enclosure movements; it could and did provide remedy for libelous and scandalous words.

Under the Stuarts, however, it had earned an infamous reputation because it had become a political instrument for imposing Anglican doctrine upon recalcitrants and for exacting compulsory loans, and that development has obscured much of its good work. If it was a cruel court, inflicting floggings, nose slittings, and ear croppings, its cruelty was less that of the court than of the age, which also witnessed such punishments at the hands of the justices of the peace under statutes of the Tudor age.

In the sixteenth century there had been established provincial councils for Wales and the Marches and for the North, and these exercised in remote parts of the country a jurisdiction that was substantially similar to that of the Star Chamber. Notorious also in the Stuart age was still another prerogative court, created initially to exercise certain of the powers of the crown as supreme head of the Church. This was the High Commission, to which was committed the task of enforcing supremacy and uniformity and suppressing movements and schisms, like Puritanism, which were dangerous to the national Church. In addition, it had supervisory powers over all the ordinary ecclesiastical courts, and it exercised within its ambit a jurisdiction comparable to that of the Star Chamber.

The ecclesiastical courts still possessed, as they had in the Middle Ages, a wide jurisdiction over several types of cases.[4] For present purposes, the most important of these courts were those which the bishop or his archdeacon held in every diocese and which concerned themselves particularly with offenses against religion and morals—blasphemy, swearing, adultery, fornication, witchcraft, absence from church, profaning the Sabbath, haunting taverns, defamation, and the utterance of heretical opinions. Their decrees were supplemented by fines and excommunication and could be enforced by royal writs ordering offenders to be imprisoned until compliance was obtained. Through the procedure of the "inquisition," conducted by the judge on his own information or on the information of apparitors or on common fame, the church courts could inquire into the most private affairs of the king's subjects. The system was an inquisition in fact as well as in name, and differed chiefly from the notorious institution of Spain in that it did not employ torture to extract confession.[5]

In addition to their corrective jurisdiction, the ecclesiastical courts also had jurisdiction over matrimonial and testamentary causes. The former involved such questions as divorce, the validity of a marriage, the legitimacy of issue. To a limited extent, the common-law courts, and Chancery, also dealt with certain of these questions in connection with rights to the possession of land and to its inheritance, and in this respect there was a dual, although not a concurrent, jurisdiction. Over divorce, however, the church courts had virtually complete control. The testamentary aspect of their work included the probate of wills, the distribution of decedents' estates and, to a limited degree, supervision over the conduct of executors and administrators.

Despite ancient and repeated claims, however, the crown was not the sole fountain of justice, and its courts had many rivals. The multitude of special and local courts had extensive and frequently overlapping jurisdiction over crime and civil disputes, either by virtue of an explicit franchise or because the tenacity of custom had not yet given way. Most important, for present purposes, among these local courts and franchises were those of the manor and the borough, which even in the seventeenth century had extraordinary vitality. What the common-law courts had won from them had been filched a little at a time through the writs of *pone, certiorari*, and false judgment, but their victory was far from complete. Large numbers of these local courts were still vigorous and active. Not only did they declare and enforce countless bylaws and ancient customs relating to such matters as land tenure and the use of common fields, but they determined liability for petty crimes, personal injuries, trespasses, and debts, and even exercised equity and probate jurisdiction.[6] Indeed, in the days before the common law had acquired its later ascendancy, and when transportation facilities were limited and travel was time-consuming, the legal center of gravity for the average Englishman was the local court.[7] There he would turn to collect a debt, sue upon a covenant, abate a nuisance, replevy a cow, and, where permitted, offer a will for probate. Moreover, many remedies not provided by the common law, or too expensive to seek in the royal courts, were easily available there, and justice speedy.

These local courts of the manor and borough were those with which the majority of the colonists had been most familiar for the remedying of civil wrongs. Indeed, it seems doubtful whether any except those with legal training had much knowledge of the law of the central courts, except on the criminal and ecclesiastical sides. As already stated, English town and manorial records of the period are replete with the same kind of orders relating to licensing, market regulation and the harboring of strangers that are contained in the colony laws;[8] those records also reveal that, as in Massachusetts, men were punished under local ordinances for idleness, tippling, and unlawful games. Equally striking is the evidence that local judicial procedures were paralleled by procedures in the colony courts and apparently relied upon in the enactments of the General Court. However, until the English custumals and other manuscript records have been studied more exhaustively, it is not possible to state with any great degree of certainty whether the colonists drew upon specific customs in particular localities, or whether their laws reflected a composite recollection or synthesis of many diverse customs. A preliminary search in the archives of London, Norwich, Boston, and Lincoln—areas from which a substantial number of the early settlers came—has provided little evidence of exact borrowing, and therefore suggests that the second alternative is the more likely.[9] On the other hand, it is tempting to suppose that the appearance in the colony of an occasional law known to have existed in a particular locality was directly borrowed. For example, the doctrine of advancements, whereby any who have received their portions in life are excluded from the intestate distribution of a decedent's estate, may have been derived directly from the English practice which Coke refers to as characteristic of distributions in London.[10]

Much of the judicial procedure in the colony courts is reflective of that employed in English manorial courts baron, as revealed in the custumals and in the numerous legal treatises and manuals of the early seventeenth century.[11] These courts frequently referred to the common-law terms for the actions brought before them— debt, trespass, replevin, and the like—but the common-law technicalities of those forms of action appear to have been regularly disregarded; judicial procedure was consequently marked by comparative simplicity and informality, in the interest of doing substantial justice.[12] For example, there was an observable tendency for litigants to rely upon trespass on the case in situations where the common law would have insisted on trespass *de bonis asportatis*.[13] At a single session of a manor court at the end of the sixteenth century, trespass on the case was brought for slander, for taking apples, and for damage to a scythe.[14] The local courts also exercised equitable jurisdiction generally supposed to have been available only in Chancery. Thus, in an action for damages in trespass in the manor of Prescot the plaintiff was denied damages but the defendant ordered to remedy the condition complained of;[15] again, in a plea of debt, the defendant was ordered to pay the plaintiff the sum due, but at a future time;[16] on another occasion, the court gave equitable relief in the form of specific performance.[17]

Disregard of the technicalities of pleading, and reliance on trespass on the case, were characteristic of early Massachusetts procedure.[18] The colonial courts likewise provided relief according to the equities of the case in hand and in disregard of the precise claims of plaintiffs.[19] Again, arbitration of suits in both jurisdictions was common, and its use in the colony may well have been suggested by manorial practice.[20] In short, the colony established a system which in many respects substantially accorded with practices that were widely prevalent in the manorial courts; at the same time, that system was adapted to the settlement of disputes in keeping with ideas of law and fair dealing and without reference to the skill of the pleader. Insofar as civil procedure was concerned, only as much formality was required as would ensure good faith, protect against harassment and inconvenience, and assure to all a rightful opportunity to be heard.

Influential as English local customs appear to have been on Massachusetts civil procedure, that influence is also apparent in the colony's substantive law. For example, the orders and adjudications of the courts leave little doubt that the colonists were influenced by the concept of nuisance as it was understood in the English local courts of the time. In England, a common nuisance was conceived of as an offense against the public, either by the commission of an act which tended to the annoyance of the king's subjects, or by the omission of an act which the common good required. The local records are filled with presentments for the same kinds of offenses that came regularly before the Massachusetts County Courts—eavesdropping, barratry, being a common scold, failing to scour ditches or mend highways [21]—all of which were comprehended within the concept of nuisance and required no specific statutory prohibition to be punishable. Moreover, nuisance jurisdiction was notably elastic and permitted inquiry into and regulation of novel kinds of anti-social conduct as the need arose. Consequently, the English local courts, like those in the colony, enjoyed a wide latitude in defining offenses and in determining punishments. However, it seems clear that they did not exercise the kind of arbitrary justice of which the Massachusetts freemen complained. On the contrary, within each community, the custumals or bylaws, or both, appear to have delineated punishable offenses with considerable minuteness and to have prescribed known penalties for their commission.[22] In the area of petty misdemeanors, therefore, the colonists had been accustomed to a marked degree of certainty, much of which resulted from the fact that the rules, and the penalties for their infraction, had generally been reduced to writing. Thus, although many of the practices of the local courts on the private law side were readily accepted by magistrate and freeman alike because conformable to what they had known and to what right conduct and fair dealing required, the magistrates' attempt to import discretionary justice into an area where certainty had been the practice in England violated inherited sentiments and was therefore strongly resisted as an encroachment upon customary liberties.

Of the instances of the influence of English local custom on Massachusetts law, few are more striking than the rules with respect to inheritance and recording. In marked contrast to English common law, whereby intestate realty passed to the eldest son by primogeniture, the colony laws provided that when a parent died intestate, that is, without a will, all the children were entitled to share in both the real and personal property, and the eldest son was to have a double portion.[23] This latter provision for the eldest son was apparently made pursuant to the Book of Deuteronomy and has led to conjectures that the intestacy law was essentially Mosaic. However, a comparison of the two systems on the basis of a seventeenth century exposition of the Hebrew law by John Selden almost certainly eliminates the possibility.[24] Conceivably, the Massachusetts scheme was derived from Plymouth Colony, where partible inheritance, including the double portion, existed as early as 1627.[25] However, its ultimate source appears to have been in English local customs under which, in numerous manors and towns, intestate land had been divided among all the children of a decedent.[26] Both the Pilgrims and the Bay colonists had been familiar with these customs, for, significantly, instances of partibility are found in districts from which both groups of settlers came, notably in the manors of eastern England.[27] The custom also prevailed elsewhere, for example, in Cambridge, Dorset, Gloucestershire, Leicestershire, Middlesex, and Nottinghamshire, not to mention other counties.[28] Partible inheritance was not confined to manors, but appears in many boroughs and towns, such as Dover, Exeter, Ispwich, Torksey, and Wareham.[29] Although much of the evidence of the existence of such customs is derived from mediaeval sources, they were well known in the sixteenth and seventeenth centuries and even persisted as late as the nineteenth.[30] Under most of these customs, land descended equally to all children, but in some places it was restricted to sons.[31] One instance has been found of a double portion for the eldest.[32] The details varied greatly from place to place, but the underlying idea of partibility maintained itself with extraordinary tenacity.[33]

It is not, of course, to be supposed that the instinct to imitate or reproduce the familiar explains the reliance on local customs in framing and developing the Massachusetts law of intestacy. The process of enactment, and particularly of revision for codification, was too selective and too well thought out for that to have been the case. In the absence of reported debates, or of drafts of legislation, it can only be supposed that ideas of economic equality, evidenced, for example, by the method of allotting land or, more probably, that practical considerations, dictated the scheme of inheritance. Because of the poor soil and configuration of the terrain, New England farming was necessarily a cooperative enterprise, requiring many hands. Hired help was scarce, after the initial terms of apprenticeship ended, and the cost, as we know from Winthrop himself, became prohibitive during the depression of the early 1640's.[34] Moreover, primogeniture would not only have encouraged the growth of accumulated estates but, more importantly, would have resulted in the impoverishment of younger children in an economy in which land was the chief form of wealth. The alternatives of seeking industrial work or other commercial opportunities were not initially available in the sparsely settled communities of Massachusetts as they had been in England. Indeed, in the next century, when the intestacy law was challenged before the Privy Council,[35] it was expressly argued that the foundation and growth of the colony depended upon equality of descent and that if younger children "were to receive no share at all of those lands which they themselves have cultivated, all future culture must cease, and the unsubdued part of the Colony eternally remain, as it is, a wilderness. . . ."[36]

A second striking example of the influence of English local custom can be seen in the colony law of 1640 providing for the recording of deeds and mortgages and their acknowledgment before a public officer.[37] The act provided that a conveyance not so recorded should be ineffective except as against the grantor and his heirs, and it empowered magistrates to commit to prison without bail any grantor refusing to acknowledge a conveyance.[38] In spite of numerous revisions, the act afforded the essential basis of the present-day Massachusetts law.[39] Although, as in the case of the intestacy law, there is a possibility that certain features of the Massachusetts recording system were derived from a Plymouth act of 1636 and ultimately, perhaps, from Dutch practices which the Pilgrims had known in Holland,[40] the Bay Colony as early as 1634 had required that all allotments and transfers of land be entered in books of possession to be kept by each town.[41] Entry therein assured legal priority to grantees, and that order was therefore the genesis of the recording system later developed by the 1640 act.

Available evidence suggests that English borough and manorial practices provided the precedent, either directly or indirectly, for recording. England had no general system of land-title registration,[42] but since the Middle Ages there had prevailed in many English boroughs a practice of recording conveyances, dower rights, leases, and wills on the court records or on books and rolls kept for the purpose. Such local customs had been jealously guarded and were not by any means defunct in the late sixteenth and early seventeenth centuries.[43] Along with recording was a practice in many boroughs of requiring that a deed be acknowledged in open court or before the mayor or other town officer.[44] A similar custom was observed in many English manors. In some parts of England, it was customary to enroll indentures before justices of the peace.[45] Unquestionably, most of the colonists were familiar with such practices and the security provided thereby in the local communities from which they had come; in this connection it is pertinent to recall that Governor Bellingham, who sat on many of the colony law committees, had been recorder of Boston, in old England, where recording also obtained.[46]

The purpose of the colony's recording system was threefold: to publicize and to maintain government control over land transfers and thus to help preserve the social and economic unity of the towns; to provide evidence of title in the event that the instrument were lost or destroyed; and to guarantee title to the recording grantee against subsequent or fraudulent transfers. The recording system, therefore, was in part an instrument of government policy, but it also fulfilled a need which many of the colonists felt for assuring titles to land. Those who came from the north and east of England had particularly felt the effects of the agricultural revolution of the sixteenth century. The characteristic tenure in these districts was the copyhold, and it was upon the copyholder that the heaviest blow fell when the traditional agricultural organization was upset by the enclosure movement. The small freehold cultivator also suffered therefrom and was frequently driven off the land, sometimes by the rise in prices, sometimes by the scarcity of agricultural produce occasioned by the substitution of sheep farming for crop raising, sometimes by direct eviction. Agricultural employment had been diminished with the graziers' consolidation of their holdings, so that men were left destitute and forced to wander about the countryside or to migrate to the towns. Those who sought work without permission were punished; those who found no work were sent to the stocks or harried as vagrants from town to town.[47]

The security of copyholders who were not driven from their lands was frequently tenuous and precarious.[48] Some legal protection against their landlords was afforded by the court rolls establishing their tenancies;[49] some they had in the Court of Chancery.[50] Yet the records of cases which came before the Star Chamber and the Court of Requests continually emphasize their insecurity.[51] It was there-

fore altogether natural, both with respect to copyholders and free-
holders, that the enclosure movement, the rise of prices, and the
widespread misery attendant thereon should create among many of
the Massachusetts colonists, as among those at Plymouth, "a deep
and abiding distrust of the ancient tenure; a noticeable distaste for
the new economic as against the old customary rents; a suspicion of
leases by which the new system of rents were put into effect, a
great solicitude for the recorded title or written evidence of right
in the land; and finally a nostalgia for the one type of landholding,
the freehold, where the risks of tenure were slight." [52] Thus, the
establishment of a general recording system undoubtedly owed as
much to the countryman's attitude, developed out of the insecurity
and uncertainties of several generations, as it did to the importance
which the colonists attached to written records and to their
familiarity with record keeping in English local communities.

The influence of local traditions, although of a different sort, is
forcefully illustrated by the machinery and administration of
criminal law, which in its broad outlines followed English patterns.
These were not, however, the patterns of the customs of the manor
and borough but of king's law, uniformly prescribed throughout
England by numerous parliamentary statutes but administered
locally and with considerable flexibility by the justices of the peace.
These justices, or magistrates as they were also called, were com-
missioned by the crown to maintain the king's peace in the counties
where they resided, and they were vested with wide discretionary
powers in the exercise of their duties. [53] The Massachusetts magistrates were their counterparts in America.

Reference has already been made to the order by which the
assistants invested several of their number with the "power that
justices of peace hath in England for reformacion of abuses and
punishing of offenders." [54] As time went on, it appears to have been
assumed that every assistant upon election was entitled to bear the
title of magistrate and to exercise the powers of English magistrates
insofar as appropriate to the colony's needs. These men rigorously
examined persons suspected of crime, administered oaths to accusers
and witnesses and took their depositions, committed the accused to
custody or admitted him to bail, after the manner of the English
justice of the peace. [55] They also exercised the broad power, so essen-

tial a part of the commission of the peace in England, to bind persons to good behavior by requiring them to execute recognizances, breach of which resulted in citations for contempt and forfeiture of the stipulated surety.[56]

Punishments inflicted by the colonial magistrates were very similar to those imposed by their English counterparts. Fines, whippings, multiple damages, and terms in the stocks were common and standard punishments, and even ear cropping and branding were not unheard of.[57] An examination of the quarter sessions records demonstrates that the extensive employment of public humiliation and confession, which is commonly ascribed to the Puritan insistence upon humbling the will as a condition precedent to repentance and reform, had close counterparts in contemporary practices of English magistrates. In Salem, in 1640, an apprentice was ordered whipped and sent before the congregation of the church "with a paper writt and sett vpon his head for breking a hous, stealing, etc. on the Lord's day;"[58] a Yorkshire girl convicted of stealing a felt hat was sentenced by an English magistrate in 1609 "to be whipped and set in the Stocks at Malton, with a paper on her head, &c."[59] A Salem woman was ordered in 1645 "to sit half an hour next lecture day at Hampton and . . . to make public acknowledgment of her slanderous speeches of Susan Perkings and Lidia Pebody;"[60] a Nottinghamshire scold was sentenced in 1622 to make public confession of her fault to Bridgett the wife of Robert Hardy on the next Lord's day "at the Church Style" in the presence and hearing of the rector and the whole congregation.[61] A Gloucester tailor, convicted of converting cloth to his own use, was sentenced by a Massachusetts court in 1652 to make treble restitution and to acknowledge his crime at a public meeting in Salem;[62] a Yorkshire laborer who stole sixpence in money and a pair of stockings was sentenced at Richmond in 1610 "that he shall publicly, in the Church of the place where he lives, repeat distinctly after the Curate, . . . his confession of and repentance for his crime. . . ."[63]

In the same way that English statutes conferred certain powers upon a single justice, others upon two justices, and reserved still others to the justices of the county assembled in their quarter sessions,[64] the colonial laws conferred substantial jurisdiction upon a single magistrate, and specified those powers that were to be exercised by two magistrates and by magistrates assembled in court.[65] In England, the justices of the peace were of two classifications: those of the quorum and those not of the quorum. Ordinarily, the quorum included those justices of a county who were possessed of comparatively greater knowledge of the legal and administrative duties of the commission of the peace, and were hence more nearly professional than were the justices not of the quorum.[66] Many of the statutes which conferred powers upon English justices acting out of sessions required that one of them be of the quorum.[67] The English distinction between types of justices also had a colonial counterpart in the distinction between magistrates and commissioners. The latter, "persons of worth," were appointed "from time to time . . . by the General Court" at the nomination of the towns of their counties; they exercised all the powers of a magistrate in the County Court; but it was provided "that no Court be kept without one Magistrate at the least," [68] so that apparently these commissioners, as distinct from the commissioners for small causes, had no power to act outside sessions of the County Courts.[69]

The colonial magistrates and commissioners, sitting in the quarterly sessions of the County Courts, like the justices of the peace in their quarter sessions, tried before a petty jury the criminal cases brought before them pursuant to indictment or presentment.[70] Like the quarter sessions,[71] both the County Courts and the Court of Assistants summarily punished contempt in open court, and punished other contempts upon indictment.[72] These similarities of function are further illustrated by the striking resemblances between the quarter sessions records and those of the colony courts. The cases which have been referred to relating to disputes between masters and servants illustrate that the procedures for dealing with cases of this type were much alike in the two jurisdictions. In Massachusetts a rebellious servant, or one who ran away, was ordered whipped [73] or to serve additional time;[74] in England, similar penalties were imposed by the justices of the peace, who had broad discretion in the punishment of apprentices under the Statute of Labourers.[75] Both jurisdictions punished masters for excessive correction or cruelty to servants,[76] and in flagrant cases canceled their indentures.[77] Moreover, both the quarter sessions and the colonial courts had extensive and similar administrative powers which have been summarized at an earlier point.[78] The two types of courts differed chiefly in the fact that the latter heard civil as well as criminal cases, whereas the English justices of the peace had no substantial jurisdiction in civil cases except insofar as disputes might lead to a breach of the peace or require arbitration.[79]

The colonists' substantial adoption of the machinery of criminal justice as administered by the English justices of the peace was apparently deliberate. It was what they were used to, and, as the system was developed initially in Massachusetts, it provided wide latitude for the exercise of magisterial discretion; consequently it comported well with the leaders' ideas about the functions of government and law. The fact that Winthrop, one of the principal architects of the judicial system, had been a justice of the peace in England, and was thoroughly conversant with the scope of their duties, assured that the machinery would work efficiently as well as in a manner to which the colonists had been accustomed. Indeed, it worked even more successfully in the colony, partly because the community was small and supervision by the central government easier, and partly because the magistrates saw to it that their orders would not be continually thwarted, as in England, by the use of prerogative writs.[80]

The adoption in the colony of the procedures and practices of the justices of the peace necessarily presupposed the introduction of another type of English law; namely, the numerous statutes which were the source of the justices' powers and which it was their duty to know. The statutes—acts of parliament having broad and general, though typically detailed, application—had become increasingly significant in the sixteenth century. Those of Elizabeth had effected profound innovations in the structure of local government, provided the manner in which the poor should be cared for and imposed conditions on the economic and even the personal conduct of her subjects. The execution of much of the statutory law was committed in the first instance to the justices of the peace and the local officials whom they supervised. The records bear ample testimony to the colonists' familiarity with such statutes, which were collected and epitomized and presumably available to them in numerous contemporary manuals and abridgements.[81]

Sumptuary and other regulatory laws enacted in the reign of

James I and enforceable by the justices of the peace included prohibitions against tippling, tobacco smoking, profane swearing, and
Sunday sports. These had their counterparts in the early orders of
the assistants and, later, in the enactments of the General Court.
The first price regulation in Massachusetts, for example, set maximum prices on the basis of those prescribed in England, plus four
pence.[82] The apprenticeship system in the colony was clearly imitative of the English system under the Statute of Artificers and the
Poor Law of 1601,[83] and, as stated, disputes between masters and
servants were handled in much the same way as that prescribed by
the English Statute of Labourers.[84] One provision of the Massachusetts theft act of 1646, relating to the robbing of orchards and
gardens, appears both from its language and its substance to have
been modeled on an Elizabethan statute whose enforcement was
likewise committed to the justices of the peace.[85] Colony legislation
prescribing treble damages for what may be termed "fringe" property crimes, falling in the penumbra between larceny and trespass,
appears likewise to have been modeled upon Elizabethan and
Jacobean statutory offenses.[86]

Other English statutes of general application were certainly
known to the colonists, notably Winthrop and Ward, who had
been trained at the Inns of Court. Compendia of the statutes were
vademecums of all English lawyers, and one or more of these were
unquestionably available in early Massachusetts. It was on the basis
of Pulton's collection that Joseph Hills revised the draft of the 1648
Code,[87] and at least two of the colony laws other than those just
referred to were clearly based upon or copied from English
statutes.[88] Of these, the most striking is that relating to the tanning
and leather trades, which, when compared with its English counterpart in a statute of James I, demonstrates that the colonists copied
verbatim several of its provisions. Moreover, conveyancing formulae
in early Massachusetts deeds indicate familiarity with Henry VIII's
Statute of Uses and presupposed that it was in force in the colony.[89]
In addition to such evidence of the availability of statutory compila-
tions, estate inventories reveal that several of the colonists had
copies thereof. For example, Governor Dudley owned an abstract
of penal statutes;[90] William Tyng, a Boston merchant, owned a copy
of the statutes at large and a book entitled "Office of Executors;" [91]

and John Harvard's gift to the College included a collection of English statutes published in 1587 and a copy of Lambarde's manual for justices of the peace known as the *Eirenarcha*.[92]

Only a small part of the national law of England was contained in statute books by the early seventeenth century. The bulk of it was the common law, enshrined in the law reports, in form books, in abridgements, and in standard treatises such as those of Littleton and Coke. How many of these texts were at the disposal of the colonists in the early period is not known, but the available deeds, wills, and other documents, to say nothing of the 1648 Code, amply demonstrate that the common law was among the important elements in their legal heritage. Several of the surviving deeds created estates for life, in fee simple and fee tail, as well as remainder and reversionary interests.[93] More than one will contains such technical expressions as "die without issue" and a "charge on a devise" and provides for cross-limitations.[94] The Code itself abounds in such common-law terms as barratry, chattels real and personal, escheat, frank-tenement, hereditaments, nonsuit, primer seisin, reversion, remainder, seisin, specialty, talesmen, and wardship. Such terms suggest that the common-law training acquired at the Inns of Court by Winthrop and Ward can hardly have been forgotten, and seems certainly to have been drawn upon in the course of their extensive service on the successive law committees that prepared the Code of 1648.

The instruments which the colonists used in their commercial transactions also show a practical familiarity both with English law and with the customs of the Law Merchant.[95] Careful study of those instruments, nearly all of which are contained in two collections compiled by Thomas Lechford and William Aspinwall,[96] reveal striking similarities to the models contained in contemporary English formbooks.[97] Colonial mortgages, as in England, were fee simple conveyances with a defeasance provision, and contain the familiar salutatory, granting, and habendum clauses.[98] Sales of ships in both countries were accomplished by conveyances drafted in the same manner as fee simple conveyances of land.[99] Bills of exchange and bills of lading are generally similar in content and purpose,[100] and the surviving examples of other types of obligations are virtually identical with those used in England.[101] Mortgages, in particular, followed English phraseology in the defeasance clauses.[102] It has not been possible, however, on the basis of the existing instruments, to ascertain which of the English mercantile or conveyancers' hand-books were available in the colony, chiefly because the colonial formulae were seldom stereotyped and were nearly always adjusted to the needs of the particular situation. However, it may be said with confidence that if a working knowledge of, and a capacity for adapting, accepted techniques is a standard of competency, that of the early Massachusetts scriveners must be rated as excellent.

Notwithstanding the great importance of local law, both customary and that administered by the justices of the peace, in the daily lives of most Englishmen of the seventeenth century, the procedures and even the doctrines of the common law were far from being unknown in rural England. Even the custumals of manors prescribed that certain pleas should follow the process of the common law.[103] The itinerant justices who traveled from county to county to hold the assizes and to hear cases under the nisi prius system were nearly always judges of the central courts who took with them and applied the common law.[104] Their appearances were the occasions for great gatherings of the local inhabitants, who watched with fascination the machinery of royal justice in motion. The working of the circuit system tended, as Holdsworth says, to strengthen the belief that the maintainance of a supreme law was the great aim of government and "caused the idea of the supremacy of the law to be no mere technicality of the lawyers or abstraction of the philosophers, but an article in political creed, and a part of the political instinct of all Englishmen." [105]

The extent to which the Massachusetts colonists drew generally upon the common law is strikingly illustrated by the provision for dower. In England, since the days of the Norman kings, the common law had assured to a wife surviving her husband certain rights in his property after his death.[106] Those rights had varied both in character and in extent, but typically they were rights in land.[107] In days when real property was the chief form of wealth, the practice of allowing the widow a share in her deceased husband's lands afforded her after his death the protection and means of livelihood which she required. The rule early became established that the widow was entitled to an estate for her life in one-third of each parcel of land of which he had been solely and beneficially seised during the marriage and to which issue of the marriage might by a possibility succeed.[108] That interest was known as dower. Dower rights attached upon marriage, unless the husband had made an adequate settlement on his bride beforehand, but once those rights had attached she could not be deprived of them by his will or by the sole act of the husband during the marriage. She was entitled to dower in addition to the land or other property he might leave her by will and to whatever personal property she might be entitled to if he died intestate.[109] She might release her rights of her own volition, and she could be barred from them if she deserted her husband or if he divorced her for adultery.[110] After the death of her husband, she was entitled to have her third or thirds assigned to her by metes and bounds by the husband's heir or other tenant of the land.[111] If no assignment were made, she was entitled to a writ of dower to enforce her rights.[112] The interest was free from the claims of the husband's creditors.

Such, generally, were the rights of a widow in the real property of her deceased husband in seventeenth century England. The extent to which analogous rights were recognized in Massachusetts in the early years is not entirely clear,[113] but in 1647 provision for dower was expressly made.[114] The principal provisions of the act were as follows: The benefits of the act extended to every woman in the colony who was either married and living with her husband, or married and not living with him as a result of his consent or inevitable providence, or divorced and she was the innocent party; the rights conferred by the act accrued upon marriage; the widow's interest was an estate for her life, after the death of her husband, in one-third of all the realty of which her husband had been seised, in an estate of inheritance, at any time during the marriage; although the estate did not come into her possession until her husband was dead, she could not be deprived of her inchoate right during the marriage by any act of her husband, or by anyone claiming under him, unless she consented thereto; her interest might be barred only by a jointure before marriage, by desertion on her part, or by divorce when she was the guilty party; her estate was free from the claims of the husband's creditors; upon her husband's death, her estate was to be assigned to her by metes and bounds by her husband's heir or other person interested; if the lands were not assigned to her within a month after her demand, she was entitled to a "writ of dower" to enforce her rights.

The resemblance of the provisions of this act to common-law dower are so obvious that no discussion is required to prove its source. The only noteworthy difference is that, in Massachusetts, contrary to English law, dower attached to reversions and remainders of which, as future estates, there could be no seisin under the common law.[115] It should be emphasized that the rights accorded the widow in Massachusetts were quite distinct from English local customs, notably that of freebench recognized in manorial courts, and which in this area appear to have had no influence on the Bay Colony. Freebench was the widow's customary right to a share of the realty of which her husband had died seised, and hence in the nature of a right of succession,[116] a survival perhaps from an age when a wife may have been her husband's heir.[117] At common law, however, the widow's right to one-third of the realty attached, as in Massachusetts, to all the lands of which her husband had been seised during marriage; and, since her right was one of which she could not be deprived by act of the husband, it was not a right of succession.

Examples of wholesale importation into the colony of common-law doctrine, as in the case of dower, are remarkably few. Nevertheless, as Professor Plucknett has observed, by 1648 there had been a voluntary reception of a considerable amount of common law, but its doctrines had been tempered or adapted to what was deemed suitable or expedient for the colony. If English terms were used for process and for types of legal actions, the technicalities thereof were not insisted upon, so that, as already emphasized, judicial procedure was much simplified and judgments more speedily rendered than in England. One of the most significant features of the common law, reflected both in the Code and in proceedings in the courts, was the guarantee of due process—open procedure, the opportunity to be heard, jury trials, and decisions according to precedent—for which the English common-law courts had come to stand.[118] Primarily, it was the deputies for whom these ideals had the greatest force, and it was they who stood out for, and helped foster, the Massachusetts ideal of a government of laws and not of men.

The precise extent to which other forms of English law—that of Chancery, Star Chamber, and the ecclesiastical courts—influenced the law of the colony must for the present remain somewhat conjectural. Equity jurisdiction was expressly provided for, but it was to be exercised in the course of an action at law rather than in a separate suit, as in England.[119] The use of the bill of review in connection with new trials after newly discovered evidence [120] suggests, although it does not prove, familiarity with Chancery practice, which permitted such a bill when new matters of fact had emerged after entry of a decree.[121] The convictions of Phillip Ratliffe and the harsh punishments which the assistants inflicted upon him and upon other dissidents for seditious speeches, slander of authority, and the like are very reminiscent of Star Chamber proceedings.[122] These were precisely the types of offenses of which that court took cognizance.[123] Indeed, in words that might have come from the lips of Winthrop himself, the Star Chamber had announced that all men should "take heede how they complayne in wordes againste any magistrate, *for they are gods*." [124] Moreover, it is significant that in the Ratliffe case, at least, the conviction, as under Star Chamber procedure, was based upon a "particular," or deposition, "proued vpon oath." [125] In any event, the advantages of the summary and flexible jurisdiction of the English prerogative courts for purposes of controlling active disaffection cannot have been lost on the magistrates, whose preference for the formulation of law through executive discretion has been the subject of extended discussion in earlier chapters.[126]

The influence of the English ecclesiastical courts is far clearer than that of Chancery or the Star Chamber, and has already been referred to in connection with the colony's supervision of religious life and moral conduct.[127] That all who emigrated to Massachusetts, particularly those who were Puritan, were familiar with one or more aspects of the law applied by the church courts can scarcely be doubted,[128] and the assumption of that jurisdiction by the magistrates and by the elders of the churches was largely an organizational change. It was a change, however, that comported with early Puritan agitation in England to transfer the entire jurisdiction of the ecclesiastical courts to the civil arm of government, largely because of their leniency in dealing with moral offenses.[129] Pursuant to English ecclesiastical practices, but with greater vigor and severity, the magistrates began at once not only to punish men for adultery, blasphemy, false opinions, drunkenness, fornication, schism, slander, and swearing,[130] but to order men to resume their conjugal duties. Among the sentences imposed were public confession and the wearing of papers to describe their offenses.[131]

Insistence upon public confession or penance was an even more common practice in the ecclesiastical courts than in the English quarter sessions. In the diocese of Ely, between July, 1954, and November, 1596, public confessions of sin were made before the congregation by at least four adulteresses, by two couples who had committed fornication before marriage, by a man who had harbored an adulteress in his house, by assorted Sabbath breakers, by a woman convicted of being "a pratlinge gossip goinge from one howse to another to tell tailes and lies," and by another who had "bene a scoulder and a slaunderous person and a sower of strife amongest my neighbors to the breach of Charity." [132] One of the adulteresses was further sentenced to stand for three hours in the bull ring in Cambridge on the next Saturday,

cloathed in a white sheete downe to the grounde, with a white wand in her hand, haveinge papers pinned, the one vpon her breste and the other vpon her backe, declaringe her abhominable offence . . . desiringe the people that so shall behould her to pray to God for her & to forgive her. . . .[133]

The act books of the ecclesiastical courts of the Archdeaconry of Essex for the late sixteenth and early seventeenth centuries likewise reveal numerous instances of public confession of sin,[134] and, like the justices of the peace, they sentenced men to wear papers. Thus a delinquent was ordered ". . . to stand in the marquet place of Brentwood in a whitt sheat, when the people are most there, with a paper uppon his hed & the detection written in the same; and in lik case in his parish church." [135]

In addition to assuming punitive and corrective jurisdiction over matters of religion and morals, the colony courts also undertook to deal with probate, intestate distribution, and divorce. Over the first two, the church courts had primary jurisdiction insofar as personal property was concerned and except as local custom decreed otherwise; over divorce they had a near monopoly. That the colonists were conversant with ecclesiastical jurisdiction over these matters does not appear open to doubt. Certainly, the more prosperous in the community were familiar with the testamentary and probate jurisdiction of the church courts to which they were obliged to repair for the appointment of executors and administrators of estates, to submit estate inventories, and to apply for decrees establishing the rights of distributees in the personal property of a decedent. With the assumption of testamentary and probate jurisdiction by the Court of Assistants, and later by the County Courts,[136] the records began to show evidence of some familiarity with ecclesiastical law, such as appointments of personal representatives *de bonis non* and *cum testamento annexo*.[137] However, in the administration of estates, the colonial courts insisted little on formalities beyond requiring the appointment of an executor or administrator and requiring inventories for the prevention of fraud. Unsigned, unwitnessed, and even oral wills were accepted by the County Courts, whose primary concern was to discover the intent of the deceased.[138] If acceptable testimony were not forthcoming, the more mechanical rules of intestate distribution were applied.[139] Even in this event, the colony courts, as distinguished from the courts of the archdeacon in England, exercised considerable discretion and took into account the needs of a widow and of minor children according to the size and nature of the estate.[140] Contrary to English practice, which, generally speaking, assigned jurisdiction over freehold lands to the common-law courts and over personal property to the church courts, in Massachusetts the two types of property were administered together, as was to become the general practice in the United States.[141]

The extent to which numerous features of the colonists' varied legal heritage were transplanted to Massachusetts demonstrates that the law was neither rude nor untechnical and that it did not operate as a popular equitable system under crude frontier conditions.[142] Obviously, the totality of that heritage was not, and could not have been, transplanted. None of the colonists, and few if any Englishmen of their day, were familiar with every aspect of English law and justice, which was too diverse and too specialized to be mastered completely by any individual. At most, those few of the colony leaders who had been trained at the Inns of Court, or had served as justices of the peace, were conversant with the main doctrines and procedures of the common law and with the statutes. They and others were also familiar, at firsthand or through legal manuals of the time, with the customary law of the manor and borough courts. Moreover, much of the law of England was ill suited or unnecessary for the relatively simple community of the Bay Colony. Trusts and elaborate settlements are phenomena of a moneyed economy, and it was to be some years before they made their appearance in Massachusetts.[143] Similarly, maritime and commercial law were of no great significance in the early years, but when in 1650 the need therefor had become apparent the General Court promptly ordered a copy of Malynes' *Lex Mercatoria* to the end that whatever was appropriate to the colony's needs should be extracted therefrom.[144] In this way, still another segment of the English legal heritage was made a part of the colony laws.

Even the colonists' adoption of English legal rules with which they were familiar was not a process of slavish reproduction. On the contrary, the process was selective and carefully planned; indeed, it was so selective, and the process of syncretization so carefully thought out, that in many areas of the law it is impossible to determine the precise sources upon which they drew. Undoubtedly, had they wished, the cumbersome machinery of the common law could have been substantially duplicated by such men as Winthrop and Ward. Instead, as the history of the first two decades amply demonstrates, they chose to construct out of their varied heritage a legal system which accorded with their ideas of fair dealing, good faith, and certainty, to the end that the "due form of government" could be achieved.

Both the magistrates and the deputies were well aware, despite their assertions to the contrary in the famous Declaration of 1646,[145] that the Massachusetts legal system was not that of the common law. Dissatisfaction with various aspects of the common law, particularly with its delays and its technical pitfalls, and distrust of lawyers as a class, were constantly voiced by Puritan writers under the early Stuarts and later in the Interregnum,[146] and it is therefore hardly surprising—or even inconsistent—that the colonists viewed some aspects of the common law with hostility and others with veneration. They were also aware that their system departed in numerous ways from the general standard, set by the charter, that they should make no laws contrary to those of England. That standard, however, was not so narrow as has frequently been supposed, and certainly did not prescribe a wholesale introduction of the common law. More importantly, from the colonists' standpoint, the Separatist principles upon which the colony had been founded had fostered ideas both of the independence and of the dignity of their body politic, and there was great alarm both in Plymouth and in Massachusetts when it was learned that William Vassal, of Scituate, had petitioned parliament that the colonists "might be wholly governed by the laws of England." [147] The magistrates and freemen alike saw themselves as engaged, not merely in establishing a subordinate adjunct of the English political and legal system, but in bringing into being a new commonwealth, having its own powers and prerogatives, and charged with a holy mission that demanded appropriate political and legal institutions. In a letter that the General Court wrote to Edward Winslow in connection with his appearance before the Commissioners for Foreign Plantations, it was stated that the colonists claimed "not as by commission, but by a free donation of absolute government." [148]

The "absolute government" which the colonists believed that they had been granted must, in their view, be exercised so as to further the commonwealth's holy purposes. As John Cotton observed, "it is one thing" for saints gathered in churches "to submit unto what they have noe calling to reforme: another thing, voluntarily to ordeyne a forme of government which . . . is expressly contrary to rule." For ". . . when a commonwealth hath liberty to mould his owne frame . . . It is better that the commonwealth be fashioned to the setting forth of Gods house, which is his church: than to accommodate the church frame to the civill state." [149] If the colonists were obligated to frame a government suited to the performance of the colony mission, they were equally obligated, and thus, in their view, morally empowered, to frame laws similarly suited to the commonwealth's needs and purposes. Hence, it was easy for Winthrop to declare that the colony government was not like that of a corporation but was "in the nature of a parliament," [150] and for the General Court, at the time of the Child Remonstrance, to declare that "our allegiance binds us not to the laws of England any longer than while we live in England." [151]

Viewed in its entirety, the process of acceptance, rejection, and adaptation of the colonists' English legal heritage was reflective of their social, political, and spiritual life, and of the interest conflicts engendered therein. Although the growth of the law, in its early stages at least, was substantially after English ways, revealing much of the image of seventeenth century England, the process was one of syncretizing, on the basis of reason and experience, traditional English ideas with the precepts of the Bible, with a view always to the urgency of fulfilling the dictates of God's special commission to His commonwealth.

XI

~

Toward New Horizons

"Noe lawes," announced the royal charter to the Massachusetts Bay Company, "shall be made contrarie to the laws of this our realme of England," yet within a short time after the founding of the colony the literal terms of this as well as other solemn injunctions of that instrument were deliberately disregarded. Although much of the colony's law developed in the first two decades comported with that of England, conscious repudiation and modification thereof was one of the signal aspects of the path of the law in early Massachusetts. Departure from English norms, however, was not limited to adoption of biblical precedent. Impelled by their determination to shape the legal structure in accordance with the purposes for which the colony had been founded and with the emerging needs of the new community, the colony leaders radically altered accepted English practices and procedures and, in addition, developed numerous legal rules entirely unknown to English law.

In the beginning, the colonists moved with caution because they were fearful of attracting the unfavorable attention of the English government.[1] Among the principal objections to reducing the colony laws to writing was that the publication of written laws would reveal colonial divergences which would be viewed as violations of the provisions of the charter. In the well known passage already quoted from Winthrop's *Journal*, the Governor insisted that the best means of retaining freedom in the framing of the colony's law was to raise up laws by custom and to adopt such rules without formal enactment and publication.[2] In 1646, however, when the government of Charles I was enmeshed in the English Civil War, the General Court openly declared that

. . . our allegiance binds us not to the laws of England any longer than while we live in England, for the laws of the parliament of England reach no further, nor do the king's writs under the great seal go any further. . . .[3]

This declaration, on its face an open repudiation of the injunction of the charter, was rationalized on the ground that

we have no laws . . . contrary to the law of God and of right reason, which the learned in [the laws of England] have anciently and still do hold forth as the fundamental basis of their laws.[4]

The position of the General Court was not entirely disingenuous. The charter provision established general standards only. They were the standards of Englishmen, as opposed, for example, to the standards of Turks. The charter expressly recognized the colonists' right to make necessary laws "for the government and ordering of the saide landes and plantacion, and the people inhabiting and to inhabite the same," and it obviously contemplated that provisions would have to be established to meet unforeseen needs and requirements.[5] There could hardly have been any objection to colonial orders which established representative government, or which provided for the registration of marriages, births, and conveyances. On the other hand, radical departures from English law, such as the abolition of primogeniture or the adoption of the civil marriage, would probably not have been tolerated by the English government in the early years of the colony, and of this probability Winthrop was undoubtedly aware in expressing his fear that the charter might be revoked. It must be emphasized, however, that the principal significance of the charter provision lay in the relationship between the colony government and the crown,[6] and its principal effect was less to deter the colonists from establishing laws contrary to those of England than to serve as a warning that they be circumspect about the methods they employed in so doing. Astute as they were to avoid occasions for unfriendly scrutiny by the English government, their determination to purify their English heritage and to execute the terms of God's covenant with Massachusetts was the major force in shaping the law of the colony. By comparison with that purpose, the injunctions of the charter were hardly more than words.

Colonial departures from English law must be appraised from the standpoint of the colonists' impulse to reform, which extended far beyond their resolution to purify church doctrine and ecclesiastical polity. The zeal to reform every aspect of human activity, including the law—both as a means to that end and even as an end in itself—was a central characteristic of Puritan thinking.[7] A similar urge to reform the laws of England was dramatically expressed in the numerous proposals advanced in tracts and debates when the Puritan party came into power in England. Few of those proposals were carried out, but they are nonetheless of great interest as indicating not only the features of English law which were the subject of discontent but the types of solutions that recommended themselves. Among the many proposals put forward by the reformers of the Interregnum were the establishment of a system of local courts for the trial of small causes, the conduct of pleading in English, the adoption of civil marriage, the abolition of benefit of clergy, and the allowance of counsel to those accused of crime.[8] The tract known as the *Examen Legum Angliae*, published in London in 1656, proposed that adultery be punished by death and theft by multiple restitution, that estates pass by partible inheritance with a double portion to the eldest son, that no man be convicted in a capital case save by the testimony of two witnesses, and many other rules which were then a part of the positive law of Massachusetts.[9] Although Puritans on both sides of the Atlantic turned constantly to the guidance of Scripture and drew upon a common fund of moral attitudes, the English proposals bear so striking a resemblance to the laws then in force in Massachusetts that it is tempting to conjecture that copies of the Code had reached the hands of the English reformers. Significantly, the author of the *Examen Legum Angliae* showed an awareness of colonial developments in referring to the laws of New England "collected into a body, and endeavoured to be made agreeable to the Jews Law morall and juditiall." [10] Moreover, Hugh Peter, some-

time minister of the church of Salem, served on a committee named
by the Council of State, and headed by Sir Matthew Hale, to submit
drafts of statutes thought necessary for the reformation of the
existing law.[11] Evidence of this kind suggests that the subject of
New England influence upon Puritan legal reformers of the Interregnum deserves more detailed exploration than it can be here
accorded.

The movement for law reform in England was not, however,
restricted to the Puritans. Dissatisfaction with the expense, delays,
and inequities of the civil law, and with the severity and capriciousness of the criminal law, was widespread, both within and without
the English legal profession in the early seventeenth century. Even
Sir Edward Coke, who was ordinarily loath to admit that any part
of the law of England was less than perfect, had recognized that
the criminal law, particularly in its statutory aspects, was in some
respects excessively harsh and in need of reform.[12] Lord Bacon, his
great rival, had introduced a bill in parliament in 1614 providing
for the appointment of commissioners "to review the state of penal
laws, to the end that such as are obsolete and snaring may be repealed, and such as are fit to continue and concern one matter may
be reduced respectively into one clear form of law."[13] Two years
later, Bacon produced a detailed *Proposition for compiling and
Amendment of our Laws*, in which he recited the "great incer-
tainties, and variety of opinion, delays and evasions" of the law as
it then stood, and proposed that work be commenced upon a
"digest or recompiling of the common laws; and . . . of the
statutes."[14] With respect to the common law, Bacon proposed the
preparation of "a perfect course of the law" based upon the Year
Books from the time of Edward I, drastically edited and abridged,
to be supplemented, first, by a book of ancient law drawn and
edited from other sources "to be used for reverend precedents, but
not for binding authorities," and, second, by new legal texts, "aux-
iliary books that conduce to the study and science of the law."[15]
With respect to the statute law, Bacon proposed a thorough
"reforming and recompiling," in which obsolete enactments would
be repealed or replaced by statutes more agreeable to the time. The
"grievousness of the penalty" would be mitigated in other statutes,
and the concurrent statutes heaped one upon another," dealing with

the same subjects, be reduced "to one clear and uniform law." [16]

Unlike the would-be reformers of the English law, however, the colonial lawmakers were not faced with the task of simplifying and bringing order into a massive, tangled corpus of local, ecclesiastical, statutory, and common law. Rejection of those features of English law which appeared to them objectionable was a relatively simple matter, since reform could be accomplished and abuses corrected by framing a new legal system, in which inherited tradition could be molded according to conscious design. The process by which those objectives were accomplished was remarkably fluid. Enactments of the General Court frequently reflected patterns which had evolved and gained prior acceptance in the community through adjudication in the courts; other laws, many of them of far-reaching importance, were established *pro re nata*, as the occasion required.[17]

Two central and closely interrelated purposes were prominent both in the laws themselves and in the manner in which they were enforced and administered. One was idealistic and reflective of the religious and political motives which had led to the foundation of the colony; the other was practical and aimed at establishing just and workable rules, appropriate to the special conditions in the colony. The idealistic element was particularly apparent in the colonial laws dealing with religion. Some of these, such as the law forbidding Jesuits to enter or remain in the colony, and the law enjoining the hospitable reception of Christians fleeing to the colony from unjust persecution, were primarily expressive of religious ideals and had little practical impact in the early years. The Bay Colony was in no sense threatened by an incursion of Jesuits, and the long-standing colonial policy of receiving refugees of proper religious persuasion needed no formal promulgation to give it the force of law. These enactments, like the fasts and days of humiliation or thanksgiving repeatedly ordered by the churches, were a means of publicly declaring sympathy with the godly victims of "the great wars, combustions and divisions which are this day in Europe." [18]

Most of the colonial laws concerning religion, however, were not only expressive of Puritan community sentiment, but had very practical aims, such as defining the spheres of civil and ecclesiastical power.[19] It is obvious, of course, that these laws created a pattern of church-state relationship that drastically modified traditional English conceptions of civil supremacy and had as their object both the establishment of the Massachusetts brand of Congregationalism and also, in John Cotton's words, the avoidance of "the churches usurpation upon civill jurisdictions, *in ordine ad spiritualia,* and the commonwealths invasion upon ecclesiasticall administrations, *in ordine* to civill peace, and conformity to the civill state." [20]

Among the significant results of the colonial definition of the respective spheres of church and state was the civil government's assumption of control over many matters, such as the recording of births, marriages and deaths, which had been the province of the ecclesiastical authorities in England. In particular, the government's assumption of jurisdiction over marriage and divorce resulted in fundamental departures from English ways. In Massachusetts, marriages were effected by a civil ceremony and depended for their validity not upon the ministrations of a priest but upon the free consent of the parties. In England, the law of marriage was entirely within the jurisdiction of the Established Church, and the performance of the marriage ceremony was a sacramental function of its ministers. By contrast, from the earliest days of the colony, civil marriage, involving no more than a simple exchange of promises by the parties in the presence of a magistrate, appears to have been the only form of marriage permitted. The source of this practice may well have been the example provided by Plymouth Colony, which had employed the civil ceremony from as early as 1621, "according to the laudable custom of the Low Countries." [21] At the same time, the English Separatists had consistently advocated civil marriage upon the authority of the Bible, and their close connection with the Calvinist church of Holland, where civil marriage had been established in 1580, reinforced their conviction that the civil ceremony should replace the forms of marriage recognized by the Church of England. However much the Separatist and non-Separatist Puritans sects differed as to the necessity of breaking the ties with the Church of England, their agreement on matters other than the issue of separatism was always substantial. The influence of Separatist ideas upon the Massachusetts colonists was therefore not merely a result of the proximity of Plymouth but was also a part of the common heritage which the two groups had brought with them from England. Nevertheless, the substantive similarity of the details of the Plymouth marriage laws to those later enacted in Massachusetts strongly suggests that the former served as a model for the latter.[22]

From the assumption of jurisdiction over marriage it was a logical step for the colony government to assume jurisdiction over divorce. Moreover, the absence of a separate ecclesiastical court in the colony almost necessarily entailed its taking jurisdiction over divorce, which in England was within the province of the Church. Divorce, under English ecclesiastical law, was either *a mensa et thoro*—roughly equivalent to the modern decree of separate maintenance—or *a vinculo*, involving the complete severance of the marriage bond.[23] The spiritual courts had no power to pronounce a divorce *a vinculo* if there had been a valid marriage, but the colonists appear to have abandoned the conception of the divorce *a mensa et thoro* and to have granted divorces *a vinculo* in the same types of situations in which the bishops' courts issued *a mensa* decrees. A decree of separation was incompatible with colonial ideas, constantly expressed in the legislation and court records, that the unattached individual was a potential danger to the community. If a marriage was effectively to be dissolved for practical purposes, it was thought wiser both for the parties and for the community that they be free to settle themselves in new marriages than to pose continual threats to the stability of other households. Unfortunately, the printed colony records for the first twenty years contain too small a number of divorce cases to warrant conclusions as to the grounds upon which divorce was granted in the colonial courts. However, the subsequent development of the law of divorce was in the direction of standards that were clearly more liberal than those of the English spiritual courts, particularly from the standpoint of the rights accorded to the wife. Further research in the unpublished court files will undoubtedly shed more light upon this area of the law and will probably substantiate the conjecture that the liberalization of divorce law had its roots in the early decades.

The idealistic element in the colony's law is particularly evident in the large number of enactments which had as their primary purpose the control of conduct through positive guidance rather than through prohibition and punishment. This attitude is manifested in laws relating to the family, which was viewed as a cornerstone of church and commonwealth alike.²⁴ Although English magistrates, by virtue of statutory authority, were much occupied with the settlement of disputes between master and servant, and although they sometimes intervened in flagrant domestic quarrels, English law contained no general statement of domestic rights, privileges, and duties such as is found in the statutory law of Massachusetts. One of the chief purposes of the colony enactments appears to have been to provide admonition and guidance to heads of households in their crucially important disciplinary duties. In conformity with the Puritan ideal of stern but loving correction as a basic principle of family government, the law proscribed cruelty to wives and children as well as to servants, and employed the characteristically English device of limiting the power of authority by defining the rights of the individual. Although suits and presentments arising out of disregard of those rights came before the courts with fair frequency, the mere declaration of the rights of family members, hortatorily announced in the colony laws, appears substantially to have ensured that the wide powers entrusted to the heads of families would not be abused.

In the same way that the colonial laws relating to religion and the family reflected typically Puritan ideals, limitations upon the power of government authority, embodied in guarantees of individual rights, reflected other ideals, related less specifically to Puritanism than to broad conceptions about the rights of Englishmen. Indeed, many of the colony laws evinced a higher regard for the rights of the individual than did the English law of the time, and for that reason merit extended discussion.

Freedom of speech and debate was subject to many limitations in Massachusetts, and the colonial authorities, like their English counterparts, were quick to punish what they deemed to be malice, presumptuousness, or sedition in public utterances. Moreover, minority interests were frequently subordinated to the overriding needs of the community as its leaders defined them. Nevertheless, the right of the colonists to be heard on matters affecting their interests was given substantial recognition. Protection against arbitrary majority action in the various public bodies of the commonwealth was afforded by the law guaranteeing "freedom of dissent" to "any member, or members of any Court, Council or civil Assemblie" in cases concerning "any cause Capital, or Wars, or subscription to any publick Articles, or Remonstrance." [25] Any such member or members as could not "in judgement and conscience consent to that way the major Vote or Suffrage goes," were given liberty "to make their *contra-Remonstrance* or *Protestation* in speech or writing, and upon their request, to have their dissent recorded in the *Rolls* of that Court, so it be done christianly and respectively, for the manner, and the dissent only be entred without the reasons therof for avoyding tediousnes." [26] To the same effect was the provision

that all and everie Freeman, and others authorized by Law, called to give any Advice, Vote, Verdict or Sentence in any Court, Council or civil Assemblie, shall have full freedom to doe it according to their true judgements and consciences, so it be done orderly and inoffensively, for the manner.[27]

This provision, extending in express terms to a juryman's freedom to return a verdict in accordance with his own conscience and judgment, appears to have eliminated the common English practice of controlling the jury's determinations through the threat of fine or imprisonment. Finally, and perhaps the most broadly phrased right protective of minority interests, was the liberty that

Every man whether Inhabitant or fforreiner, free or not free . . . to come to any publique Court, Councel, or Towne meeting, and either by speech or writeing to move any lawfull, seasonable, and materiall question, or to present any necessary motion, complaint, petition, Bill or information, whereof that meeting hath proper cognizance, so it be done in convenient time, due order, and respective manner.[28]

These three constitutional guarantees may not often have affected substantially the course of decision of public questions, but their existence undoubtedly lessened the likelihood of arbitrary or ill considered majority action. Of equal importance was their effect in guiding politically dangerous dissent into lawful and manageable channels, where the proponents of a majority position could meet it with reasoned arguments. Unquestionably, the requirements that the petitioner state his case at a "convenient time," in "due order," and in a "respective manner," and that the dissenter register his protest "christianly and respectively," gave the colonial authorities much practical control over the exercise of the right to be heard on public questions. Nevertheless, whatever their effect in practice, these provisions expressed an ideal of freedom of discussion on public issues, and of positive encouragement of responsible, popular participation in their resolution, that was much in advance of any practices then current in England.

The ideal of equal protection of the laws was forcefully expressed in the Massachusetts law declaring that "every person within this Jurisdiction, whether Inhabitant or other," was to have "the same justice and law . . . which wee constitute and execute one towards another, in all cases proper to our cognisance without partialitie or delay." [29] Although the purchase of land by strangers intending to settle in the colony was subject to the approval of a magistrate,[30] the law of Massachusetts did not impose a general disability upon aliens with respect to the ownership of property; "all persons" were declared capable of disposing of property by will or testament, and to alien lands and estates.[31] By contrast, in England at this time, an alien could not inherit land, and, although he could purchase it, it was subject to confiscation by the crown; as a corollary of that rule, he could not bring a real action in the king's courts.[32] Moreover, the colonial right of petition to, and debate in, public meetings of the colony extended to "every man whether Inhabitant or fforreiner," so that the stranger in Massachusetts enjoyed a general freedom to participate in public affairs that exceeded even the rights of most native-born Englishmen of the time.[33]

The Massachusetts provisions as to bail, appeal, double jeopardy, and confrontation of accursers show varying degrees of improvement upon English practices. In seventeenth century England, the right of a person accused of a crime to be released on bail was governed by strict statutory rules whose intricacies occupy page after page of contemporary manuals prepared for the guidance of justices of the peace. Confessed felons and thieves "openly defamed and known," were not bailable, but bail was allowed to one who was only "lightly" suspected of felony or accused of petty larceny but not previously convicted.[34] Bail was denied to persons accused of murder, but it was allowable in cases of manslaughter.[35] Treason, arson, counterfeiting, prison breaking, and contempt were among other nonbailable offenses.[36] In Massachusetts, by contrast, bail was guaranteed as a positive right except in "Crimes Capital, and Contempts in open Court," or when denial of bail was ordered by "some expresse act" of the General Court.[37] In every other case, no man who could "put in sufficient securitie, bayle or mainprise, for his appearance and good behaviour in the meane time" was to "be restrained or imprisoned by any Authority whatsoever, before the law hath sentenced him thereto. . . ."[38] In the simplicity of its administration, as well as in the protection that it afforded to the accused, the colonial practice was certainly far in advance of the English.

Another distinct innovation in Massachusetts law was the availability of an appeal from a conviction for a capital crime as a matter of right. Appeal to the County Court from the judgment of a single magistrate empowered to hear small causes of a criminal nature was also allowed in any case as a matter of right.[39] In England at that time, and for many years after, there was no "right" of appeal in criminal cases. The writ of error was applicable only in cases involving some procedural irregularity apparent upon the record of the proceedings.[40] Its issuance was entirely discretionary, and the writ was in fact ordinarily issued only when the crown wished to reverse a conviction.[41]

In two other respects, Massachusetts criminal law was well in advance of that of England. The rule against double jeopardy, in the sense that no man's life ought twice to be placed in jeopardy for the same offense, was an accepted part of English law in the seventeenth century. In general, a plea of *autrefoits acquit, autrefoits convict, or autrefoits attaint* was an absolute defense in a subsequent prosecution for the same offense.[42] The comparable Massachusetts rule was far broader than the English rule, which was applicable only when the offense was punishable with death, because it extended not only to all types of criminal prosecutions but to civil trespasses as well.[43] Again, every person accused of a capital crime in Massachusetts was entitled to confront his accuser, and the testimony of witnesses in such cases was required to be made in person.[44] In noncapital criminal cases, testimony by deposition was acceptable if the witness lived more than ten miles from the place of trial;

otherwise his testimony was required to be given orally at the trial.[45] In England, the use of depositions without affording the accused an opportunity to face or question his accusers was a common practice in the great state trials as well as in ordinary felony actions.[46]

In recognizing a limited privilege against self-crimination, the colonial law roughly paralleled English practice. In England, it was the duty and the invariable practice of the justice of the peace to conduct a close examination, not under oath, of every person brought before him for crime, and his record of this examination was customarily read to the jury at the trial.[47] "Speak him fair to the end that you may get him to confess," wrote one justice to another about a man charged with theft in seventeenth century England.[48] During the trial, the accused was questioned freely and pressed strongly to answer, but he was not permitted the privilege of answering upon his oath. Such practices appear to have been followed by the colonial magistrates.[49] Although the last decades of the sixteenth century and the first of the seventeenth had witnessed much agitation about self-crimination in England, discontent focused not upon the common-law practice of judicial examination before and during trial but upon the use of the ex officio oath by the prerogative courts as a means of forcibly extracting incriminating evidence from an accused.[50] The controversy over that oath reached its height in John Lilburne's trial before the Star Chamber in 1637.[51] He had, however, expressed his willingness to answer questions "about the thing laid to my charge"—a willingness, in other words, to submit to the judicial examination customary in common-law criminal prosecutions.

The use of an oath or torture to compel incriminating testimony from accused persons was vigorously disapproved of in Massachusetts. The sensitiveness of the colonists to any hint of the use of the ex officio oath is forcefully illustrated by the examination of the Antinomian minister, John Wheelwright, before the General Court in 1637 for an allegedly seditious sermon. Wheelwright was told that since a copy of the offending sermon was in Court, and since he had acknowledged it, the Court "might thereupon proceed, *ex officio*." [52] At the mere mention of the hated words, there was a violent reaction among some members of the Court:

at this word great exception was taken, as if the Court intended the course of the High Commission, &c. It was answered that the word *ex officio* was very safe and proper, signifying no more but the authority or duty of the Court, and that there was no cause of offence, seeing the Court did not examine him by any compulsory meanes, as by oath, imprisonment, or the like, but onely desired him for better satisfaction to answer some questions. . . .[53]

Wheelwright's friends "cried out, that the Court went about to ensnare him, and to make him to accuse himselfe," [54] but the historian of the trial insists that "The reason why the Court demanded that question of him, was not to draw matter from himselfe whereupon to proceed against him. . . ." [55] Implicit in this explanation, no less than in the objections of Wheelwright's friends, was a common belief that forcible self-crimination by administration of an oath was unlawful. Also implicit in the attempt to justify the Court's procedure is an acceptance of the lawfulness of self-crimination unaccompanied by "any compulsory meanes." [56] Like Lilburne, the colonists appear to have had no objections to judicial examination of an accused about the "thing" laid to his charge.

Four years later, when the colony was troubled by a wave of vicious criminality, Governor Bellingham consulted the elders of the New England churches on the question "how far a magistrate might exact a confession from a delinquent in capital cases?" [57] The consensus of the elders, as recorded by Winthrop, was that

where such a fact is committed, and one witness or strong presumptions do point out the offender, there the judge may examine him strictly, and he is bound to answer directly, though to the peril of his life. But if there be only light suspicion, &c. then the judge is not to press him to answer, nor is he to be denied the benefit of the law, but he may be silent, and call for his accusers. But for examination by oath or torture in criminal cases, it was generally denied to be lawful.[58]

It is not surprising, therefore, that a limited privilege against self-criminating evidence from an accused by means of an oath or physical compulsion was embodied in the Massachusetts laws of 1641 and 1648 which provided that no person be required to take any oath or subscribe to any articles except "such as the General

Court hath considered, allowed and required." [59] Since the Court would not, at this time, have conceivably allowed the use of an ex officio oath, the colonial provision effectively barred the use of that device without expressly naming it.

A second aspect of the colonial privilege against self-crimination was a prohibition of the use of torture to extract confessions of crime except under strictly limited conditions. Torture, if not "barbarous and inhumane," was permitted only after conviction for a capital crime "by clear and sufficient evidence," and then only for the purpose of disclosing the names of accomplices and conspirators.[60] The records of the colony during the first two decades, however, reveal no instance of torture having been applied.[61] In England, on the other hand, torture of prisoners during interrogation was frequently authorized by the Privy Council in connection with offenses against the state during the reigns of Elizabeth and the first two Stuarts, and it appears to have been ordered occasionally in the investigation of other crimes such as murder, larceny, and robbery.[62] Moreover, the orders authorizing its use indicate that torture was employed before the victim's trial to extort confessions and evidence to be used for his conviction.[63]

Because of present-day concern about the "right to travel," special interest attaches to the colony laws with respect to freedom of movement. The Massachusetts Bay colonists were permitted that freedom to a far greater degree than their English contemporaries. The Body of Liberties had included a "free libertie" of every man "(notwithstanding any civil power) to remove both himself and his familie at their pleasure out of [the colony]. Provided there be no legal impediment to the contrary," and this provision was carried forward into the Code of 1648.[64] In England, however, the prerogative of the crown to prevent the departure of any person from the kingdom by the writ *ne exeat regno* went unquestioned as a power necessary for reasons of state.[65] In an age when the writ was principally used to control the movements of Jesuits and others regarded as subversive of the safety of the kingdom, this prerogative was not viewed as a menace to the liberty of law-abiding Englishmen. Nevertheless, although the writ had not been used to halt or to hamper the flood of emigration to Massachusetts, it was a potential

threat to the colony's development during the early years. Moreover, men who had torn up their roots once to seek a new life in a
new country could envisage the possibility of doing so again and be
jealous of their right to remove when they wished.

Within the colony, too, the residents of Massachusetts enjoyed
substantial freedom of movement. Letters of demission, given to
church members upon their departure from one town for another,
appear with remarkable frequency in the church records, and indicate a considerable degree of mobility within the colony. In
England, factors not operative in Massachusetts restricted movement at least among the poorer classes. Because of the system under
which the various craft guilds enjoyed local monopolies in their
respective trades and could call upon the courts to enforce them
against outsiders, even the skilled journeyman found it exceedingly
difficult to establish himself in a new locality. If his own trade were
depressed, he could not take up a new one without first serving the
requisite apprenticeship; and he was usually prevented from resum-
ing his own trade in a new locality by the jealous hostility of established craftsmen.[66] Mobility among all classes of laborers and craftsmen was further hampered by the operation of the poor laws, which
prescribed that a pauper was to be maintained by his own parish
and which empowered the parish authorities to expel any outsider
before he became settled in the parish.[67] This was often done even
in the case of a healthy, industrious stranger who had assurance of
employment, on the ground that he might become a charge upon
the parish ratepayers in the future.[68] By the same token, parish
officers were reluctant to allow a resident to depart the parish for
another, lest he later be sent back to them impoverished.

Most of the colony's improvements on English law in the area of
civil liberties were not radical innovations but embodied ideals
which were widely held, both in England and in Massachusetts, to
be the rights of Englishmen. Many of those rights were not legally
recognized in England, but most of them were claimed at one time
or another there, and their denial was widely regarded as a grievous
wrong. The legal recognition of such rights in Massachusetts Bay
owed much to the influence of the deputies, whose distrust of
arbitrary powers in the hands of the magistrates had its roots in

unhappy memories of disregard of due process, particularly by the prerogative agencies of the crown. The magistrates, for the most part, were unwilling to admit the necessity of such guarantees in a commonwealth governed by godly men. In their view, the powers of government were properly limited, not by the enactments of human lawmakers, but by the law of God embodied in the social covenant and interpreted by the magistrates alone. The disagreement in this matter was less as to substance than as to method, for there is little evidence that even the most authoritarian of the magistrates were opposed to the particular civil liberties enumerated and defined. The guarantees for which the ancient charters, the statutes, and the common law had come to stand were as much a part of their own inheritance as they were of the freemen generally, and it is not without significance that the limitations imposed by the General Court upon the powers of government were framed "in resemblance to a Magna Charta," [69] and echo more than one of its famous provisions.

Closely connected with the colonists' concern for the individual were their conceptions of punishment, and no more striking or important example of the influence of Puritan beliefs upon the law can be found than in the procedures developed for dealing with criminal offenses. The evidence of the court records provides notable illustrations of the extent to which the magistrates directed the criminal law of the colony away from traditional concepts of retribution which permeated English criminal law, toward practices which emphasized moral persuasion in order to reform the offender. Puritan theology posited that the law of nature, in the form of immutable moral principles, was engraved by God upon the human soul at its creation. In terms of individual conduct the natural law was conceived of as serving an accusatory function through the medium of the conscience, with divinely instilled principles providing the basis for the moral assessment of every human act. Melanchthon had said that the primary utility of the natural law was in its function of accusing and terrifying the conscience.[70] This point of view was also emphasized in the *Decades* of Heinrich Bullinger, a sixteenth century Swiss reformer whose writings were well known and much respected by English Puritans:

The law of nature is an instruction of the conscience, and, as it were, a certain direction placed by God himself in the minds and hearts of men, to teach them what they have to do and what to eschew. And the conscience, verily, is the knowledge, judgment, and reason of a man, whereby every man in himself and in his own mind . . . doth either condemn or else acquit himself.[71]

To be sure, the traditional Protestant natural-law doctrine which infused the Puritan ethic stressed that man's divinely instilled moral principles were partially effaced by original sin, so that the conscience, unaided, could not be relied upon to order human behavior. But it was a further tenet of Puritanism that the force of logic and persuasion, exerted in public preaching and in private exhortation, and aided by an infusion of divine grace, could restore the innate human sense of right and wrong from a "dimme aged picture," to something like its original brightness.[72] The human conscience, thus restored to its proper and effective accusatory function, was capable of affording a "True Sight of Sin." [73] Thomas Hooker summarized this position in a sermon by stating:

We must see sin, 1. Cleerly. 2. Convictingly, what it is in it self, and what it is to us, not in the appearance and paint of it, but in the power of it; not to fadam it in the notion and conceit only, but to see it with Application. . . . It's one thing to say sin is thus and thus, another thing to see it to be such. . . .[74]

The rejection of the guidance of the restored conscience was seen as an act of the will in rebellion against the reason, and a central feature of Puritan thinking about sin and crime was therefore its emphasis upon the evil pride of soul that knowingly rejected the dictates of the offender's conscience. John Cotton took the position that

. . . an *Erronious* and *blind Conscience*, (even in fundamentall and weighty Points) It is not lawfull to persecute any, till after *Admonition* once or twice: . . . And then if any one persist, it is not out of *Conscience*, but against *his Conscience*, . . .[75]

If the offender "knew" the law in the narrow sense that he was aware that society had forbidden his act, and in the deeper sense that his own conscience accused him for it, then the offender, no less than the magistrate who punished him, bore witness to the justice of his punishment. The process of conviction and punishment became significant, not merely from the familiar retributive standpoint of attempting to redress an imbalance resulting from a wrongful act, but from the further and more sophisticated standpoint of ensuring, to the extent that it was possible, that the person punished was himself an active participant in the punitive process.

As in other aspects of their lives, the colonists sought to make criminal punishment bear witness to God's goodness and justice. This aim was plainly stated by the General Court in remitting a fine upon the offender's acknowledgment of the error of his act and the justice of his punishment. The remission was granted

to manifest the Corts ready inclination to shew all due incuragment to delinquents to confes their errors, & acknowledg the iustice of the Corts proceedings, rather then put any to such temptation as should either dishonor God or wound their owne consciences, by hardening of them selves in their evill courses.[76]

On the other hand, when the offender stubbornly refused to acknowledge his fault after the application of due means of conviction, the justification for rigorous punishment was patently clear. The hardness of heart of the wrongdoer who dishonored God and wounded his own conscience by persevering in evil courses justified his punishment and bore witness to God's goodness and reasonableness in a way that punishment not preceded by efforts directed at "clear conviction" of sin could possibly have done. John Winthrop provides an example of this attitude in his account of the whipping of a Hingham man who refused to allow his child to be baptized. "[M]uch patience and clear conviction of his error, etc." was applied in his case, but he remained obdurate; whereupon "he was ordered to be whipped." He was punished, Winthrop carefully noted, "not for his opinion, but for reproaching the Lord's ordinance, and for his bold and evil behavior both at home and in the court." [77]

"Conviction" of sin, in the sense that the word is derived from "convince," was thus a part of the procedure employed by the colonial courts in conjunction with conviction in its legal sense. It was an emotional as well as an intellectual process, and involved both the reason and the will. In many cases the courts seem to have tried to "convince" the wrongdoer of the validity and justice of the law he rejected, and so to repent of his wrong doing.[78] The offender's free acknowledgment of the justice of the court's proceeding thus appears to have been sought as evidence both of his recognition of the evil of his act and of the enlistment of his will in its repudiation.

Punishments inflicted pursuant to this rationale had, of course, the further and commonly recognized effect of deterring others from similar wrongful conduct. The effectiveness of the convicted murderer's public expression of repentance at the foot of the gallows, or of the proud slanderer's abject submission before his neighbors, can hardly be doubted. It must be emphasized, however, that submission and acknowledgment would not save a capital offender from the gallows. "Conviction" in such cases might help to bring the condemned man's soul to grace, but it could not alter a punishment which was enjoined by God's word. In noncapital cases, however, once the offender's submission was obtained, and its sincerity undoubted, the court was likely to be inclined toward leniency. If he recognized the justice of the prescribed penalty, and if his reason and his will afforded him a "true sight" of his particular sin, then his punishment was often mitigated or even dispensed with entirely.[79] As a general rule, retraction and submission were sufficient to exempt even highly dangerous sectaries from punishment. Roger Williams and John Wheelwright were given repeated opportunities to recant before they were banished, and the sentences imposed upon the followers of Wheelwright, who were fined for signing a petition on his behalf, were promptly remitted upon admission of error and submission to the Court.[80] Submission and acknowledgment also inclined the courts toward leniency in other types of cases. John Endecott, who was ordered committed to prison by the General Court in 1635 "for his contempt in protesting against the proceedeing of the Court" in connection with his cutting the cross from the Salem militia's colors, was dismissed

"vpon his submission, & full acknowledgement of his offence." [31]
George Story was committed in 1642 "vpon his miscarriage"—
presumably to one of his betters—but later, "vpon his submission, &
acknowledgement of his fault, hee was discharged." [82] Even Joell
Jenkin, bound over to the next court in 1640 for getting his
master's daughter with child, was discharged at the next court "upon
his repentance." [83]

As explained at an earlier point, the magistrates often referred
offenders to the ministers for "conviction." [84] Mr. Ambrose Marten,
who called the church covenant "a stinking carryon and a humane
invention," and accused the ministers of dethroning Christ, and
setting up themselves, was "counselled" by the General Court in
1639 "to go to Mr. Mather to bee instructed by him." [85] A Boston
schoolmaster, accused of brutally beating his usher, was "openly
convict . . . by the oaths of four or five witnesses," yet he continued to justify himself; "so, it being near night, he was committed
to the marshall till the next day." [86] The next morning, "many of
the elders" appeared in court, and reported that, "the evening before, they had taken pains with him, to convince him of his faults;
. . . but, in the end, he was convinced, and had freely and fully
acknowledged his sin, and that with tears; so as they did hope he
had truly repented. . . ." [87]

Consistent with this emphasis upon "conviction," several of the
criminal statutes of the colony included obstinacy in the face of
"due conviction," or its equivalent, as an element of the offense. For
example, an Anabaptist could be banished for propounding the
heresy, but only if he appeared "to the Court wilfully and
obstinately to continue therin, after due meanes of conviction. . . ." [88] Again, children or servants might be removed from
the custody of heads of households who neglected their education,
but only if the neglect continued "after admonition [by the town
selectmen] given to such masters of families." [89] Also related to the
Puritan emphasis upon "conviction" of offenders was the insistence
that every person in the commonwealth should know the laws. It
was expressly ordered that children be taught to read in order that
they might understand the capital laws of the commonwealth, and
the Code of 1648 particularly stressed the importance of sufficient
publication of the colony's laws.[90] Even Winthrop, for all his

opposition to the prescription of penalties by statute, was insistent upon "the necessitye of declaringe and statinge [the laws], so as all the people may knowe them, for I ever held it vniust, to require of men the obedience to any Lawe, which they may not (by common Intendment) take notice off." [91]

The extensive use of the admonition as a civil punishment in Massachusetts is another aspect of the emphasis upon "conviction." The printed quarter sessions records do not indicate that the admonition was employed in the English secular courts of the seventeenth century, but it was one of the penalties commonly imposed by the ecclesiastical courts of the period.[92] "Monition" was the mildest of the ecclesiastical censures; more serious offenses were punished by penance, by suspension from participation in the sacraments, or by excommunication. The church records suggest that in many cases the admonition was a perfunctory exhortation to "go and sin no more;"[93] but if the presiding official were a stern moralist, the admonition may have involved an investigation of the guilt of the offender.[94] In Massachusetts, however, the admonition was no mere *pro forma* proceeding, but a solemn inquiry into the conduct of the accused with a view to his seeing his sin "Cleerly" and "Convictingly." [95] One of John Winthrop's chief objections to the prescription of fixed penalties was that they "take away the vse of Admonition, which is allso a divine sentence and an Ordinance of God, warranted by Scripture. . . ." [96] "The Words of the wise are as goads, and as nayles fastened by the masters of Assemblys—by these (my sonne) be admonished, Pro.29:1: Isay. 11:4 Pro.17:10. A Reproofe entereth more into a wise man, then 100 stripes into a foole." [97] The colonial court records provide numerous instances of the use of the admonition. For example, William Browne, "for his obscean, & filthy speaches," was "sharply reprehended, & admonished not to use such base speaches," by the Court of Assistants;[98] Mr. James Downing, admonished "to take great heed" of the company of drunkards, "manifested great remorse which gladdened the hearts of his friends;" [99] and Weybro Lovell, the wife of Captain William Lovell, presented for "light and whoarish behavior" by a Boston grand jury, "was seriously admonished to repent, & walke humbly, chastly, and holily." [100]

Closely akin to solemn public admonition was the practice of enjoining offenders to make public confession of sin, or to make public apology to one who had been injured. Thus, Mr. John Wooldrige was fined three pounds by the Court of Assistants in 1642 "for his drunkenesse, & swearing," and "enjoyned vpon paine of 5^lb. to acknowledge his offence, at Boston, Charlestowne, & Cambridge, reading an acknowledgment written. . . ." [101] Ralfe Fogge, who was convicted at Salem in 1650 of "lying in face of open congregation on a Lord's day, slandering the church," and reproaching the Governor, "saying that the Governor was the grand jury, and the grand jury, the Governor," was ordered to confess publicly in words prescribed by the court on the next Lord's day.[102] Likewise, when lack of sufficient proof prevented conviction under one of the capital laws, the magistrates imposed a particularly cogent form of public penance. In 1641 Thomas Owen and Sara Hales, accused but not convicted of adultery, were found guilty of "adulteros practises" and sentenced "to bee sent to the gallos with a roape about his [her] neck & to sit upon the lather an houre the roapes end throwen over the gallos & so to returne to prison." [103]

Such punishments, like that prescribing the wearing of papers or other emblems which announced the offense,[104] emphasized the importance of humbling the will as a means of "conviction" of sin; but they were also a particularly effective means of moral persuasion in a community that placed a high premium upon public esteem. A reputation for godliness was, of course, a principal criterion for the visible sainthood so prized by serious Puritans; but to the colonists generally personal honor was no less important, and the frequency of slander actions in the courts attests as much to the colonists' dislike of opprobrium as to their penchant for litigation.[105] Punishments of this kind were essentially a species of social excommunication, varied in method and duration, but having the common effect of setting off the offender from respectable society and from the approval of his fellows.

Implicit in the battery of punitive devices of admonition, referral to church discipline, public confession and humiliation is an attitude of hopefulness for the wayward which, despite the endless sermonizing on the depravity of man, was among the most vital forces in Puritanism. If the Puritan magistrate abhorred the criminal act, he respected the offender to whom, no less than to himself, God's promise of grace was freely proffered, and whose soul, however disordered in its faculties, could not be regarded as hopelessly lost. As practical men, the magistrates recognized that there were those who "must be helde in by feare of punishment," and, like their English counterparts, they did not hesitate to deal with such persons severely. Although Winthrop might urge that a reproof to a wise man was more effective than one hundred stripes inflicted upon a fool, he would have heartily agreed that "correccion is ordained for the ffooles back." [106] Much of the apparent contradiction between whippings, brandings, and ear croppings on the one hand, and "due means of conviction" on the other, can be resolved in terms of a balance which the criminal law struck between the correction that was suitable for the rational and the coercion required for the obstinate.

To characterize the Puritan attitude toward criminal punishment as humanitarian in any modern sense would be misleading. Although the laws of Massachusetts proscribed the use of punishments "that are in-humane, barbarous or cruel," the colonists' standards of in-humanity were decidedly not ours, and they had little compassion for the plight of the criminal as such. Their innovations in this area of the law reflect Puritan objections to the English criminal law, whose punishments were meted out irrationally and in defiance of conceptions of righteousness and justice implicit in the law of God. The colonial laws extended the penalty of death to several offenses which were not capitally punishable in England, yet at the same time they prescribed relatively mild punishments for crimes such as theft and burglary for which many hundreds of Englishmen were sent to the gallows every year. The capriciousness of the English system which, through the device of benefit of clergy, allowed many felons with a modicum of literacy to escape the rigors of an outworn criminal law was particularly objectionable to the Puritans, who argued that God had "appointed Magistracy for the punishment of evil-doers, without respect of persons in Judgement." [107] Their adoption of what they conceived to be just criminal laws and penalties not only eliminated much that was capricious in English law but, more importantly, helped to establish a system that accorded with their own convictions of righteousness. Yet, to the extent that their innovations did away with excessively harsh punishments for numerous minor offenses and emphasized the reform of the criminal, the colonists were humanitarian in the sense that they were greatly concerned with the welfare of the human soul and entirely opposed to the taking of human life without the clearest of warrants in God's word.

If the colony's departures from English norms in the area of crime and punishment were particularly reflective of Puritan ideals, other aspects of the law emphasized practical attitudes and the influence of local conditions. Here, the growth of the law was characterized less by repudiation of English ways than by selectiveness and adaptation. Few better examples of this feature of the colony's legal development can be pointed to than the system of judicial procedure, which ensured easy accessibility to the courts and prompt and inexpensive justice.

Early in the seventeenth century Bacon had observed that the subjects of England "do already fetch Justice somewhat far off," more than in any nation that he knew,[108] and his criticism was echoed in the cry of the Interregnum pamphleteer, "Let the people have right at their own doors." [109] Although the English local courts partially supplied the need for a cheap, nearby forum, they were often hampered by royal writs ordering the transfer of cases before the king's courts, where litigants would be faced with all the expense and delay for which those courts had become notorious. In Massachusetts, each town had its own court for the trial, without jury, of civil cases in which the "debt, trespasse or damage doth not exceed fourty shillings." [110] These courts ensured the expeditious dispatch of the numerous small claims that make up the bulk of judicial business in a simple rural community. In addition, the quarterly sessions of the County Courts provided a convenient forum for trial by jury of those cases which involved sums above forty shillings. Appeals were allowed as a matter of right, both from decisions of the courts for small causes and from the County Courts.[111] Procedures were informal, and a plaintiff was allowed to withdraw his action or be nonsuited before a verdict had been given in, with a right to "renew his sute" at a later court.[112] Fees were reasonable: each town was supplied with a clerk of writs who was authorized to grant summons at twopence, attachment and replevin at threepence, and to take bond to prosecute a suit at fourpence.[113] A fee of ten shillings was required for entry of an action in a County Court or in the Court of Assistants, but provision was made for suits *in forma pauperis*.[114] Apparently no fee was required for entry of an action in a court for small causes.

Ease of access to the courts and liberality of procedure created inevitable problems. Trivial, unfounded, or vexatious suits were apparently common, and the ready availability of appeals, voluntary nonsuits, and new trials tempted the dogged litigant unreasonably to drag out the settlement of a lawsuit. A number of enactments sought to prevent abuses of this nature by prescribing penalties for common barratry, for falsely pretending "great damages or debts to vex his adversary" and for taking an appeal or seeking a new trial without "just cause of any such proceeding." [115]

By comparison with England, the Massachusetts jury enjoyed considerable freedom. A grand juror was not required to "inform, present or reveal any private crime or offence wherin there is no perill or danger to this Colonie, or any member therof, when any necessarie tye of conscience, grounded on the word of God bindes him to secresie;" [116] grand jurors and petty jurors alike were allowed to bring in a "*Non liquet* or a special verdict" in any case "wherin evidence is so obscure or defective that the Jurie cannot clearly and safely give a positive verdict," and the judgment in such a case was to be made by the court.[117] If the jury was unable to "finde the *main issue*," they nevertheless had liberty to bring in a partial verdict, finding such facts as they were able.[118] Control or intimidation of the jury by the bench, such as was common in England at this time, was impossible under the Massachusetts system; if the court could not accept the jury's verdict, the only course was to refer the issue to the General Court for determination.[119] This procedure, however, could be invoked by the jury as well as by the court, since it applied whenever "the Bench and Jurors shall so differ at any time about their verdict that *either* of them cannot proceed with peace of conscience." [120] Moreover, whenever a petty jury was "not clear in their judgements or consciences, concerning any Case wherin they are to give their verdict," any member was allowed "in open Court to advise with any man they shall think fit to resolve or direct them, before they give in their verdict." [121] This startling deviation from English practice reflected the characteristically Puritan reluctance to force the conscience, but its incidental effect may well have been to afford members of the clergy who were present in court an opportunity to be heard on matters of conscience.

Among the numerous ways in which the law of Massachusetts improved upon that of England was in the effectiveness of the control which the colony courts exercised over the course of administration of estates following the grant of probate. In England, realty was not ordinarily subject to administration.[122] Although, in theory, personal property was fully subject thereto, in fact, the ecclesiastical courts could often do little more than grant probate, since the courts of common law readily issued writs of prohibition to prevent the spiritual courts from proceeding further.[123] As a result, the English executor was in many, if not in most, cases enabled to do as he wished, free from effective control by any court. By alleging false debts, admitting liability in collusive suits against the estate, and similar fraudulent practices, the executor often prevented legacies from being paid.[124] Because in the colony land was subject to administration on the same basis as personal property, and because jurisdiction over all phases of probate and administration were vested in the same court, the colonial courts could and did insist that each person entitled to a portion of the testator's estate receive his portion and no more. The record in one case shows the court ordering a guardian selected for the testator's children to put up a bond, and later foreclosing the bond to safeguard the children's legacies;[125] in other cases, the court would order the payment of debts, the sale or partition of property, and otherwise exercise active control over all aspects of administration.[126]

In the distribution of intestates' estates, the colony courts exercised wide discretion with a primary view to the needs of the surviving spouse and children. This practice, which was a clear departure from that of the ecclesiastical courts, had statutory foundation in sections of the Body of Liberties which provided for partible inheritance among the children and declared that a widow who was not left a "competent portion" of her husband's estate should be "relieved" "upon just complaint made to the Generall Court." [127] It was to be nearly three hundred years before legislatures of the modern world perceived the wisdom of the principle involved and began to enact similar provisions into statutes affecting testate distributions.[128] An enactment of 1647 gave the widow, in addition to dower, a one-third share in her husband's personal property, thereby anticipating by almost thirty years the principle of an assured share under the English Statute of Distribution.[129] The discretionary rule was restored in 1649, when the 1647 provision as to personalty was repealed and the County Courts ordered to assign to the widow such portion of her husband's personal estate as "they shall conceive iust and equall."[130] Without reference, however, to the particular statutory rule in effect, the courts continued to distribute intestate property in accordance with family needs. In 1646 a widow with three small children was assigned all her husband's property and charged with their upbringing;[131] again, in 1649, a widow with two small children was given the whole estate, and the children nothing.[132] In still another case, approximately five-sixths of the estate was given outright to the widow, and one-sixth reserved for bringing up an unborn child which she was then carrying.[133] In 1647 a widow with no children to raise was given roughly one-fourth of the estate;[134] in 1650 an estate of more than one hundred pounds was distributed among the children only, with nothing to the widow.[135] Analysis of cases in the probate records indicates that when the estate was very small, the widow received virtually everything, whether or not there were minor children to support.[136] When larger estates were involved, her share was likely to be less, and portions were reserved for minor children to be paid at their majority or marriage.[137]

A further example of the interplay of the ideal and the practical, of Puritan attitudes and community needs, is provided by the laws governing the debtor-creditor relationship. The depression that struck and nearly shattered the colony's economy in the early 1640's immediately resulted in the enactment of laws to provide remedies to the creditor against the debtor's fraud or evasion, and at the same time to protect the debtor's person and property from the full consequences of the scarcity of money and the collapse of the price structure.

Among the enactments in aid of creditors was a statute of 1641 giving creditors an option of commencing an action for recovery of a debt by summons or by attachment in a number of situations which involved opportunities for fraud or evasion.[138] In the earliest years of the colony, attachment, as at common law, appears to have been issued only against a defendant who failed to respond to a summons. An order of 1630 had provided that all suits be instituted with a summons, to be followed, if the defendant did not answer, by an order to attach his goods or his person.[139] By contrast, the 1641 statute allowed a suit to be begun with an attachment when the defendant was "a stranger, not dwelling amongst us," or was "going out of our iurisdiction," or was "going about to make away his estate to defraude his creditors," or was a person "doubtfull in [his] estates," [140] The provision thus gave the creditor a hold upon the goods or the person of the debtor, or a bond to ensure his appearance to answer, from the beginning of the action; it minimized the possibility of his fleeing the jurisdiction, concealing his property, or divesting himself of his assets upon learning of the commencement of the suit. Presumably this procedure, resembling in some respects the modern process by which attachment commences a *quasi in rem* suit, worked out well in practice, for it was extended in 1650 to every civil action, with the result that attachment could be used to commence a suit without a showing of circumstances conducive to fraud or evasion.[141] A second enactment of 1650 broadened the effect of attachment by providing that it should remain in force, not merely until the defendant appeared or judgment was issued by default, but until the execution was either satisfied or discharged.[142] Thus, within twenty years, attachment had evolved from the common-law device to compel the defendant's appearance in court into a procedure which ensured both an initial and a continuing effectiveness of the court's process against the defendant's property and person.

Moreover, by 1648, in contrast with the common-law procedures and with the earlier colonial rule, both of which distinguished between writs attaching the goods of the defendant and those attaching his person, the writ of attachment directed the marshal or constable "to attach the body and goods of (WF) and to take *Bond* of him . . . with sufficient Suertie or Suerties for his appearance at the next Court . . ." thereby in effect combining the English writs of *capias* and *distringas* into a single process. In further contrast with the common law, a Massachusetts creditor appears to have been allowed to attach goods of the defendant in the hands of a third person, and also to attach debts owed the defendant.[143]

The earliest of the colony's laws dealing generally with the procedure to be followed in levying execution upon a judgment was enacted in 1647 in response to complaints of "Marshals and other Officers" "that they are oftentimes in great doubt how to demean themselves in the execution of their offices. . . ." [144] In the light of the complaint, it is probably safe to assume that the statute embodies a declaration and clarification of what the General Court deemed to be the proper existing procedure. Under the statute, officers charged with levying execution were to levy first upon the goods of the defendant; if the judgment could not be satisfied from the defendant's personal property, he was to levy upon the "land or person according to law." [145] Since arrest or imprisonment "for any debt or fine" was prohibited "if the law can finde any competent meanes of satisfaction otherwise from [the debtor's] estate," [146] the effect of the statute was to authorize and require the levying officer to levy, apparently pursuant to a single writ, upon the personal property, real property, and body of the defendant, in that order.[147] If the defendant escaped imprisonment by an oath that he was not concealing property, the creditor could require him to satisfy his debt by service, either to the creditor or to such other person "of the English nation" to whom he might be sold on the creditor's behalf.[148] This procedure, like that of attachment, was a significant simplification and expansion of the English common-law rule, under which a creditor seeking to levy execution had to choose among three writs, some of which were exclusive and barred the employment of any other writ if the first proved ineffectual.[149] The colonial rule which allowed execution successively and in one proceeding against the defendant's goods, lands, and person, together with the provision—which had no English counterpart—for the satisfaction of a judgment debt by service, afforded the Massachusetts creditor remedies for the recovery of his debt that were relatively cheap, efficient, and uncomplicated.

The colony laws relating to the debtor-creditor relationship were not limited to protecting only the interests of creditors. On the contrary, it is one of the remarkable features of the colony's legal

development that, in an economic depression which afforded opportunities for exploitation of the debtor class, members of the General
Court, whose economic interests for the most part were identified
with the creditor class, should develop an impressive array of rules
for the protection of the debtor.

Most of those rules were far in advance of contemporary English practice. In the beginning, as in England, a debtor could discharge his debt only by payment in full.[150] Unless other means were
stipulated by the parties, the common law required payment in
money.[151] By contrast, a 1640 enactment of the General Court,
recognizing "that there is a great stop in trade & commerce for
want of money," declared that "no man shalbee compelled to
satisfye any debt, legacy, fine, or any other payment in money, but
satisfaction shalbee accepted in corne, cattle, fish, or other commodities. . . ."[152] This act was followed by a second, which
provided that payment to the creditor in an execution was to be
directly from the debtor's goods rather than from the sum realized
from their sale. The preamble sets forth the situation that gave rise
to the statute:

> Whereas many men in the plantation are in debt, & heare is not
> money sufficient to discharge the same, though their cattle & goods
> should bee sould for halfe their worth, as experience hath shewed vpon
> some late executions, wherby a great part of the people in the country
> may bee undone, & yet their debts not satisfied, though they have
> sufficient upon an equall valewation to pay all, & live comfortably
> upon the rest . . .[153]

Moreover, the colonial law exempted from execution a debtor's
bedding, clothing, tools, arms, and household necessities—a principle
now widely accepted in modern American law—whereas in England, at that time, the only exemptions other than clothing were
land and, under one type of execution, beasts needed for plowing.[154]

Although many of the colonial laws as to debtors and creditors
departed from common-law practices and procedures, several are
paralleled in some degree by English local customs. The rule permitting the use of an attachment to commence an action of debt had

precedent in the local custom of London whereby a debt action might be commenced with a writ of *capias* requiring the sheriff to arrest the defendant to ensure his appearance; moreover, there is evidence indicating that the *capias* sometimes was being issued even at common law without the summons having first been ignored.[155] The applicability of attachment to land is comparable with the London custom allowing the sequestration of land as a means of bringing the debtor into court after his goods had been exhausted by successive writs of distress.[156] Still another London custom, also found in other English cities, permitted the attachment of debts or goods owed the debtor when the debtor was out of the jurisdiction; this custom had a counterpart in the colonial rule of garnishment.[157] Levy of execution upon land, followed by sale for the creditor's benefit, existed in at least one English borough during the mediaeval period.[158] These parallels again suggest the influence of English local customs, which has been discussed at an earlier point, but at the same time it must be recognized that the colony laws in this area were enacted to meet, and were given impetus by, the challenge of specific and immediate problems, and their adoption unquestionably owed as much thereto as to the persuasive force of English experience.

The colonial laws as to debtor and creditor were essentially the outcome of a severe economic crisis. Yet the form of the law's response to that situation was not determined by the cause. Tawney's characterization of the Puritan as one who sees the poverty of those who fall by the wayside as a moral failing, and in riches the rewards of a triumph of energy and will,[159] provides only a partial explanation. These attitudes were undoubtedly present in the mind of the Massachusetts Puritan, and may serve to explain the legislature's concern for the rights of creditors. Something more, however, is needed to explain the equally striking legislative concern for the rights of the debtor, and it seems more than probable that much of the explanation is to be found in the colonists' view of their mission as an undertaking that required the effort and co-operation of the whole community, committed to bearing one another's burdens. In their eyes, as a passage from the Code already quoted so vividly recites:

. . . obedience to them [the laws] must be yeilded with respect to the common welfare, not to thy private advantage, and as thou yeildest obedience to the law for common good, but to thy disadvantage: so another must observe some other law for thy good, though to his own damage; thus must we be content to bear one anothers burden and so fullfill the Law of Christ.[160]

The Massachusetts debtor, deprived by the law of attachment and execution of many of the loopholes available to the English debtor at common law, yielded obedience to the law for the common good, but to his own disadvantage; and the creditor, forced to accept fish in payment of a money debt, and to forego the money proceeds of a forced sale in favor of satisfaction from the debtor's goods, "observed," in the wor 's of the Epistle, "some other law" for the good of the debtor, "though to his own damage." To this idea of bearing one another's burden, enforced by the law of the colony, is assignable much of the credit for the fact that the colony's first economic depression did not, like many later depressions, give rise to lawlessness and strife between the "haves" and the "have-nots." The conditions in Massachusetts in the 1640's were similar in many ways to those that gave rise to the Shays Rebellion a century and a half later. However, unlike the Puritan leaders, the Massachusetts government in 1786 refused to accommodate creditor and debtor interests for the good of the whole community and helped to pauperize hundreds of farmers by an insistence that creditors receive their full due, whatever the consequences.[161]

Within short compass it is impossible adequately to summarize, much less to detail, the numerous ways in which the laws of the Bay Colony ignored, adapted, and improved upon their English legal inheritance. If the practices of the courts were largely reflective of English experience, conscious and deliberate design characterizes the legislation, which drew upon or rejected that experience according to what seemed most suitable to the well-being of the community. Responsive to, yet not overly hampered by, tradition, the law developed into a coherent, workable, and comprehensive system. By mid-century, Massachusetts law, like its literature, education, and theology, had acquired a character of its own that was to endure far beyond the period in which it was formed. Framed to meet the conditions of a new society, built to carry out the purposes for which the colony had been founded, many of its laws were nevertheless copied in other colonies and survived to form the basis of much of the present-day law of the United States.[162] That this should prove so bears eloquent testimony to the wisdom, foresight, and idealism of the founders of the Bay Colony.

XII

~

Of Law and Liberty

Few problems of government have so absorbed the serious attention of statesmen and political thinkers as has that of accommodat-
ing the liberty of individuals and the collective interests of the
community at large. Since at least the end of the eighteenth century,
it has been one of the postulates of American government that individuals should be accorded the maximum degree of freedom of
initiative and expression consistent with a like freedom on the part
of others and with the welfare of the social or political groups to
which they belong. Indeed, in modern times this optimum individual freedom is very frequently equated with the word "liberty" in
its widest sense. So accustomed are people to accepting as axiomatic
the importance of promoting individual freedom that they are
ready, almost instinctively, to condemn any form of government
whose laws narrow or suppress its expression. Hence, the very title
of this chapter may easily appear to be incongruous. How is it
possible to speak of liberty in colonial Massachusetts, which
deliberately suppressed freedom of speech, banished men for their
political opinions, and executed Quakers for their religious beliefs?
How can liberty be said to have existed under a form of government in which office, power, and authority were concentrated in
an oligarchy of a dozen magistrates who denied the right to vote to
perhaps two-thirds of the population?

To denounce the early government of Massachusetts on the
ground that it was undemocratic and did not share ideals which

others have come to prize is not only to close the mind and fetter historical inquiry but to inhibit understanding of early New England society. There can be no question that intolerance was stamped upon the face of the Bay Colony in the seventeenth century and that nearly every aspect of the colonists' lives was closely supervised and regimented. Unquestionably, also, the government of Massachusetts was undemocratic in the modern sense and was, in fact, a dictatorship of a small group of zealous men who exercised extensive powers of discipline and coercion over the several thousand inhabitants within their jurisdiction. Yet this same government, building upon and purifying its English heritage, constructed within twenty years a commonwealth in which were achieved not only the high religious purposes of its establishment but important social goals that command admiration. Through its legislation the colony government fostered family life, promoted education, and stimulated trade and manufacturing. Many of its laws protecting the lives and property of its citizens were far in advance of those of contemporary England. By 1650 Massachusetts had become the dominant political and ecclesiastical influence in New England, the center of its trade, and the leader in resistance to the policies of the English government. These achievements alone, within a twenty-year period, are indeed remarkable.

There can be little doubt that many of the colony's achievements were accomplished at the expense of individual personal liberty. It must again be emphasized, however, that the men of that time had ideals which were very different from our own and that the word "liberty" had very different connotations from what it has today. John Norton defined liberty as "a Power, as to any external restraint, or obstruction on mans part, to walk in the Faith, Worship, Doctrine and Discipline of the Gospel, according to the Order of the Gospel." [1] Winthrop, it will be recalled, defined liberty in much the same terms in his "little speech" at the time of the Hingham militia affair, but he had gone further and emphasized that this form of liberty was "the proper end and object of authority" to be "maintained and exercised in a way of subjection to authority." [2] Authority, that is, government and law, were thought to have been made necessary by man's fall from grace, and subjection thereto was regarded as a religious duty. The end of law was thus seen as the accomplishment of God's will in a regenerate society bound together by both a religious and a political covenant. Explicit in Puritan thinking was the familiar mediaeval principle that the welfare of the whole, rather than individual advantage, was the mainspring of the state. Government, therefore, was conceived as having full power to coerce the wayward and the recalcitrant in the interest of what its officers defined as the common good.

Winthrop classified men as belonging in one or the other of two categories: "they who are godly and vertuous" who observe law "for Conscience, and Vertues sake," and those who "must be helde in by feare of punishment." [3] The latter were a principal source of concern to the magistrates, and against them were directed an impressive number of legal and other governmental sanctions developed during the first two decades. If the community was to remain a unit and to carry out God's purposes, sin of all kinds must be sought out and extirpated; and the temper of the leaders, as well as of the freemen generally, was eminently suited to the performance of that task with respect both to themselves and to the non-Puritan elements in the community. "Holy watching" of his neighbor was as characteristic of the Puritan as his habit of mercilessly scrutinizing his own conduct, and the injunction that the colonists bear one another's burdens entailed precisely this kind of neighborly vigilance. To the Puritans, "brotherly love" characteristically took the form of correction and admonition rather than of toleration, which led neither to improvement nor to regeneration.

Dean Fordham has observed that "In the very broadest sense, the indispensable element of sanction in any legislation designed to order human behavior is the willingness of the members of the community at large to conform, whether by reason of approval of or acquiescence in the policy itself or by reason of a social character which impels the desired compliance with a measure which may be distasteful." [4] The regenerate in Massachusetts were within the social covenant, and this fact, together with their general agreement with the purposes for which the colony had been founded, substantially ensured their compliance with the laws established by the commonwealth. The reprobate, on the other hand, were under, although not within, the covenant by having come to live within the commonwealth and by having subscribed to the oath which every resident was required to take. Against them, moral and social sanctions were somewhat less effective than were governmental sanctions, particularly those of the laws which carried open threats of penalties and prosecution for their infraction. Nevertheless, as the Epistle to the Code recites, the laws were made "with respect to the whole people, and not to each particular person: and obedience to them must be yeilded with respect to the common welfare. . . ." [5]

The end of law as viewed by the colonists was less alien to our own conceptions than a first impression might suggest. In politically organized society, law operates as a restraint on individual action for the benefit of some other individual or of the group as a whole. Conformity is imposed to the extent necessary to subserve the ideals upon which a particular society is organized, and the extent of individual freedom allowed by law depends upon the definition of what constitutes the welfare of the community. When the ideals of a society are defined as they were in early Massachusetts, there is, of course, little room for the nonconformist, for the man who does not keep pace because he hears a different drummer.

In nearly all societies, many legal rules find their basis in religious and ethical ideas, but even in the Puritan state such ideas were by no means the sole foundation of the law. It has been observed that in a society of any complexity, law is a necessity of life, needed by the individual to maintain an inner balance between his aggressive and his social instincts. Impelled by the former, he seeks to satisfy his own demands at the expense of others; driven by the latter he seeks to secure the advantages of group life.[6] To the extent that law is a means for effecting the adjustment of these essentially conflicting human instincts, it is not only a highly important agency of social control but a product of individual and social forces. Law is thus something more than the command of the state,[7] more than an embodiment of a common will [8] or of idealized ethical custom,[9] and more than a standardized set of rules and procedures for the settlement of controversies in the courts.[10] The studies of anthropologists and sociologists have developed a recognition that law is the product of, or the response to, exceedingly complex actions and interactions operating within an environment of social and psychological factors whose influence is only beginning to be understood.[11]

One of the most notable features of politically organized society is what jurists refer to as the "legal order," that is, a regime for regulating and adjusting the relations of men, particularly their desires and claims with respect to one another and to things and to the community generally. Law is the central feature of this regime, and consists of the body of authoritative precepts, guides, and received ideals, and the techniques of using them, consciously established or implicitly recognized by particular societies for the delimitation and securing of social as well as individual interests. These interests reflect the demands or desires which human beings, either individually or in groups, seek to satisfy, and which are consequently of the essence of what the ordering of human relations in civilized society must take into account.[12] The law does not create interests, but it classifies them and recognizes or refuses to recognize them in accordance with policies and purposes of differing communities and civilizations. Moreover, the law defines the extent to which it will give effect to the interests which it recognizes, in the light of other interests and of the possibilities of effectively securing them through law; it also devises means for securing those that are recognized and prescribes the limits within which those means may be employed.[13] Dean Pound has observed that the interests which the legal order secures may be individual, public, or social.[14] Analytically, the three types are distinct, but they are frequently interlocking in the sense, for example, that social interests necessarily include or take account of individual interests.

In terms of this analysis, it seems clear that, in a broad sense, one of the most important of the public and social interests recognized and fostered by the Massachusetts legal system was that of maintaining the purity of the colony churches so that the commission which God had given to His commonwealth might be carried out in all its articles. That interest found its clearest expression in the imposing series of laws enacted to ensure religious orthodoxy, attendance upon and respect for the word of God, and the constitutional protection of the churches' political position. When the colony leaders resorted to such devices as the negative vote and discretionary penalties to promote and ensure the safety of this overriding community interest, there came into prominence a countervailing pressure for the express recognition of such individual interests as those of personality, substance, and freedom of association. This pressure was especially evident in the agitation of the deputies for written laws and for clearly prescribed penalties, which resulted in the enactment of the Body of Liberties and the Code of 1648. The civil liberties expressly assured therein contain a remarkable array of individual interests guaranteed by law in a social system primarily committed to the securing of broad social and public interests. Although many types of individual interests, particularly in the area of personal conduct, gave way to, or were displaced by, the public interest of regimenting men's lives in accordance with the purposes of the Puritan state, others were given clear recognition under the Massachusetts legal system. For example, the colonists were left relatively free to pursue their chosen trades and callings, to buy and sell, to own and dispose, to give and inherit and, above all, to secure and protect in the courts these individual interests of substance and personality.

In primitive societies, but also to some extent in more advanced civilizations, law usually consists of customary rules of action or inaction, declared or undeclared in an authentic form, but effective to order men's conduct because community sentiment so dictates. At later stages of political development, law tends to consist primarily of rules declared or developed by persons having official authority for that purpose and therefore includes, in addition to custom, the enactments of legislatures, the orders of public officials, and the decisions of judicial tribunals. In some societies, as for instance in early Massachusetts, religious, no less than civil, groups may be invested with authority to regulate human conduct. Because in any advanced stage of civilization law is both a product of the society within which it operates, and because it is also an agency for social control, it is seldom static but responds to, as well as regulates, new and emerging desires and claims of men with respect to one another and to the state. In early Massachusetts the law appears both as an anchor to tradition and as a vehicle for change. Influential as was the force of biblical precedent and of English law and custom, local conditions and the emerging needs of the community were among the significant determinatives of the path of the law. No more cogent illustration of the use of law as a device for effecting needed adjustments can be found than in the enactments relating to debtors and creditors which resulted from the depression of the 1640's.

Legal rules in advanced stages of civilization are a function of time and place, for the desires and claims which press for recognition and adjustment are ever changing. Whether particular rules for adjusting human relations and regulating human conduct are the outcome of custom, legislation, or judicial decision, they reflect by and large some need or needs of society, or of some segment of society, at particular times. Very often these rules, or the techniques of applying them, become outmoded and linger on beyond their periods of usefulness. For this reason the law frequently contains elements which can be understood only in terms of what has gone before. Yet the past is also significant because law is responsive to received ideals, such as the sense of justice or injustice, ethics and religion, which men inherit from an earlier day. Legal rules, therefore, also reflect in some measure, as they did in Massachusetts, the picture of what men of a particular time regard as the ideal of relations among men, thereby further illumining from an ethical or moral standpoint the patterns of the society in which they operate. The colonists' identification of man-made rules with the law of God, the law of nature and the law of reason is only one manifestation of the ideal element in their law. Hortatory injunctions, such as those contained in the capital laws, provide vivid examples of this ideal element that infused the laws and supplemented its regulatory effect upon human conduct.

The foregoing exposition of the role of law in society has been stated in somewhat broader terms than those to which the legal profession is ordinarily accustomed. Lawyers tend to think of law as consisting of the rules applied or enforced by judicial or other official bodies in the settlement of justiciable controversies, and to view the history of law as the evolution of those rules and of the doctrines and precedents associated therewith. Such views can be misleading. In their emphasis upon official acts, they center attention upon parties, procedures, and doctrines, and discount the impact of political and economic pressures, as well as the influence of ethical and philosophical ideas. If, however, law is viewed both as a reflection of social forces and as an agency of social control, the history of law is not an arid exposition of the development of doctrines and rules but a vehicle for describing, and demonstrating the interrelation of, social structures and the pressures that bear upon them.

The continuing interplay of tradition and design in early Massachusetts affords convincing proof of the intimate connection that existed between law and social organization. Legal rules continually reflected individual and group sentiments, as well as the purposes of the organization to which they belonged, and the interaction between the two.[15] Traditional elements in the colonists' legal heritage were reflected, accepted, or modified according as they appeared objectionable or suitable to the colony's needs and purposes. The integrated pattern that resulted was the outcome of careful planning, justified by Puritan ideals, by human logic, and by practical experience. The ideal and the practical constantly affected each other. Thus, if criminal statutes were enacted to conform to Scripture, or to mitigate the harshness of English criminal law, others were framed to deal with such specific and harassing problems as petty thievery and housebreaking on the Sabbath.

If much that is encountered in Puritan social theory seems foreign to modern conceptions of law and liberty, it must not be forgotten that the political and legal arrangements instituted by the colonists, as well as the assumptions that underlay them, contained the seeds of ideas that later became and still remain part of the American heritage. Notably, the conception of the social covenant and the emphasis upon a God-given fundamental law were the genesis of ideals which flowered in the eighteenth century and shaped political and legal thinking in the early days of the Republic.

From its inception, the government of the Bay Colony was authoritarian in operation but consensual in origin. Its officers were considered to derive their authority not from the people who selected them, but directly from God, "in way of an ordinance." [16] As late as 1669, John Davenport affirmed the orthodox position in saying that ". . . in one and the same action, God, by the Peoples suffrages, makes such an one Governour, or Magistrate, and not another." [17] As the century wore on, however, and the intensity of religious orthodoxy was dimmed, this doctrine became progressively more difficult for men to understand or accept, as did the idea of the social covenant as a commitment of society to the will of God. An inevitable result of the subsidence of the religious impetus was a tendency, which became steadily more evident, to turn away from theological justifications toward rational explanations for political and legal theory. Yet the conception of the social covenant survived, although it took new form. The beginnings of the transformation are apparent in the election sermon preached by Samuel Willard in 1690, wherein he stated, "A People are not made for Rules, But Rulers for a People." [18]

The roots of Willard's emphasis upon the preservation of the liberties and rights of the people as an end of government not only stemmed from Puritan ideas of the social covenant but went far back into the seventeenth century and beyond to ideas born of the earliest efforts of Englishmen to place limits on the power of a government that did not derive its authority from the people. Out of the English Civil War developed changed conceptions of the basis and purpose of government, illustrated by Sir Orlando Bridgman's instructions to the jury for the trial of the Regicides in 1660: "the people, as to their properties, liberties, and lives, have as great a privilege as the king." [19] In colonial thinking, such conceptions were carried much further, and by 1717 John Wise, of Ipswich, could argue from "several Principles of Natural Knowledge; plainly discovering the Law of Nature," that "The formal Reason of Government is the Will of a Community." [20] "For, as [the people] have a Power every Man over himself in a Natural State, so upon a Combination they can and do bequeath this Power unto others. . . ." [21] In contrast with John Cotton's belief that democracy was not a "fitt government eyther for church or commonwealth," [22] Wise stated that democracy "is a form of Government, which the Light of Nature does highly value, & often directs to as most agreeable to the Just and Natural Prerogatives of Humane Beings." [23] The progressive acceptance of the idea that the people are the source of governmental power, whose object is the preservation of popular liberties, is summarized by Professor Miller, who writes that

. . . men perceived the charms and usefulness of claiming that the compact had been an agreement of the people, not to God's terms, but to their own terms. The divine ordinance and the spirit of God, which were supposed to have presided over the political process, vanished, leaving a government founded on the self-evident truths of the law of nature, brought into being by social compact, instituted not for the glory of God, but to secure men's "inalienable rights" of life, liberty, and the pursuit of happiness.[24]

So out of old fields was to come the new harvest. In legal as well as in political thinking, eighteenth century America also drew upon and modified conceptions of an earlier day. Foremost among the problems with which men were to become preoccupied at the end of the century was that of assuring that governmental power would not be abused. The solution was found in the idea developed by Coke, but mediaeval in origin, of applying fundamental law as a check upon governmental action. The idea was carried out in the Federal Constitution, which was "framed and adopted under the influence of that dread of royal power which had dictated the line of English constitutional development during two preceding centuries." [25] "A written constitution," observes John Dickinson, "is in itself the most effective possible application of the idea of a law sovereign over all laws which emanate merely from government." [26] This was precisely the device, also born of the idea of the rule of law, to which the deputies of the General Court had resorted in pressing for the enactment of the Body of Liberties and the Code of 1648 to curb the powers of government and to accommodate law and liberty in early Massachusetts.

Notes

LIST OF ABBREVIATIONS

Assistants Records   *Records of the Court of Assistants of the Colony of the Massachusetts Bay* (ed. J. Noble and J. F. Cronin: Boston, 1901–1928) 3 vols.

Body of Liberties   *The Colonial Laws of Massachusetts* (ed. W. H. Whitmore: Boston, 1889) 29–64. Citations are to Liberties.

Col. Soc. Mass.   The Colonial Society of Massachusetts.

Essex Records   *Records and Files of the Quarterly Courts of Essex County, Massachusetts* (ed. G. F. Dow: Salem, 1911) 8 vols.

Laws and Liberties   *The Laws and Liberties of Massachusetts* (ed. M. Farrand: Cambridge, Mass., 1929). Citations are to pages.

Mass. Hist. Soc.   The Massachusetts Historical Society.

Mass. Records   *Records of the Governor and Company of Massachusetts Bay* (ed. N. B. Shurtleff: Boston, 1853–1854) 6 vols.

N.E.Q.   *New England Quarterly.*

Winthrop, *Journal*   *Winthrop's Journal: History of New England* (ed. J. K. Hosmer) New York, 1908) 2 vols.

Winthrop Papers   *Winthrop Papers* (Massachusetts Historical Society: Boston, 1929–1947) 5 vols.

Preface

1. T. F. T. Plucknett, Book Review, *N.E.Q.* III, 576–577 (1930).
2. See H. Kantorowicz, *Rechtswissenschaft und Soziologie* (Tübingen, 1911) 30–34.
3. F. C. Von Savigny, *Vom Beruf unsrer Zeit für Gesetzgebung und Rechtswissenschaft* (Heidelberg, 1814) 8.
4. M. Howe, Book Review, *N.E.Q.* XIX, 245 (1946).
5. *Id.*, *Readings in American Legal History* (Cambridge, Mass., 1949) 232.
6. See, however, J. Goebel, "King's Law and Local Custom in Seventeenth Century New England," *Columbia Law Review* XXXI, 416 (1931); G. L. Haskins, "The Beginnings of the Recording System in Massachusetts," *Boston University Law Review* XXI, 281 (1941); *id.*, "The Beginnings of Partible Inheritance in the American Colonies," *Yale Law Journal* LI, 1280 (1942).
7. This problem still awaits detailed investigation. See the preliminary study of G. L. Haskins and S. E. Ewing, 3rd, "The Spread of Massachusetts Law in the Seventeenth Century," *University of Pennsylvania Law Review* CVI, 413 (1958).
8. G. L. Haskins, "Codification of the Law in Colonial Massachusetts: A Study in Comparative Law," *Indiana Law Journal* XXX, 1 (1954); *id.*, "De la codification du droit en Amérique du Nord au xviiᵉ siècle: une étude de droit comparé," *Revue d'histoire du droit* XXIII, 311 (1955).
9. *Id.*, *Indiana Law Journal*, 11; *Revue d'histoire du droit* 324.

Chapter I *THEIR HIGHEST INHERITANCE*

1. H. Adams, *History of the United States of America* (New York 1889) I, 133.
2. G. L. Haskins, "De la codification du droit en Amérique du Nord au xviiᵉ siècle: une étude de droit comparé," *Revue d'histoire du droit* XXIII, 311 (1955). *Id.*, "Codification of the Law in Colonial Massachusetts: A Study in Comparative Law," *Indiana Law Journal* XXX, 1 (1954).
3. J. T. Adams, *The Founding of New England* (Boston, 1921) 120–121, and authorities there cited.
4. *Ibid.*
5. W. S. Churchill, *A History of the English-Speaking Peoples* (London, 1956) II, 142.
6. See G. L. Haskins, "Law and Colonial Society," *American Quarterly* IX, 354 at 356–357 (1957), and authorities there cited.
7. C. Lofft, *Principia cum Juris Universalis tum Praecipue Anglicani* (London, 1779) I, 123.
8. Per Chase, J., in U.S. v. Worrall, 2 Dallas' Federal Reports 384 at 394 (1798).
9. Per Story, J., in Van Ness v. Pacard, 2 Peters' U.S. Supreme Court Reports 137 at 144 (1829).
10. J. M. Zane, *The Story of Law* (New York, 1927), 358.
11. Thus, the Massachusetts Bay charter, *Mass. Records* I, 12.
12. *Ibid.*

13. See J. Kent, *Commentaries on American Law*, 12th edition (ed. O. W. Holmes, Jr.: Boston, 1873) I, 472-473 [537-538]. See, e.g., Doe, ex dem. Patterson, v. Winn, 5 Peters' U.S. Supreme Court Reports 233 at 241-242 (1831) per Story, J.; Carter & Wife v. Balfour's Administrator, 19 Alabama Supreme Court Reports 814 at 829 (1851). See also, generally, J. H. Smith, *Appeals to the Privy Council from the American Plantations* (New York, 1950) 465-522.

14. E.g., Morris v. Vanderen, 1 Dallas' Pennsylvania Reports 64 at 66 (1782) per McKean, C. J.: ". . . [T]he common law of England has always been in force in Pennsylvania; . . . all statutes made in Great Britain, before the settlement of Pennsylvania, have no force here, unless they are convenient and adapted to the circumstances of the country; and . . . all statutes made *since* the settlement of Pennsylvania, have no force here, unless the colonies are particularly named. . . ." See also Respublica v. Mesca, 1 Dallas' Pennsylvania Reports 73 at 74 (1783) per McKean, C. J.: "We know . . . that many statutes, for near a century, have been practiced under, in the late province, which were never adopted by the legislature; and that they might be admitted by usage, and so become in force, was the opinion of the British parliament, declared in a statute passed in the year 1754, enabling legatees to be witnesses to wills and testaments."

15. The Guardians of the Poor v. Greene, 5 Binney's Pennsylvania Reports 554 at 558 (1813).

16. See the masterly historical exposition of Chief Justice Harlan Fiske Stone, speaking for the Supreme Court, in C. J. Hendry Co. v. Moore, 318 U.S. Supreme Court Reports 133 (1943).

17. *Abridgement of the Laws in force and use in Her Majesty's Plantations, viz.: of Virginia, Jamaica, Barbadoes, Maryland, New-England, New-York, Carolina, etc.* (London, 1704).

18. J. Goebel and T. R. Naughton, *Law Enforcement in Colonial New York* (New York, 1944) xxxv.

19. P. S. Reinsch, "The English Common Law in the Early American Colonies," *Select Essays in Anglo-American Legal History* (Boston, 1907) I, 367 at 370.

20. C. J. Hilkey, "Legal Development in Colonial Massachusetts," *Columbia Studies in History, Economics and Public Law* XXXVII, 68 (1910).

Chapter II *CREEDS AND PLATFORMS*

1. The charter is printed in *Mass. Records* I, 3-20.

2. *Id.* at I, 7.

3. *Id.* at I, 12.

4. *Id.* at I, 11. For the early activity of these courts, see *id.* at I, 42-44.

5. For discussion of this and other early grants in New England, see H. L. Osgood, *The American Colonies in the Seventeenth Century* (New York, 1904) I, 98-137; F. Rose-Troup, *The Massachusetts Bay Company and Its Predecessors* (New York, 1930); R. E. Moody, "A Re-Examination of the Antecedents of the Massachusetts Bay Company's Charter of 1629," *Mass. Hist. Soc. Proc.* LXIX, 56 (1956).

6. *Mass. Records* I, 383–385.

7. *Id.* at I, 397; see also *id.* at I, 386–387.

8. *Id.* at I, 405, 406, 407.

9. *Id.* at I, 387.

10. See note 55, *infra*.

11. The steps by which these men became associated with the first entrepreneurs are sketched in S. E. Morison, *Builders of the Bay Colony* (Cambridge, Mass., 1930) 33 *et seq*. See also C. B. Park, "Friendship as a Factor in the Settlement of Massachusetts," *American Antiquarian Society Proceedings*, XXVIII, 51–62 (1918).

12. Writing several years after the event, Winthrop said of the residence clause, "with much difficulty we gott it abscinded." *Winthrop Papers* IV, 470. This statement has often been taken to mean that the omission was obtained by greasing the palm of some official. See e.g., S. E. Morison, *op. cit. supra* n. 11, at 66. However, against other facts, notably concern among the members during the summer of 1629 as to whether the removal of the company to New England would be legal, Winthrop's statement does not appear conclusive. *Mass. Records* I, 52. It seems at least possible that the antecedent of the pronoun "it" may have been the customary understanding that the management of the company would remain in England. For discussion of the question, see J. T. Adams, *The Founding of New England* (Boston, 1921) 139–140; Rose-Troup, *op. cit. supra* n. 5, at 75–79; C. M. Andrews, "Historic Doubts," *Col. Soc. Mass. Publ.* XXVIII, 280 at 288 (1935); C. Deane, "The Forms Used in Issuing Letters-Patent by the Crown of England," *Mass. Hist. Soc. Proc.* XI (1st ser.), 166 (1871); J. Parker, "Remarks," *id.* at 188.

13. *Mass. Records* I, 51.

14. *Id.* at I, 59.

15. *Id.* at I, 60 *et seq*.

16. See Chap. VII, pp. 99 *et seq. infra*.

17. It has been estimated that by 1650 there was at least one university-trained man to every forty or fifty families in New England. S. E. Morison, *The Puritan Pronaos* (New York, 1936) 16. Of these the greater proportion were Cambridge men, long nourished on Puritan doctrine. Cf. J. B. Prizer, "Some Aspects of the Influence of Cambridge Men and their University in the American Colonies," *Historical Publications of the Society of Colonial Wars in the Commonwealth of Pennsylvania* VII, No. 9, 4 (1956).

18. P. Miller, *Orthodoxy in Massachusetts, 1630–1650* (Cambridge, Mass., 1933) 73.

19. For a careful discussion and analysis of Separatist and non-Separatist Congregationalism, see *id.*, at Chaps. 3 and 4.

20. *Id.* at 85–92.

21. *Id.* at Chap. 5.

22. *Id.* at 99–100.

23. J. Allin and T. Shepard, *A Defence of the Answer made unto the Nine Questions or Positions sent from New-England* (London, 1648) 4.

24. See, e.g., *Winthrop Papers* III, 10–14.

25. Miller, *op. cit. supra* n. 18, at 105 *et seq*. This thesis rejects the view that the Bay colonists acquired their Congregationalism by a species of contagion from Plymouth. See *id.* at 125, 127 *et seq*. Cf. S. E. Morison, *By Land and by Sea* (New York, 1953) 234.

26. *Winthrop Papers* II, 177–178.
27. Miller, *op. cit. supra* n. 18, at 144.
28. *Winthrop Papers* II, 231.
29. R. B. Perry, *Puritanism and Democracy* (New York, 1944) 627.
30. Cf. A. S. P. Woodhouse, *Puritanism and Liberty* (London, 1938) 44.
31. R. Baxter, *Christian Directory* (London, 1678), reprinted in *The Practical Works of Richard Baxter* (London, 1854) I, 376.
32. Winthrop, *Journal* II, 238–239.
33. *Id.* at I, 239.
34. G. W. Prothero, *Select Statutes and Other Constitutional Documents Illustrative of the Reigns of Elizabeth and James I* (Oxford, 1913) xxx.
35. P. Miller and T. H. Johnson, *The Puritans* (New York, 1938) 182–183.
36. J. W. Allen, *A History of Political Thought in the Sixteenth Century* (New York, 1928) 76.
37. C. H. McIlwain, ed., *The Political Works of James I* (Cambridge, Mass., 1918) xvii.
38. *Ibid.*
39. P. Miller, "The Marrow of Puritan Divinity," *Col. Soc. Mass. Publ.* XXXII, 247 at 294 (1937).
40. *Id., The New England Mind: The Seventeenth Century* (Cambridge, Mass., 1954) 412, referring to the classic statement published as early as 1579 in the *Vindiciae Contra Tyrannos*. Elsewhere, McIlwain, *op. cit. supra* n. 37, at xvi, has pointed out that, despite easy generalizations about Tudor absolutism, in England, as on the Continent, there was much discussion of the nature and extent of royal power, of election, of contract, of restrictions imposed by the coronation oath and of assertions of the right of the people collectively to judge, to dispose, and even to kill the king. This outburst of political thought and radical opinion was an inevitable feature of the sixteenth century, and is attributable in large part to the diversity of religious views stimulated and made possible by the Reformation.
41. Miller, *op. cit. supra* n. 40, at 418.
42. *Winthrop Papers* II, 292–293.
43. *Id.* at II, 293.
44. E.g., *id.* at II, 172–173, 199.
45. Morison, *op. cit. supra* n. 11, at Chap. 2.
46. *Id.* at 71–72.
47. C. E. Banks, *The Planters of the Commonwealth* (Boston, 1930) 13–15; *id., Topographical Dictionary of 2885 English Emigrants to New England, 1620–1650* (Baltimore, 1957).
48. H. A. L. Fisher, *The Bay Colony: A Tercentenary Address* (Boston, 1930) 17.
49. See C. E. Banks, "Religious 'Persecution' as a Factor in Emigration to New England, 1630–1640," *Mass. Hist. Soc. Proc.* LXIII, 136 (1931). The idea of religious groups seeking refuge outside England was not new. Roman Catholics had considered emigrating early in the seventeenth century. C. M. Andrews, *loc. cit. supra* n. 12, at 287.
50. *Winthrop Papers* II, 91.
51. E. D. Mead, "Thomas Hooker's Farewell Sermon in England," *Mass. Hist. Soc. Proc.* XLVI, 253 at 261 (1913).
52. Miller, *op. cit. supra* n. 18, at 43 *et seq.*

53. *Winthrop Papers* II, 91.

54. *Id.* at II, 139.

55. *The Planters Plea* (London, 1630) 23 *et seq.*

56. *Winthrop Papers* II, 126, 148–149.

57. See the summary in N. M. Crouse, "Causes of the Great Migration 1630–1640" *N.E.Q.* V, 3 at 8–15 (1932). The author particularly emphasizes the crisis in the wool trade of East Anglia.

58. *Winthrop Papers* II, 139.

59. G. L. Beer, *The Origins of the British Colonial System, 1578–1660* (New York, 1908) 41–42, 51.

60. R. Hakluyt, "Discourse on Western Planting," *Maine Historical Society Collections* (2d ser.) II (1877).

61. *Winthrop Papers* II, 139.

62. *Johnson's Wonder-Working Providence* (ed. J. F. Jameson: New York, 1910) 35.

63. How many of the colonists were Puritans has been a subject of disagreement. James Truslow Adams, for example, has asserted that four out of every five were non-Puritan (Adams, *op. cit. supra* n. 12, at 121). Thomas Lechford, writing from firsthand knowledge in or about 1640, stated that "three parts of the people of the Country remaine out of the Church" (T. Lechford, "Plain Dealing: or Newes from New-England," *Mass. Hist. Soc. Coll.* [3rd series] III, 55 at 122–123 [1833]). This latter statement, however, is not to be interpreted as meaning that three-quarters of the colonists were non-Puritan, for they might be Puritans in their beliefs and yet not qualify in the eyes of a congregation for admission to a church. Nevertheless, it seems clear that many of the colonists who were neither Puritans nor church members probably had little sympathy with, certainly little understanding of, the objectives of the colony leaders. See Osgood, *op. cit. supra* n. 5, at I, 221.

64. E.g., *Winthrop Papers* II, 192, 202.

65. C. E. Banks, *The Winthrop Fleet of 1630* (Boston, 1930) Chap. 4; *Winthrop Papers* II, 171–172.

66. Osgood, *op. cit. supra* n. 5, at I, 146–147.

67. See Chap. III, n. 6, *infra.*

68. *Winthrop Papers* II, 225.

69. Cf. Winthrop, *Journal* II, 290 *et seq.*

70. P. Miller, "The Cambridge Platform in 1648," *The Cambridge Platform of 1648* (ed. H. W. Foote: Boston, 1949) 60 at 74.

71. *Mass. Records* I, 408.

72. *Winthrop Papers* II, 231–232.

73. Banks, *op. cit. supra* n. 65, at 34.

74. J. G. Palfrey, *History of New England* (Boston, 1865) I, 313.

75. *Winthrop Papers* II, 295.

Chapter III   *FOUNDATIONS OF POWER*

1. H. L. Osgood, *The American Colonies in the Seventeenth Century* (New York, 1904) I, 150–152. It was partly as a result of the land system that quit-rents were not established in Massachusetts. See B. W. Bond, Jr., *The Quit-Rent System in the American Colonies* (New Haven, 1919) Chap. 2.

2. *Mass. Records* I, 87.

3. *Winthrop Papers* II, 295.

4. *Commonwealth History of Massachusetts* (ed. A. B. Hart: New York, 1927) I, 120.

5. See W. H. Whitmore, *The Massachusetts Civil List for the Colonial and Provincial Periods, 1630–1774* (Albany, 1870) 21. Whitmore lists eleven assistants for the year 1630. Of these, William Vassall appeared at a meeting of the assistants on board the *Arbella* on the outward voyage, but he is not listed as having attended any of the meetings after his arrival in Massachusetts. In any event, he returned to England very shortly. Of the remaining ten, Thomas Sharp also returned to England soon afterward, and Isaac Johnson died. Thus, by October, 1630, there appear to have been only eight assistants in the colony. See J. G. Palfrey, *History of New England* (Boston, 1865) I, 323 n. 1, in which it is stated that there appears to have been only one freeman, John Glover of Dorchester, in addition to the governor, the deputy-governor, and the assistants.

6. *Mass. Records* I, 75; *Commonwealth History, supra* n. 4, at 103.

7. *Mass. Records* I, 11.

8. *Id.* at I, 79; at this meeting the question was also propounded whether the freemen should not have the power to elect the assistants, and this "was fully assented vnto by the generall vote of the people, & ereccion of hands" (*ibid.*). If the sentence means what it says, since the assistants were the freemen and the freemen were the assistants, the latter were asking for confirmation of existing practice, Professor Morgan argues that the word "freemen" as here used must have had a broader meaning than the technical one and that the question presages the admission of those who requested it. See E. S. Morgan, *The Puritan Dilemma: The Story of John Winthrop* (Boston, 1958) 91. See also comment on this point in Book Review, *Amer. Hist. Rev.* LXIV, 186 (1958).

9. *Mass. Records* I, 79.

10. *Id.* at I, 74.

11. Milton, "Tetrachordon," *The Prose Works of John Milton* (ed. C. Symmons: London, 1806) II, 120–121.

12. *Mass. Records* I, 16–17.

13. *Id.* at I, 76.

14. *Id.* at I, 82–83.

15. H. M. Dexter, *As to Roger Williams and His "Banishment" from the Massachusetts Plantation* (Boston, 1876) 17. Dexter points out, *ibid.*, that in banishing persons from the colony the magistrates were acting as a company having a right to exclude and to decline to admit incompatible and unsuitable members. In this connection, it should be noted that the charter expressly provided that the patentees might "expulse" all persons who should attempt any "detriment, or annoyance to the said plantation or inhabitantes" (*Mass. Records* I, 18).

16. *Id.* at I, 88.

17. *Id.* at I, 94.

18. E.g., *id.* at I, 74, 76, 77–78, 85, 92.

19. *Id.* at I, 84, 100–101, 109.

20. *Id.* at I, 79–80.

21. *Id.* at I, 387.

22. Morgan, *op. cit. supra* n. 8, 93 *et seq.*, explains the decision on the basis of the Puritan conception of the social compact.

23. *Mass. Records* I, 366.

24. *Id.* at I, 87.

25. For discussion of the qualifications for church membership, see Chap. VI, *infra*.

26. See *Mass. Records* I, 366–379; an alphabetical list of freemen is printed at *id.* I, 471–479.

27. See Chap. I, note 4, *supra*.

28. *Mass. Records* I, 87.

29. *Id.* at I, 95.

30. *Id.* at I, 117.

31. B. and S. Webb, *English Local Government from the Revolution to the Municipal Corporations Act: The Manor and the Borough* (London, 1908) 294 *et seq.*

32. Winthrop, *Journal* I, 74.

33. *Ibid.* It is noteworthy that as early as 1631 the freemen are referred to as the "commons" of the General Court (*Mass. Records* I, 87).

34. Winthrop, *Journal* I, 79; see also *Mass. Records* I, 95.

35. Winthrop, *Journal* I, 122–123.

36. *Id.* at I, 122.

37. *Mass. Records* I, 117.

38. *Id.* at I, 118–119.

39. In 1634 there were 24 deputies for eight towns (J. Winthrop, *History of New England* [ed. J. Savage: Boston, 1825] I, 129, n. 1, and *Mass. Records* I, 116–117). In 1644 there were 39 deputies for 24 towns (*id.* at III, 1–2). No town was permitted to send a deputy unless there were ten freemen therein (*id.* at I, 178).

40. *Id.* at I, 119.

41. See, however, the statement of the elders in 1644 that "there is a three-fold power of magistratical authority, viz., legislative, judicial, and consultative or directive. . . ." (Winthrop, *Journal* II, 212). In several respects the General Court was not unlike the High Court of Parliament in England. See G. L. Haskins, *The Growth of English Representative Government* (Philadelphia, 1948) 94.

42. E.g., *Mass. Records* I, 291, 306.

43. E.g., *id.* at I, 207, 309, 346; II, 60, 90, 102, 104, etc. By 1638 the number of petitions had so greatly increased that it was ordered that a committee should hear and determine "all particuler petitions & suites, & of other private business" (*id.* at I, 223). In some respects, the petitions are reminiscent of those presented to the English parliaments in the Middle Ages, when little distinction was drawn between legislative, judicial, and administrative functions. See G. L. Haskins, "The Petitions of Representatives in the Parliaments of Edward I," *English Historical Review* LIII, 1 (1938).

44. *Mass. Records* I, 167, 179, 186, 221. The provision for life terms was adopted to comply with the biblical precept that magistrates should serve for life (Winthrop, *Journal* I, 178).

45. *Ibid.*; *Mass. Records* I, 195.

46. See generally E. E. Brennan, "The Massachusetts Council of the Magistrates," *N.E.Q.* IV, 54 (1931).

47. Osgood, *op. cit. supra* n. 1, at I, 177.

48. *Mass. Records* I, 74.

49. *Id.* at I, 239. See also n. 67, *infra*.

50. *Laws and Liberties*, 30–31, 45, 35, 5, 19, 20.

51. T. Lechford, "Plain Dealing: or Newes from New England," *Mass. Hist. Soc. Coll.* (3rd series) III, 55 at 84 (1833); E. Washburn, *Sketches of the Judicial History of Massachusetts* (Boston, 1840) 30.

52. *Mass. Records* I, 169.

53. *Ibid.* These four courts had jurisdiction over suits arising in neighboring towns as follows: Ipswich (Newbury), Salem (Saugus), Newtown (Charlestown, Concord, Medford, and Watertown), Boston (Roxbury, Dorchester, Weymouth, and Hingham).

54. *Id.* at II, 38.

55. *Id.* at I, 169. By 1639 the business of the Court of Assistants had so increased that further special courts were established. For their composition and jurisdiction, see *id.* at I, 276.

56. *Laws and Liberties* 15. Osgood's statement to the contrary, *op. cit. supra* n. 1, at I, 190, does not appear to be supported. See, in this connection, the 1650 case in *Essex Records* I, 191, in which the Salisbury Court ordered that "Mr. Bacherler and Mary his wife shall live together . . . and if either desert the other, the marshal to take them to Boston to be kept until next quarter Court of Assistants, to consider a divorce."

57. *Mass. Records* I, 169; *Laws and Liberties* 15.

58. *Mass. Records* I, 169, 325–326. Judicial practice permitted extensive re-examination of questions of fact and law upon appeal, with the result that an appellant customarily obtained a second jury trial in the appellate court. See discussion in M. Howe, *Readings in American Legal History* (Cambridge, Mass., 1949) 125–127.

59. E.g., writs of dower, idleness, and highway disputes (*Laws and Liberties* 17–18, 25–26).

60. *Mass. Records* II, 279. Cf. *id.* at I, 239.

61. *Id.* at I, 169. After the colony was divided into counties in 1643, this requirement was changed to "magistrates living in the respective Counties." In accordance with seventeenth century usage, the terms "magistrate" and "assistant" are used interchangeably.

62. E.g., *Essex Records* I, 5, 7, etc. See also *Mass. Records* I, 197.

63. See p. 32, *supra*.

64. See *Essex Records* I, index, 446–449.

65. Osgood, *op. cit. supra* n. 1, at I, 190–191.

66. See *Laws and Liberties* 8–9, 13.

67. *Mass. Records* I, 239. See also *id.* at I, 327. The limit was raised to forty shillings in 1647 (*id.* at II, 208, 209). In 1649 the jurisdiction of the Commissioners' Courts in such actions was made compulsory (*id.* at II, 279).

68. *Id.* at II, 188.

69. *Laws and Liberties* 8.

70. In 1646 the selectmen were authorized to hear and determine small causes to which the magistrate in charge was a party. *Mass. Records* II, 162–163. For the duties of the selectmen with respect to colony laws, see Chap. V, p. 74, *infra*.

71. *Mass. Records* I, 264.

72. *Laws and Liberties* 15.
73. See, however, *Mass. Records* I, 79, 87.
74. E.g., in 1642 Winthrop expressed resentment at the deputies sitting too often as a court "in judging private Causes, to which they have no ordinary callinge" (*Winthrop Papers* IV, 359).
75. *Supra*, n. 61.
76. *Mass. Records* II, 16.
77. *Infra*, p. 38.
78. *Mass. Records* IV, *passim*. Several cases were also heard on transfer from the Court of Assistants. *Id.* at IV (Part 2), 197, 329, 405–406. Note the provision in *Laws and Liberties* 32, to the effect that, if the court and the jury disagreed about a verdict, the case shall be referred to the General Court for determination.
79. The General Court had concurrent jurisdiction with other courts in specified situations, e.g., with the Court of Assistants power to appoint persons to perform marriages, and with that court and the County Courts' power to appoint searchers for powder (*id.*, at 38, 45).
80. *Mass. Records* II, 285; IV (Part 1), 82.
81. *Winthrop Papers* IV, 477. Arbitrary penalties were the subject of adverse comment by Thomas Hooker in 1638, See his letter to Winthrop in *Winthrop Papers* IV, 75 *et seq.*, esp. 81–82.
82. Particularly for theft and burglary. See Chap. IX, p. 154, *infra*.
83. See Chap. VIII, *infra*.
84. Winthrop, *Journal* I, 151; *Mass. Records* I, 147.
85. *Id.* at I, 174–175.
86. See Winthrop, *Journal* I, 323–324.
87. Printed in *The Colonial Laws of Massachusetts* (ed. W. H. Whitmore: Boston, 1889) 29–61.
88. In 1641 several deputies expressed their conviction that penalties should be fixed for lying and swearing. Winthrop recorded at that time arguments foreshadowing his more elaborate discourse three years later (Winthrop, *Journal* II, 49–52). See note 91, *infra*.
89. *Mass. Records* II, 61.
90. *Mass. Records* II, 90; Winthrop, *Journal* II, 217.
91. *Winthrop Papers* IV, 468 *et seq.*
92. *Mass. Records* II, 92–93. See also W. C. Ford, "The Negative Vote," *Mass. Hist. Soc. Proc.* XLVI, 276 (1913); Thomas Hooker had, however, expressed his concern about the magistrates' discretionary powers as early as 1638, stating that he looked upon it "as a way which leads directly to tyranny" (*Winthrop Papers* IV, 75 at 81).
93. *Mass. Records* II, 95–96.
94. This was *The Book of the General Lauues and Libertyes* (Cambridge, Mass., 1648), reprinted as *The Laws and Liberties of Massachusetts* (Cambridge, Mass., 1929). See generally Chap. VIII, *infra*.
95. See p. 31, *supra*.
96. Winthrop, *Journal* II, 170–171.
97. *Mass. Records* II, 92 *et seq.*
98. *Id.* at II, 94–95.
99. *Supra*, n. 91.
100. Osgood, *op. cit. supra* n. 1, at I, 182.

101. Winthrop, *Journal* I, 133-134.
102. *Mass. Records* II, 12. The question of the negative vote had its origin in an act of 1636 (*id.* at I, 170). A detailed account of the case of Sherman v. Keayne may be found in Winthrop, *Journal* II, 64-66, 116-120. For a thorough discussion of the legal and political issues, see M. Howe and L. F. Eaton, Jr., "The Supreme Judicial Power in the Colony of Massachusetts Bay," *N.E.Q.* XX, 291 (1947). As already indicated, the General Court had judicial as well as legislative and administrative functions, although these functions were seldom differentiated by contemporaries. See, however, Winthrop, *Journal* II, 212. By 1644 it had become the highest judicial court in the colony insofar as it exercised appellate jurisdiction.
103. Winthrop, *Journal* II, 120.
104. *Mass. Records* II, 58-59.
105. *Ibid.;* also Howe and Eaton, *loc. cit. supra* n. 102.
106. Principally Saltonstall and Bellingham. Winthrop, *Journal* II, 117.
107. *Id.* at II, 229 *et seq.*
108. *Id.* at II, 235.
109. *Id.* at II, 236-237.
110. *Id.* at II, 237-239.
111. See P. Miller, "The Marrow of Puritan Divinity," *Col. Soc. Mass. Publ.* XXXII, 247 at 292 (1937). Cf. *Laws and Liberties,* Epistle.
112. Despite the fact that Winthrop and several other magistrates were freemen of the original company, they were formally admitted as freemen of the colony in 1636 (*Mass. Records* I, 372).
113. *Id.* at I, 117.
114. For certain of these controversies, see Winthrop, *Journal* I, 78, 84-88, 169-172. See also n. 106 *supra.*
115. See especially Chap. V, *infra.*

Chapter IV   *A DUE FORM OF GOVERNMENT*

1. Chap. II, *supra,* pp. 17-18 Cf. W. Lambarde, *Archeion, or a Discourse upon the High Courts of Justice in England* (ed. C. H. McIlwain and P. L. Ward: Cambridge, Mass., 1957) 9-11. *Laws and Liberties,* Epistle.
2. *Winthrop Papers* II, 292-293.
3. P. Miller, *The New England Mind: The Seventeenth Century* (New York, 1939) 420.
4. *Winthrop Papers* IV, 476. See W. Perkins, *The Order of the Causes of Salvation and Damnation* (Cambridge, 1957) Chap. 24.
5. P. Miller and T. H. Johnson, *The Puritans* (New York, 1938) 183.
6. *Ibid.*
7. *Laws and Liberties,* Epistle.
8. *Mass. Records* I, 115.
9. J. Dorfman, *The Economic Mind in American Civilization, 1606-1865* (New York, 1946) I, 69 *et seq.*
10. Winthrop, *Journal* I, 78.
11. *Winthrop Papers* IV, 54. See generally S. Gray, "The Political Thought of John Winthrop," *N.E.Q.* III, 681 at 692-693 (1930).

12. *Winthrop Papers* IV, 383.

13. T. Hutchinson, *The History of the Colony and Province of Massachusetts Bay* (ed. L. S. Mayo: Cambridge, Mass., 1936) I, 415.

14. *Ibid.*

15. W. C. Ford, "The Negative Vote," *Mass. Hist. Soc. Proc.* XLVI, 283 (1913).

16. *Winthrop Papers* IV, 162.

17. But, said Ward, "I question whether it be of God to interest the inferiour sort in that which should be reserued inter optimates penes quos est sancire leges" (*ibid.*).

18. *Laws and Liberties,* Epistle. B. K. Brown, "A Note on the Puritan Concept of Aristocracy," *Miss. Valley Historical Rev.* XLI, 105 (1954). See also H. L. Osgood, "The Political Ideas of the Puritans," *Political Science Quarterly* VI, 1 at 28 (1891).

19. This was particularly true in cases of contempt of civil or church authority. Thus, Israel Stoughton, a deputy from Dorchester who had allegedly said that the assistants were not magistrates, was assailed by Winthrop as a "troubler of Israel" and barred by the General Court from holding office for three years (*Mass. Records* I, 135, 136). He was, however, "restored to his former libertie" slightly over a year later (*id.* at I, 175).

20. *Winthrop Papers* IV, 348.

21. Chap. II, pp. 14–15, *supra.*

22. E.g., Winthrop, *Journal* I, 66, 71–72.

23. The phrase is Winthrop's. *Winthrop Papers* III, 12.

24. Winthrop, *Journal* I, 162–163; *Mass. Records* I, 160–161. Williams' personal friendship with Winthrop nevertheless persisted and is attested by the letters which they continued to interchange.

25. For a recent evaluation of this episode, see E. S. Morgan, *The Puritan Dilemma: The Story of John Winthrop* (Boston, 1958) Chap. 10. See also *id.,* "The Case Against Anne Hutchinson, *N.E.Q.* X, 635 (1937).

26. One of the best expositions is that of C. F. Adams, *Three Episodes of Massachusetts History* (Cambridge, Mass., 1892) I, 363 *et seq.* Two consequences of Antinomian principles were particularly opposed and resisted by the Puritans. One was an egalitarianism of anarchical proportions; the other was their belief that they had the right to ignore or to shape events according to their "better" insight. The Antinomian arrogated all right and justice to himself alone. Such claims and pretensions ran counter to the whole trend of post-Reformation political thought. See G. Huehns, *Antinomianism in English History* (London, 1951) 89–105.

27. *Mass. Records* I, 207. An account of the trial will be found in C. F. Adams, *Antinomianism in the Colony of Massachusetts Bay, 1636–1638* (Boston, 1894).

28. *Id.* at 176.

29. *Id.* at 284.

30. Winthrop, *Journal* I, 264.

31. *Id.* at I, 324.

32. H. L. Osgood, *The American Colonies in the Seventeenth Century* (New York, 1904) I, 254. See also Winthrop, *Journal* II, 138.

33. J. T. Adams, *The Founding of New England* (Boston, 1921) 174, 210.

34. W. S. Holdsworth, *A History of English Law* (London, 1924) V, 192.

35. *Id.* at IX (1944) 233.
36. *Id.* at V, 192–193.
37. *Id.* at IX, 228.
38. *Id.* at IX, 229.
39. *Ibid.* Cf. J. H. Wigmore, *A Treatise on the Anglo-American System of Evidence in Trials at Common Law* (3d ed., Boston, 1940) VIII, 298, 301.
40. Holdsworth, *op. cit. supra* n. 34, at IX, 224–225.
41. *Id.* at IX, 225.
42. *Id.* at IX, 227. For an extensive extract from Sir Thomas Smith's contemporary account of a sixteenth century trial for robbery in *De Republica Anglorum*, see *id.* at IX, 225 *et seq.*
43. J. T. Adams, *op. cit. supra* n. 33, at 174.
44. E.g., *Laws and Liberties* 26; Osgood, *op. cit. supra* n. 32, at I, 264, 269 *et seq.*
45. J. T. Adams, *op. cit. supra* n. 33, at 148.
46. On the banishment of rogues, see stats. 39 Elizabeth I, c. 4; James I, c. 7; E. Coke, *Institutes* (Part III) Chap. XL, 103. Recusants to abjure the realm, stat. 35 Elizabeth I, c. 1, Coke, *supra*, Chap. XXXVIII, 102. For instances of transportation of convicted felons to Bermuda and the West Indies early in the seventeenth century, see *Middlesex Sessions Records* (ed. W. L. Hardy: London, 1936) II (new series), 22, 25, 38, 108, 114.
47. P. Miller, *Orthodoxy in Massachusetts* (Cambridge, Mass., 1933) 163.
48. C. F. Adams, *op. cit. supra* n. 27, at 256.
49. T. Weld, *An Answer to W. R.* (London, 1644) 13.
50. J. Cotton, *The Bloudy Tenent* (London, 1647) 35.
51. Weld, *op. cit. supra* n. 49, at 13.
52. E.g., *Mass. Records* I, 223, 126, 205; *Laws and Liberties*, 24, 6, 45, 53. See Chap. II, *supra*, p. 16.
54. R. Burton, *The Anatomy of Melancholy* Pt. III, Sec. 4, Memb. 1, Subs. 1 (ed. F. Dell and P. J. Smith: New York, 1951) 875.
55. E. A. J. Johnson, *American Economic Thought in the Seventeenth Century* (London, 1932) 123. See Cotton's rules for trading in Winthrop, *Journal* I, 315–318, and Chap. VI, *infra*, n. 54.
56. *Mass. Records* I, 111.
57. See Johnson, *op. cit. supra* n. 55, at 15–21.
58. See *id.* at 208–209.
59. See, for example, the proscription of dice and cards (*Mass. Records* I, 84), the penalties imposed for excesses in dress (*id.* at I, 126, 183, 274), for drunkenness (*id.* at II, 100), for lying (*Laws and Liberties* 35), for profanity (*id.*, at 45).
60. *Mass. Records* I, 18.
61. See Chap. III, p. 33, *supra*; Chap. VIII, pp. 127, *et seq.*, *infra*.
62. J. Dickinson, "Social Order and Political Authority," *Amer. Pol. Sci. Rev.* XXIII, 293 at 627 (1929).
63. W. H. Whitmore, *The Massachusetts Civil List for the Colonial and Provincial Periods, 1630–1774* (Albany, 1870) 21–22.
64. *Id.*, at 21–26.
65. C. M. Andrews, *The Colonial Period of American History* (New Haven, 1934) I, 496. J. T. Adams says that there were about 14,000 inhabitants by 1640. J. T. Adams, *op. cit. supra* n. 33, at 120.

66. See the detailed treatment of Puritan casuistry in G. L. Mosse, *The Holy Pretense: A Study in Christianity and Reason of State from William Perkins to John Winthrop* (Oxford, 1957). Professor Mosse concludes that Winthrop practiced "policy," in the Machiavellian sense, but that he was enabled to do so by the flexibility inherent in Puritan theology. The position which Machiavelli reached from "realistic presuppositions" was thus attained by Winthrop through religious ideas, sincerely applied without thought of deceit (*id.*, at 101–102).

67. *Essex Records* I, 35.

68. See particularly, Winthrop, *Journal* I, 84, 86–87, 169–171.

69. See, for example, *id.* at II, 117.

70. J. T. Adams, *op. cit. supra* n. 33 at 137.

71. See Winthrop, *Journal* I, 171–172. According to Thomas Hutchinson, Dudley reputedly pressed Winthrop on his deathbed to sign an order of banishment, and he refused, saying that "he had done too much of that work already" (Hutchinson, *op. cit. supra* n. 13 at I, 129).

72. See J. R. Seeley, *Introduction to Political Science* (London, 1896) 191–197.

73. Dorfman, *op. cit. supra* n. 9 at I, 43.

74. Chap. VII, p. 98, *infra.*

75. *Winthrop Papers* IV, 385.

76. Winthrop, *Journal* II, 271–272, 289, 295–296, etc.

77. See the exhaustive and scholarly treatment of this episode by G. L. Kittredge, "Dr. Robert Child the Remonstrant," *Col. Soc. Mass. Publ.* XXI, 1, especially at 18. For a more favorable view, see S. E. Morison, *Builders of the Bay Colony* (Cambridge, Mass., 1930) Chap. 8.

78. Kittredge, *loc. cit. supra* n. 77, at 37, 50 *et seq.*

79. See G. L. Haskins, "Executive Justice and the Rule of Law," *Speculum* XXX, 529 at 531–532 (1955).

80. C. H. McIlwain, *The High Court of Parliament and Its Supremacy* (New Haven, 1910) 75 *et seq.* Cf. Haskins, *loc. cit. supra* n. 79.

81. Winthrop, *Journal* I, 151; see Chap. III, p. 36, *supra.*

82. *Laws and Liberties*, Epistle.

83. See *Mass. Records* I, 355: "according to the lawes of God, & . . . the lawes of this land."

84. See generally Chap. VIII, *infra.*

85. See Chap. III, notes 84, 85, *supra.*

86. *Mass. Records* I, 16.

87. See Chap. III, pp. 36–37, *supra.*

88. See especially Winthrop's discourse on arbitrary government. *Winthrop Papers* IV, 468 *et seq.*

89. *Laws and Liberties* 24.

90. *Id.*, at 45. Cf. also the freemen's oath binding him to give his vote as "may best conduce & tend to the publique weale of the body, without respect of persons, or favor of any man" (*Mass. Records* I, 117). Other legislation provided "that all Towns shall take care from time to time to order and dispose of all single persons, and In-mates within their Towns to service, or otherwise. And if any be grieved at such order or dispose, they have libertie to appeal to the next County Court" (*Laws and Liberties* 51). It was further provided that "If any parents shall wilfully, and unreasonably deny any

childe timely or convenient marriage, or shall exercise any unnaturall severitie towards them such children shal have libertie to complain to Authoritie for redresse in such cases" (*id.*, at 12).

91. Chap. VII, *infra.* Sermons were also given to support economic programs. Hugh Peter urged the congregations of Boston and Salem "to raise a stock for fishing" (Winthrop, *Journal* I, 165). He also urged employment for women and children (*id.* at I, 179–80).

92. C. Gross, *The Gild Merchant* (Oxford, 1890) I, 122–124.

93. W. R. Scott, *The Constitution and Finance of English, Scottish and Irish Joint-Stock Companies to 1720* (Cambridge, Mass., 1912) I, 3.

94. *Id.* at I, 10, 152.

95. For example, the Boston shoemakers and coopers were organized as crafts in 1648 (*Mass. Records* II, 249, 250). On the connection between the English guilds and the Massachusetts company, see I. B. Choate, "The Town Guild," *New England Historical and Genealogical Register* LVII, 168, 172–173 (1903).

96. See Chap. V, *infra.*

97. *Mass. Records* I, 115; *id.* at I, 167.

98. *Supra*, pp. 48–49.

99. Andrews, *op. cit. supra* n. 65, at I, 496.

100. See generally Osgood, *op. cit. supra* n. 32, at I, 217 *et seq.* and 222–223.

101. See B. M. Levy, *Preaching in the First Half Century of New England History* (Hartford, 1945) 70.

102. For a detailed and impartial account of the Williams controversy, see H. M. Dexter, *As to Roger Williams and His Banishment from the Massachusetts Plantation* (Boston, 1876).

103. *Winthrop Papers* IV, 493.

104. *Mass. Records* I, 87.

105. See Chap. VI, *infra.*

106. E.g., Winthrop, *Journal* I, 116, 119, 128–129, 130, 143–144.

107. *Id.* at II, 279.

108. E.g., *Mass. Records* II, 179. What would today be considered violations of a moral code (e.g., willful lying, gaming for money) were made statutory crimes. Cf. *Laws and Liberties* 24, 35. In 1651, in a single day, the Essex Quarterly Court fined five persons for lying (*Essex Records* I, 224–227).

109. *Laws and Liberties*, Epistle.

110. T. Lechford "Plain Dealing: or Newes from New-England," *Mass. Hist. Soc. Coll.* (3rd ser.) III, 74 (1833).

111. See *Winthrop Papers* III, 505.

112. *Id.* at III, 505 *et seq.*, especially at 505.

113. J. W. Allen, *A History of Political Thought in the Sixteenth Century* (London, 1928) 220: "All the Puritan writers agree that magistrates . . . must be subject to excommunication."

114. *Mass. Records* I, 168.

115. *Ibid.* Also, the magistrates were given the power to call synods. *The Cambridge Platform of Church Discipline* (Boston, 1855) XVI, 3.

116. E.g., Winthrop, *Journal* II, 179–180.

117. P. Miller, *op. cit. supra* n. 47, at 252–253. See also Winthrop, *Journal* I, 169.

118. *Id.* at I, 179. See, however, the excerpt from Richard Mather's treatise in M. Howe, *Readings in American Legal History* (Cambridge, Mass., 1949) 180–181.

119. *Cambridge Platform, supra* n. 115, at XVII, 6. For recent discussion of the significance of the Cambridge Platform, see H. W. Foote, "The Significance and Influence of the Cambridge Platform of 1648," *Mass. Hist. Soc. Proc.* LXIX, 81, especially 82 *et seq.* (1956).

120. "Excommunication . . . doth not prejudice the excommunicate in, nor deprive him of his civil rights, and therefore toucheth not princes, or other magistrates, in point of their civil dignity or authority. . . ." (*Cambridge Platform, supra* n. 115 at XIV, 6). A similar provision appears in the Code of 1648. See *Laws and Liberties* 20, and, further, Chap. VI, *infra.*

121. See generally, H. E. Ware, "Was the Government of the Massachusetts Bay Colony a Theocracy?" *Col. Soc. Mass. Proc.* X, 151 at 163 (1907).

122. Winthrop, *Journal* II, 20–21.

123. *Commonwealth History of Massachusetts,* (ed. A. B. Hart: New York 1927) I, 495. Relations with other colonies are discussed in A. H. Buffinton, "The Isolationist Policy of Colonial Massachusetts," *N.E.Q.* I, 158 (1928).

124. Notwithstanding the northern limits of the colony as described in the charter, the colony extended its jurisdiction over parts of present Maine and New Hampshire. See Osgood, *op. cit. supra* n. 32, at Chaps. I, IX. Opportunities to dominate other Puritan colonies were afforded by the establishment of the New England Confederacy (*id.* at I, 397 *et seq.*).

125. Winthrop, *Journal* I, 324.

126. Miller, *op. cit. supra* n. 47, at 148.

127. *Winthrop Papers* III, 148.

128. J. H. Smith, *Appeals to the Privy Council From the American Plantations* (New York, 1950) 45 *et seq.*

129. See G. D. Scull, "The 'Quo Warranto' of 1635," *New England Historical and Genealogical Register* XXXVIII, 209 (1884). A transcript of the *quo warranto* proceedings may be found in *The Hutchinson Papers* (Prince Society: Albany, 1865) I, 114–116.

130. Winthrop, *Journal* I, 130.

131. *Mass. Records* I, 125.

132. See p. 55, *supra.* Professor Morgan has characterized the Child affair as the greatest challenge the colony ever faced from foreign intervention. Morgan, *op. cit. supra* n. 25, at 202.

133. A. P. Newton, *The Colonising Activities of the English Puritans* (New Haven, 1914) 283.

134. *Winthrop Papers* II, 293.

Chapter V *THE INSTRUMENTS OF CIVIL GOVERNMENT*

1. *Travels and Works of Captain John Smith* (ed. E. Arber: Edinburgh, 1910) I, 204: ". . . heere are many Iles all planted with corne; groues, mulberries, saluage gardens. . . ."

2. The word "Massachusetts" means "at the Great Hill." Until 1630 it was applied only to the region of Boston Bay (S. E. Morison, *Builders of the Bay Colony* [Cambridge, Mass., 1930] 10).

3. Cf. Hubbard's description, quoted in T. Hutchinson, *The History of the Colony and Province of Massachusetts Bay* (ed. L. S. Mayo: Cambridge, Mass., 1936) I, 405.

4. *Mass. Records* I, 358.

5. *Winthrop Papers* IV, 492, speaks of the "great store of Codd . . . Sea Fowle . . . Partridge and heathe geese . . . and Deare."

6. Hutchinson, *op. cit. supra* n. 3, at 405.

7. Winthrop, *Journal* I, 54; A. Young, *Chronicles of the First Planters of the Colony of Massachusetts Bay* (Boston, 1846) 320.

8. For this reason, many of the inhabitants of Charlestown and Boston owned farms in the outlying country (W. Wood, *New Englands Prospect* [London, 1634] 38).

9. Winthrop, *Journal* I, 54.

10. Young, *op. cit. supra* n. 7, at 313–314. For a brief description of the first towns, prepared in 1633, see Wood, *op. cit. supra* n. 8, at 36 *et seq.*

11. *Mass. Records* I, 76.

12. *Id.* at I, 117.

13. *Id.* at I, 167.

14. For examples see A. B. Maclear, *Early New England Towns* (New York, 1908) 14–16. One of the important consequences of raising a plantation to the status of a town was the granting of permission to elect a deputy to the General Court (*Mass. Records* II, 44).

15. Grants of land to private persons were few. Such as were made were chiefly on the basis either of interest in the stock of the company (e.g., grants to Winthrop and Dudley) or of services rendered (e.g., to teachers). See M. Egleston, *The Land System of the New England Colonies* (Johns Hopkins Studies in Historical and Political Science: Baltimore, 1886) 24–25.

16. H. L. Osgood, *The American Colonies in the Seventeenth Century* (New York, 1904) II, 17 *et seq.*

17. *Mass. Records* I, 79.

18. *Id.* at I, 87.

19. *Id.* at I, 84.

20. *Id.* at I, 116.

21. *Id.* at I, 172. As early as 1634, the towns had been empowered to enact regulations about swine (*id.* at I, 119). Note the towns' powers to make prudential and noncriminal rules (*Body of Liberties* 66).

22. *Mass. Records* II, 49.

23. *Id.* at II, 39.

24. *Id.* at II, 6.

25. E.g., *The Early Records of the Town of Dedham, Massachusetts, 1636–1659* (Dedham, 1892) III, 4–5; *The Early Records of the Town of Rowley, Massachusetts, 1639–1672* (Rowley, 1894) I, 1–51.

26. *Proprietors' Records of the Town of Cambridge* (Cambridge, Mass., 1896) I, 11–12.

27. See generally H. L. Gray, *English Field Systems* (Cambridge, Mass., 1915) 17–49, and especially 305 *et seq.*

28. English mediaeval practices are summarized in G. C. Homans, *English Villagers of the Thirteenth Century* (Cambridge, Mass., 1941) 59 *et seq.* For their survival in the seventeenth century see S. and B. Webb, *English Local*

Government From the Revolution to the Municipal Corporations Act: The Manor and the Borough (London, 1908) 75 *et seq.*

29. E.g., *The Records of the Town and Selectmen of Cambridge* (Cambridge, Mass., 1901) 19, 30, 35, 72.

30. O. E. Winslow, *Meetinghouse Hill* (New York, 1952) 19.

31. *Dedham Records,* supra n. 25, at III, 2.

32. J. Dickinson, "Economic Regulations and Restrictions on Personal Liberty in Early Massachusetts," *Pocumtuck Valley Memorial Assoc. Proc.* 485 at 488 (1927).

33. E.g., *Dedham Records, supra* n. 25, at III, 5, 17.

34. *Id.* at III, 8.

35. *Id.* at III, 12, 15.

36. *Id.* at III, 17–18.

37. Dickinson, *loc. cit. supra* n. 32, at 489.

38. *Watertown Records* (Watertown, 1894) 4.

39. *Second Report of the Record Commissioners of the City of Boston, Containing the Boston Records, 1634–1660* (Boston, 1877) 5. See also *Dedham Records, supra* n. 25, at III, 32, 33.

40. *Boston Records, supra* n. 39, at 10–11, 12, 37. The increase in the fine suggests difficulty in enforcing the order.

41. E.g., *Cambridge Records, supra* n. 29, at 50; *Dedham Records, supra* n. 25, at III, 20, 24.

42. E.g., *Cambridge Records, supra* n. 29, at 24.

43. See references in J. H. Benton, *Warning Out in New England* (Boston, 1911) Chap. 2.

44. See *Boston Records, supra* n. 39, at 37; C. F. Adams, *Three Episodes in Massachusetts History* (Boston, 1893) II, 648–649.

45. *Mass. Records* I, 76.

46. See Chap. IV, pp. 48–49, *supra.*

47. By the "council" is meant the standing council for life established in 1636 (*Mass. Records* I, 167). See Chap. III, p. 31, *supra.*

48. *Mass. Records* I, 196.

49. For general discussion of the parish in England in the sixteenth and seventeenth centuries, see M. Campbell, *The English Yeoman Under Elizabeth and the Early Stuarts* (New Haven, 1942) Chap. 9; E. Trotter, *Seventeenth Century Life in the Country Parish* (Cambridge, 1919).

50. See *Mass. Records* I, 186. Important as the group was, the individual was not forgotten. See Chap. IV, p. 57, *supra.* Note also the right of single persons to object to families to which they were disposed in *Laws and Liberties* 51.

51. See Chap. III, *supra.*

52. It should be noted that no magistrate was permitted to serve as a ruling elder of a church while he held civil office. See Winthrop, *Journal* I, 83.

53. *Mass. Records* II, 14, 225.

54. Winthrop, *Journal* II, 158–159.

55. *Dedham Records, supra* n. 25, at III, 4, 30; *Cambridge Records, supra* n. 29, at 4; *Rowley Records, supra* n. 25, at I, 57.

56. G. Sheldon, *A History of Deerfield Massachusetts* (Deerfield, 1895)

I, 207. This description relates to the second half of the seventeenth century but is equally applicable to the earlier period.

57. *Mass. Records* I, 161.

58. Thus Edward Alleyne and Samuel Morse served on committees, and John Hayward and Thomas Wight as officers, of the town of Dedham (*Dedham Records, supra* n. 25, at III, 30, 35, 93).

59. Osgood, *op. cit. supra* n. 16, at I, 213, 464.

60. *Mass. Records* II, 197. Morison, *op. cit. supra* n. 2, at 261 *et seq.*, attributes the enactment of this legislation to the controversy arising out of the Child Remonstrance. However, the enabling legislation was prepared in 1646 and appears to have been deliberately shelved lest it appear to have been prompted by Child's petition. See G. L. Kittredge, "Dr. Robert Child the Remonstrant," *Col. Soc. Mass. Publ.* XXI, 1 at 20 (1919).

61. *Laws and Liberties* 23. See the 1643 act on the problem of "members that refuse to take their freedom" (*Mass. Records* II, 38).

62. *Laws and Liberties* 35.

63. The origin of the selectmen has been traced to the "select vestry" of the English parish. See E. Channing, *Town and County Government in the English Colonies of North America* (Johns Hopkins Studies in Historical and Political Science: Baltimore, 1884) 19–20.

64. E.g., *Dedham Records, supra* n. 25, at III, 5; *Rowley Records, supra* n. 25, at I, 55–56.

65. See generally Maclear, *op. cit. supra* n. 14, at Chap. 3.

66. E.g., *Boston Records, supra* n. 39, at 11, 19, etc.

67. G. E. Howard, *An Introduction to the Local Constitutional History of the United States* (Johns Hopkins Studies in Historical and Political Science: Baltimore, 1889) 83.

68. J. F. Sly, *Town Government in Massachusetts* (Cambridge, Mass., 1930) 35–38.

69. A general summary of the selectmen's duties may be found in Howard, *op. cit. supra* n. 67, at 79–82.

70. E.g., *Boston Records, supra* n. 39, at 76, 78.

71. *Id.*, at 93.

72. *Id.*, at 78.

73. *Id.*, at 76.

74. *Id.*, at 53.

75. *Id.*, at 75.

76. *Id.*, at 91.

77. *Id.*, at 10.

78. E.g., *Cambridge Records, supra* n. 29, at 54–56; *Watertown Records, supra* n. 38, at 19, 33.

79. *Boston Records, supra* n. 39, at 12, 14.

80. *Id.*, at 61.

81. *Id.*, at 91.

82. *Mass. Records* II, 162–163; *Laws and Liberties* 9.

83. Howard, *op. cit. supra* n. 67, at 89. In 1636 it was ordered that every town have two constables (*Mass. Records* I, 172). See also *Laws and Liberties* 13.

84. *Mass. Records* IV (Part 1), 324–327.

85. *Id.* at IV (Part 1), 121, 138.

86. Howard, *op. cit. supra* n. 67, at 89–91.
87. *Boston Records, supra* n. 39, at 80; *Cambridge Records, supra* n. 29, at 91.
88. E.g., *Dedham Records, supra* n. 25, at III, 19.
89. *Id.* at III, 5, 6, 9, 19.
90. *Boston Records, supra* n. 39, at 13.
91. *Id.*, at 80.
92. *Id.*, at 74, 98.
93. *Id.*, at 96.
94. *Mass. Records* V, 240–241; *A Report of the Record Commissioners of the City of Boston Containing the Boston Records from 1660 to 1701* (Boston, 1881) 206, 226.
95. See the extensive list in Howard, *op. cit. supra* n. 67, at 97–98.
96. See Webb, *op. cit. supra* n. 28, at 9, 13–30, 70 *et seq.*
97. A. B. White, *Self-Government at the King's Command* (Minneapolis, 1933). See also G. L. Haskins, *The Growth of English Representative Government* (Philadelphia, 1948) Chap. 3.
98. See generally Campbell, *op. cit. supra* n. 49, at Chap. 9; E. P. Cheyney, *A History of England from the Defeat of the Armada to the Death of Elizabeth* (New York, 1926) II, Chaps. 37–41; W. Notestein, *The English People on the Eve of Colonization, 1603–1630* (New York, 1954) Chaps. 19, 20.
99. It is noteworthy that in East Anglia the parish was known as the town meeting. S. and B. Webb, *English Local Government from the Revolution to the Municipal Corporations Act: The Parish and the County* (London, 1906) I, 39.
100. See E. G. Kimball, "A Bibliography of the Printed Records of the Justices of the Peace for Counties," *University of Toronto Law Journal* VI, 401 (1946).
101. Compare Webb, *op. cit. supra* n. 28, at 117, n. 3, with *Mass. Records* I, II, *passim.*
102. Webb, *op. cit. supra* n. 28, at 285; *id., op. cit. supra* n. 99, at 40–41. See the provision by which laborers could be demanded of a town for "all ordinary publick works of the Common-weal" (*Laws and Liberties* 9). Also see the provision compelling towns of fifty or more families to provide one within the town to teach the children and those with 100 or more to provide a school (*id.*, at 47).
103. Osgood, *op. cit. supra* n. 16, at I, 470. The system of yearly audit appears also to have been adopted from trading company practice. *Id.* at I, 493.
104. *Mass. Records* I, 120, 168, 240. Income taxes, introduced in 1646, were, however, based upon the ability to pay. See Osgood, *op. cit. supra* n. 16, at I, 472.
105. The Massachusetts financial system is fully described in *id.* at I, Chap. 12. Discussion of relevant English practices may be found in Webb, *op. cit. supra* n. 99, at 306 *et seq.*
106. Osgood, *op. cit. supra* n. 16, at I, 500, 502. For general discussion of the militia system in Massachusetts, see *id.* at I, Chap. 13. Liability for military service fell upon all inhabitants, including servants, except those expressly

exempted, notably magistrates, deputies, elders, officers, and students of Harvard College (*Laws and Liberties* 41–42).

107. For a summary of such regulations in the mediaeval period, many of which had survived in Tudor and Stuart England, see *Munimenta Gildhallae Londoniensis* (ed. H. T. Riley: London, 1859) I, xii, liii *et seq.* Compare legislative efforts to secure uniformity in the conditions of employment. See G. Unwin, *Industrial Organization in the Sixteenth and Seventeenth Centuries* (Oxford, 1904) 119 *et seq.*

108. Webb, *op. cit. supra* n. 28, at 27.

109. *Mass. Records* I, 76, 79, 223.

110. *Id.* at II, 168, 280.

111. *Laws and Liberties* 9. See also *Mass. Records* I, 124.

112. *Mass. Records* II, 180.

113. E.g., *id.* at I, 84, 126, 214.

114. *Id.* at I, 106, 205, 213.

115. *Id.* at I, 101, 136.

116. *Id.* at I, 214.

117. *Id.* at I, 208, 214.

118. *Id.* at I, 126, 183, 274.

119. *Id.* at I, 84; II, 195.

120. See Chap. VII *infra.*

121. *Mass. Records* I, 168, 341.

122. *Id.* at I, 196.

123. *Laws and Liberties* 11.

124. E.g., Stats. 1 Elizabeth I c. 9, 39 Elizabeth I c. 12, 1 James I c. 20. On regulation of trades and occupations see G. W. Prothero, *Select Statutes and Other Constitutional Documents Illustrative of the Reigns of Elizabeth and James I* (Oxford, 1894) 50 *et seq.*

125. See H. G. Hudson, *A Study of Social Regulations in England under James I and Charles I: Drink and Tobacco* (Chicago, 1933) 7, 22–23. For proscription of the wearing of velvet and satin, see R. Steele, *Tudor and Stuart Proclamations, 1485–1714* (Oxford, 1910) I, 140. Although English sumptuary legislation owed its origins to mediaeval regulatory ideas, by the sixteenth century it also reflected English mercantile policies, notably a wish to stimulate English trade and manufacture.

126. Hudson, *op. cit. supra* n. 125, at 9. See also Stat. 1 James I c. 9.

127. Stat. 21 James I, c. 20.

128. Stat. 1 Charles I, c. 1.

129. Stat. 2 and 3 Philip and Mary, c. 9; *Select Cases Before the King's Council in the Star Chamber* (Selden Society: London, 1911) II, xxiii.

130. Stat. 1 Charles I, c. 1.

131. Webb, *op. cit. supra* n. 28, at 20; see also *Records of the Borough of Leicester* (ed. M. Bateson: Cambridge, 1905) III, 156; *Munimenta Gildhallae Londoniensis, supra* n. 107, at III, 86; Mss., *Boston Corporation Minutes* (Boston, England) II, 167.

132. See Chap. VI, *infra.*

133. See H. D. Foster, *Collected Papers* (privately printed, 1929) 16–17.

134. See Chap. VI, pp. 89–90 *infra.*

135. Dickinson, *loc. cit. supra* n. 32, at 487.

136. See G. L. Haskins, "De la codification du droit en Amérique du Nord

au xviie siècle: une étude de droit comparé," *Revue d'histoire du droit* XXIII, 311 at 324–329 (1955); *id.*, "Codification of the Law in Colonial Massachusetts: A Study in Comparative Law," *Indiana Law Journal* XXX, 1 at 11–16 (1954).

137. Dickinson, *loc. cit. supra* n. 32, at 487.

138. "Boston Sermons," quoted in E. S. Morgan, *The Puritan Family* (Boston, 1944) 84.

139. *Mass. Records* I, 397.

140. *Id.* at I, 186.

141. See *Town Records of Salem, 1634–1659* (Essex Institute: Salem, 1868) 61.

142. *Laws and Liberties* 53.

143. E.g., *The Probate Records of Essex County, Massachusetts* (Salem, 1916) I, 50, 67, 91, 188.

144. See *Mass. Records* II, 211–212.

145. *Id.* at I, 92.

146. E.g., *id.* at I, 225; Winthrop, *Journal* II, 161–163.

147. E.g., *Mass. Records* II, 243; *Assistants Records* II, 108; Winthrop, *Journal* II, 257–259.

148. E.g., *Essex Records* I, 50, 51, 58, 59, 123–124.

149. *Assistants Records* II, 100, 105; see also the case of "Mr. Bacherler and Mary his wife" in *Essex Records* I, 191.

150. *Mass. Records* II, 211–212.

151. See Winthrop, *Journal* II, 239.

152. E.g., *Mass. Records* I, 265.

153. See *Laws and Liberties* 15.

154. *Assistants Records* II, 138.

155. Hutchinson, *op. cit. supra* n. 3, at I, 375.

156. *Mass. Records* II, 179–180.

157. *Id.* at I, 155; *Essex Records* I, 19. For later cases see *Assistants Records* III, 138–139, 144–145, both involving extreme circumstances at a time when the capital law was supposedly in effect, but in which the delinquents involved were only "whipt seuerely" and sentenced to stand on the gallows or pillory.

158. *Essex Records* I, 11. See also the order that "Dorcas Humfrey . . . bee privately severely corrected by this Court, Mr. Bellingham & Increase Nowell to see it done" (*Mass. Records* II, 13). See, in this connection, J. Winthrop, *History of New England* (ed. J. Savage: Boston, 1826) II, 45–48. By a statute of 1646, children convicted of theft were punishable directly by the courts, unless the parent paid the fine (*Mass. Records* II, 180).

159. *Laws and Liberties* 37.

160. *Watertown Records, supra* n. 38, at 64.

161. *Laws and Liberties* 11.

162. Morgan, *op. cit. supra* n. 138, at 39.

163. *Laws and Liberties* 12.

164. Stats. 5 Elizabeth I, c. 4; 43 Elizabeth I, c. 2.

165. See the example of an indenture in *Winthrop Papers* III, 199.

166. *Laws and Liberties* 38–39.

167. *Mass. Records* II, 6; see also *Cambridge Records, supra* n. 29, at 47; *Laws and Liberties* 11.

168. E.g., *Assistants Records* II, 86; *Essex Records* I, 35. See also the theft statute, n. 158 *supra*, which applied to servants as well as to children.

169. *Laws and Liberties* 39; *Assistants Records* II, 80.

170. Morgan, *op. cit. supra* n. 138, at 77. See R. F. Seybolt, *Apprenticeship and Apprenticeship Education in Colonial New England and New York* (New York, 1917) Chap. 2.

171. Morgan, *op. cit. supra* n. 138, at 77.

172. See Chap. VI, *infra*. Secular love had an important place in family life, but it was regarded as a product of, rather than a reason for, marriage. Spouses were warned not to become so transported with affection for each other, or for their children, as to forget that their highest love must be reserved for God (Morgan, *op. cit. supra* n. 138, at 12–15).

173. B. Adams, *The Emancipation of Massachusetts* (New York, 1919) 5.

174. E.g., *Essex Records* I, 128, 136, 9, 25, 59.

175. See generally Seybolt, *op. cit. supra* n. 170. Cf. the indenture printed *id.*, at 29, with that in *Records of the City of Norwich* (ed. W. Hudson and J. C. Tingey: London, 1910) II, 28–29, and in *Winthrop Papers* III, 199.

176. E.g., *Nottinghamshire County Records* (ed. H. H. Copnall: Nottingham, 1915) 68; *Middlesex Sessions Records* (ed. W. L. Hardy: London, 1936) II (new series), 238. See Chap. X, notes 73–77, *infra*.

177. *Nottinghamshire County Records, supra* n. 176, at 40–41.

178. *Id.*, at 41.

179. *Id.*, at 47.

180. *Ibid.* Cf. Stat. James I, c. 4 (viii).

181. W. H. Hale, *Precedents and Proceedings in Criminal Causes, 1475–1640* (London, 1847) 161 (CCCCLXXXVII).

182. *Ibid.*

183. *Id.*, at 207 (DCXXXVIII).

184. Haskins, *loc. cit. supra* n. 136, *Revue d'histoire du droit* XXIII, at 329; *Indiana Law Journal* XXX, at 15.

185. C. M. Bowra, *The Greek Experience* (London, 1957) 67–68.

186. F. Pollock and F. W. Maitland, *The History of English Law* (Cambridge, 1895) I, 678.

Chapter VI *COMMUNITIES OF VISIBLE SAINTS*

1. For a contemporary description, see *Johnson's Wonder-Working Providence* (ed. J. F. Jameson: New York, 1910) 215–216. See also O. E. Winslow, *Meetinghouse Hill* (New York, 1952) Chap. 2.

2. Quoted in Winslow, *op. cit. supra* n. 1, at 24. See also the Boston covenant printed in *Winthrop Papers* III, 223–225.

3. For descriptions of early meetinghouses, see Winslow, *op. cit. supra* n. 1, at Chap. 4. Cf. J. F. Kelly, *Early Connecticut Meetinghouses* (New York, 1948).

4. *Mass. Records* I, 168. No member of a church gathered without such approval was eligible to be admitted a freeman (*ibid.*).

5. See the description in S. E. Morison, *Builders of the Bay Colony* (Cambridge, Mass., 1930) 112–114.

6. *The Cambridge Platform of Church Discipline* (Boston, 1855) VIII, 9. However, when possible, neighboring churches were to be called upon for advice (*id.* at VIII, 8).

7. See Winthrop, *Journal* II, 121.

8. *Cambridge Platform, supra* n. 6, at VII, 2; X, 8, 9. See also C. E. Park, "Two Ruling Elders of the First Church in Boston," *Col. Soc. Mass. Publ.* XIII, 82 at 86–88 (1912).

9. *Cambridge Platform, supra* n. 6, at XII; C. E. Park, "Excommunication in Colonial Churches," *Col. Soc. Mass. Publ.* XII, 321 at 323–324 (1911). For a contemporary description of receiving members into the churches, see T. Lechford, "Plain Dealing: or Newes from New-England," *Mass. Hist. Soc. Coll.* (3rd ser.) III, 55 at 65–68 (1833).

10. Diffident women were frequently excused from the embarrassment of public confession (Park, *loc. cit. supra* n. 9, at 323).

11. E.g., *A Report of the Record Commissioners Containing the Roxbury Land and Church Records* (Boston, 1881) 77 *et seq.* Winthrop, *Journal* II, 26, reports that a Negro maid servant, "for sound knowledge and true godliness," was admitted to the Dorchester church in 1641.

12. *Records of the First Church at Dorchester in New England* (Boston, 1891) 2. See also the covenant of the Boston church in *Winthrop Papers* III, 224.

13. *Cambridge Platform, supra* n. 6, at XIII.

14. *Id.* at XIII, 8, 9.

15. *Id.* at XVI, 3.

16. *Id.* at XVI, 4.

17. *Ibid.*

18. *Laws and Liberties* 19.

19. See generally, Chap. IV, *supra.* The aid of the civil government was welcomed by the clergy. See *Cambridge Platform, supra* n. 6, at XVII.

20. *Mass. Records* I, 240; *Laws and Liberties* 20.

21. *Mass. Records* I, 181.

22. *Id.* at I, 140; II, 177–178.

23. Winslow, *op. cit. supra* n. 1, at 100. See also B. M. Levy, *Preaching in the First Half Century of New England History* (Hartford, 1945) 60–61.

24. T. Shepard, *Subjection to Christ in All His Ordinances and Appointments* (London, 1652) 130 *et seq.*

25. Winthrop, *Journal* I, 165, 179–180.

26. *Id.* at I, 317–318.

27. See L. Swift, "The Massachusetts Election Sermons," *Col. Soc. Mass. Publ.* I, 388 (1895).

28. See the cases of Robert Keayne (oppression), Winthrop, *Journal* I, 315–317, and Stephen Batchellor (attempted adultery), *id.* at II, 45–46.

29. See Chap. IV, p. 49, *supra.*

30. *Roxbury Records, supra* n. 11, at 83.

31. See, for example, the Nathaniel Eaton episode reported in Winthrop, *Journal* I, 310 *et seq.*

32. *Essex Records* I, 83, 88, 92.

33. Winthrop, *Journal* I, 279.

34. *Mass. Records* I, 274–275.

35. *Cambridge Platform, supra* n. 6, at XVII, 8.

36. For the jurisdiction of the ecclesiastical courts over offenses against morals, see W. Holdsworth, *A History of English Law* (London, 1938) I, 619–621.

37. See proceedings in the Archdeaconry of Essex printed in W. H. Hale, *Precedents and Proceedings in Criminal Causes, 1475–1640* (London, 1847) 188–189 (DLXXVIII), 208 (DCXL), 218 (DCLXIX), 239 (DCCXLV), 245 (DCCLXVI), 248–249 (DCCLXXVI).

38. *Id.*, at 196–197 (DCVI), 220 (DCLXXVII), 223 (DCLXXXVIII), 250 (DCCLXXXII).

39. *Id.*, at 221 (DCLXXIX), 247–248 (DCCLXXII), 257–258 (DCCCV).

40. *Id.*, at 240–241 (DCCL).

41. *Id.*, at 254 (DCCXCIII).

42. *Id.*, at 236 (DCCXXXIV).

43. *Id.*, at 243 (DCCLVII).

44. *Id.*, at 231 (DCCXV), 219–220 (DCLXXV).

45. D. Ogg, *England in the Reign of Charles II* (Oxford, 1934) II, 497. See also S. and B. Webb, *English Local Government from the Revolution to the Municipal Corporations Act: The Parish and the County* (London, 1906) 21.

46. The requirement that nonmembers attend church (see n. 22, *supra*) subjected them at least to the moral influence of the church community. In the beginning, children of members were treated as within the fold until they came of age, when they were expected to make a public profession of faith if they were to continue members of the congregation. See P. Miller, *Orthodoxy in Massachusetts, 1630–1650* (Cambridge, Mass., 1933) 201–202.

47. *First Church Records, Boston* (Mass. Hist. Soc. Mss.) 8.

48. *Id.* at 23. See also *Roxbury Records, supra* n. 11, at 85–86.

49. *First Church Records, supra* n. 47, at 24.

50. *Roxbury Records, supra* n. 11, at 85.

51. See Chap. III, p. 38, *supra*.

52. Winthrop, *Journal* I, 317.

53. *Id.* at I, 317–318. See Chap. VIII, p. 125, *infra*.

54. J. Dorfman, *The Economic Mind in American Civilization* (New York, 1946) I, 5–6.

55. E.g., *Dorchester Church Records, supra* n. 12, at 2.

56. *Cambridge Platform, supra* n. 6, at XIV, 9.

57. J. Cotton, *Gods Promise to His Plantation* (London, 1630) 19.

58. *Essex Records* I, 17.

59. W. Hudson, *Leet Jurisdiction in the City of Norwich During the Thirteenth and Fourteenth Centuries* (London, 1892) lxxv.

60. See F. Pollock and F. W. Maitland, *The History of English Law* (Cambridge, 1895) I, 568.

61. See generally, Park, *loc cit. supra* n. 9, at 321.

62. *Id.*, at 328–329.

63. For a description of the procedure employed at a slightly later period, see Winslow, *op. cit. supra* n. 1, at 175 *et seq.*; also C. F. Adams, "Some Phases of Sexual Morality and Church Discipline in Colonial New England," *Mass. Hist. Soc. Proc.* (2d ser.) VI, 477 (1891).

64. See *Cambridge Platform, supra* n. 6, at XIV, 4.

65. Park, *loc. cit. supra* n. 9, at 327–328.

66. E.g., *Roxbury Records, supra* n. 11, at 83, 85.
67. Park, *loc. cit. supra* n. 9, at 330.
68. *Mass. Records* I, 242.
69. See Chap. IV, p. 63, *supra*.
70. *Cambridge Platform, supra* n. 6, at XIV, 6.
71. See I Corinthians 12:26.
72. *Cambridge Platform, supra* n. 6, at XIV, 1.
73. T. Weld, *An Answer to W. R.* (London, 1644) 15.
74. *Ibid.*
75. Miller, *op. cit. supra* n. 46, at 210.

Chapter VII THE SORTS AND CONDITIONS OF MEN

1. For photographs illustrating the English influence, see G. F. Dow, *Every Day Life in the Massachusetts Bay Colony* (Boston, 1935) plates facing 16 *et seq.*; M. S. Briggs, *The Homes of the Pilgrim Fathers in England and America, 1620–1685* (London, 1932) Chaps. 4, 5, and 7. A noted architectural historian has observed that "the Colonial style of the seventeenth century is . . . essentially mediaeval: . . . form and details continue traditions of the Middle Ages." F. Kimball, *Domestic Architecture of the American Colonies and of the Early Republic* (New York, 1922) 14. See the illustrations *id.*, at 11, 13.

2. Winthrop states that 240 cows and about 60 horses were shipped in 1630 (*Winthrop Papers* II, 225). For a short description of livestock in this period, see P. W. Bidwell and J. I. Falconer, *History of Agriculture in the Northern United States, 1620–1860* (Washington, 1925) 18–32.

3. *Winthrop Papers* IV, 492. W. Wood, *New Englands Prospect* (London, 1634) 13, states that he visited Massachusetts Bay in 1633 and reported: "whatsoever growes well in *England*, growes as well there, many things better and larger." For a discussion of crops and agriculture, see R. R. Walcott, "Husbandry in Colonial New England," *N.E.Q.* IX, 218 (1936).

4. Bidwell and Falconer, *op. cit. supra* n. 2, at 16–17.

5. For the English diet at this time, see *Social England* (ed. H. D. Traill: London, 1895) III, 394–395.

6. S. E. Morison, *Builders of the Bay Colony* (Cambridge, Mass., 1930) 135, 140. Only the ministers wore black (*ibid.*). See Dow, *op. cit. supra* n. 1, at Chaps. 3, 5, 6. See also the lists in the Port Book entries, many of which are printed in *Winthrop Papers* III *passim*.

7. Winthrop, *Journal* I, 47; Morison, *op. cit. supra* n. 6, at 332. For descriptions of daily life in the colony, see *id.*, at Chap. 5; Dow, *op. cit. supra* n. 1.

8. G. M. Trevelyan, *Illustrated English Social History* (London, 1950) II, 65. For an admirable, though brief, sketch of England in the early seventeenth century, see W. Notestein, *The English People on the Eve of Colonization, 1603–1630* (New York, 1954), especially Chaps. 2 and 3.

9. G. M. Trevelyan, *England Under the Stuarts* (New York, 1910) 4–7.

10. See generally F. J. Fisher, "State of England Anno Dom. 1600 by Thomas Wilson," *Camden Miscellany* XVI, 1 (1936).

11. B. Smith, *Bradford of Plymouth* (Philadelphia, 1951) 25.

12. W. Harrison, *Elizabethan England* (ed. L. Withington: London, 1902) 12–13.

13. *Id.*, at 13. For a recent discussion of English social classes, see Notestein, *op. cit. supra* n. 8, Chaps. 4–10.

14. V. Pareto, *Traité de sociologie générale* (Paris, 1933) II, 1293 *et seq.*

15. *Paradise Lost* IX, 445.

16. For example, John Winthrop, while he held his position as attorney in the Court of Wards, regularly attended to his duties as lord of Groton Manor.

17. *Winthrop Papers* II, 282. See also *The Cambridge Platform of Church Discipline* (Boston, 1855) VII, 2, where it is stated to be a duty of the ruling elders of the churches "To see that none in the church live inordinately, out of rank and place. . . ."

18. *Laws and Liberties* 1; *Body of Liberties*, Preamble.

19. Lady Arbella Fiennes, wife of Isaac Johnson, was a sister of the Earl of Lincoln. She died in the late summer of 1630. Sir Richard Saltonstall, who came with Winthrop, and Sir Henry Vane, who came slightly later, were the only other titled individuals in the early years of the colony. See C. E. Banks, *The Winthrop Fleet of 1630* (Boston, 1930) 51–52.

20. Much valuable information has been collected, *id.*, at Chap. 6. See also the miscellaneous list of trades, crafts, and professions among the early grantees of Newbury in J. Coffin, *A Sketch of the History of Newbury, Newburyport and West Newbury* (Boston, 1845) 368. For a sampling, based on English records, see J. Savage, "Gleanings for New England History," *Mass. Hist. Soc. Coll.* (3d ser.) VIII, 243 at 253 *et seq.*

21. C. M. Andrews, *The Colonial Period of American History* (New Haven, 1934) I, 500.

22. *Report of the Record Commissioners of the City of Boston* X, 47 (1886). Thomas Flint is also reported to have brought £2000 with him to Massachusetts. J. Winthrop, *History of New England* (ed. J. Savage: Boston, 1826) II, 47.

23. *Note-Book Kept by Thomas Lechford, Esq.* (Cambridge, Mass., 1885) *passim.*

24. The English titles of "Master," "Esquire," "Gentleman," and "Goodman" frequently appear in the local records, as do heraldic devices and family crests on tombstones. The niceties of precedence appear to have been observed in the seating of the meetinghouses. See *Town Records of Salem, 1634–1659* (Essex Institute: Salem, 1868) 201.

25. Cf. Andrews, *op. cit. supra* n. 21, at I, 502. Although the Indians constituted a social group and were the object of considerable class legislation (see, e.g., *Laws and Liberties* 28–29), discussion thereof has been reserved for the second volume of this work.

26. Morison, *op. cit. supra* n. 6, at 214 *et seq.* See also the case of Josias Plastowe, who lost the title of "Master" for stealing from the Indians (*Mass. Records* I, 92).

27. E.g., provisions for the support of ministers (*id.* at I, 55, 73, 82); exemptions with respect to road work (*id.* at I, 124); exemptions from military training (*id.* at II, 31, 221).

28. *Body of Liberties* 43.

29. N. H. Dawes, *Social Classes in Seventeenth Century New England* (unpublished thesis, Harvard College Library, 1941) 386. This work contains valuable analysis and discussion of social classes, supported by detailed references and examples.

30. E.g., *Mass. Records* I, 264; II, 15. The law relating to provision for the poor is printed in *Laws and Liberties* 44.

31. For cases of men ordered into debt "slavery," see *Assistants Records* II, 32, 94.

32. *Mass. Records* I, 76; *Laws and Liberties* 38.

33. *Essex Records* I, 18, 20.

34. See Chap. V, p. 82, *supra.*

35. *Laws and Liberties* 25–26, 38–39.

36. E.g., *Essex Records* I, 44, 49.

37. *Id.* at I, 5, 6, 7, 9, 10, etc.

38. Winthrop, *Journal* II, 228. Servants convicted of stealing were punished by whipping if their masters did not pay the treble damage penalty (*Laws and Liberties* 5).

39. An example of sentencing to slavery for crime may be found in *Mass. Records* I, 246. See also the provision in John Cotton's proposed Code. *Mass. Hist. Soc. Coll.* (1st ser.) V, 173 at 184 (1798). See Morison, *op. cit. supra* n. 6, at 294.

40. *Calendar of State Papers, Colonial Ser., America and West Indies, 1675–1676* (London, 1893) 465.

41. E.g., *Essex Records* I, 196, 287, 323.

42. B. Adams, *The Emancipation of Massachusetts* (Boston, 1887) 258.

43. A detailed discussion of evidence relating to social mobility in the New England colonies may be found in Dawes, *op. cit. supra* n. 29, Chaps. 11 and 12.

44. For the background of these ideas, see V. Brants, *Esquisse des théories économiques des xiii²- et xiv²-siècles* (Louvain, 1895).

45. *Winthrop Papers* II, 282.

46. *Id.* at II, 283 *et seq.*

47. *Cambridge Platform*, quoted n. 17, *supra.*

48. See notes 32, 35, *supra.*

49. See the preamble to the law of 1639. *Mass. Records* I, 274. Simple attire was also viewed as a badge of modesty. Cf. *id.* at I, 126. See also Coffin, *op. cit. supra* n. 20, at 58.

50. W. D. Chapple, "Public Service of John Endecott," *Essex Institute Coll.* LXV, 403 at 415 (1929); Savage, *loc. cit. supra* n. 20, at 323.

51. Cf. *Laws and Liberties*, Epistle.

52. *Id.*, at 35.

53. See Chap. III, p. 29, *supra.*

54. See Chap. V, notes 58, 59, 60, *supra.* It should again be emphasized that among the nonfreemen were many persons of standing in the community who might be members of the churches and yet not be freemen. Cf. *Laws and Liberties* 23. Morison, *op. cit. supra* n. 6, at 340–341, has estimated that at least a half of the adult male population were church members. However, Thomas Lechford, writing in or about 1640, stated that "three parts of the people" were outside the churches (T. Lechford, "Plain Dealing: or Newes from New-England," *Mass. Hist. Soc. Coll.* [3rd ser.] III, 55 at 122–123 [1833]).

55. This statement is made on the basis of the list of freemen printed in *Mass. Records* I, 471–479.

56. E.g., in the framing of the 1648 Code. Thus, Joseph Hills and Nathaniel Duncan served on one of the committees to draft the laws (*id.* at II, 128, 169).

57. This statement is made on the basis of a study of the lists of deputies printed *id.* at I, II, III *passim.*

58. E.g., *id.* at I, 116, 137, 201, 276.

59. E.g., *Body of Liberties* 10.

60. See Chap. IV, pp. 43–44, *supra.*

61. The most recent evaluation of Winthrop will be found in E. S. Morgan, *The Puritan Dilemma: The Story of John Winthrop* (Boston, 1958).

62. *Winthrop Papers* I, 7–11.

63. *Id.* at I, 178, 195, 207; II, 3.

64. *Id.* at II, 3.

65. See G. W. Robinson, *John Winthrop as Attorney* (Cambridge, Mass., 1930). He was attorney in the Court of Wards from January, 1627, to June, 1629, a fraction over ten terms. For a recent study of the Court of Wards, see H. E. Bell, *An Introduction to the History and Records of the Court of Wards and Liveries* (Cambridge, 1953).

66. See Winthrop's notebook of cases before the Court of Wards, printed in *Winthrop Papers* II, 4 *et seq.* Winthrop was also responsible for the drafts of bills and petitions to Parliament. *Winthrop Papers* I, 295–310, 371–374, 418–419. The subject matter of these bills included provisions for supervising inns and taverns, suppression of drunkenness, and limitations on the number of practicing attorneys.

67. *Id.* at IV, 382.

68. W. Hubbard, *A General History of New England from the Discoveries to 1680* (Cambridge, Mass. 1815) 519.

69. A. Jones, *The Life and Work of Thomas Dudley* (Boston, 1899) 25.

70. *Winthrop Papers* II, 55 n.

71. Morison, *op. cit. supra* n. 6, at 269; *id.,* "William Pynchon, the Founder of Springfield," *Mass. Hist. Soc. Proc.* LXIV, 67 at 69 (1932).

72. F. Rose-Troup, "John Humfry," *Essex Institute Coll.* LXV, 293 (1929). A. P. Newton, *The Colonising Activities of the English Puritans* (New Haven, 1914) 45, states categorically that Humfry was an attorney in the Court of Wards.

73. See Chaps. II, III, *supra.*

74. See Chap. VI, *supra.*

75. See Chap. VIII, *infra.*

76. Winthrop, *Journal* I, 196.

77. Chap. VIII, pp. 124 *et seq. infra.*

78. Winthrop, *Journal* II, 49. According to Matthias Candler, a contemporary, Ward had been an utter barrister. See J. W. Dean, *A Memoir of the Rev. Nathaniel Ward, A.M.* (Albany, 1868) 126.

79. N. Ward, "The Simple Cobler of Aggawamm," *Publ. Ipswich Historical Soc.* XIV, 66 (1905).

80. See Chap. VIII, *infra.*

81. W. B. Weeden, *Economic and Social History of New England, 1620–1789* (Boston, 1890) I, 130 *et seq.* ˋ

82. Winthrop, *Journal* I, 65, 187.
83. *Id.* at I, 102, 131.
84. Weeden, *op. cit. supra* n. 81, at I, 110 *et seq.*
85. *Mass. Records* I, 112, 127, 241.
86. The extent of barter in commodities is illustrated by the fact that taxes were normally paid in kind. H. L. Osgood, *The American Colonies in the Seventeenth Century* (New York, 1904) I, 469.
87. Andrews, *op. cit. supra* n. 21, at I, 496 *et seq.*
88. See M. H. Gottfried, "The First Depression in Massachusetts," *N.E.Q.* IX, 655 (1936).
89. Such exportable commodities as fish and grains competed with English produce and hence there was no market for them in England. Forest products could not compete with those sold to England by the Baltic countries until the Dutch War began in 1652.
90. Winthrop, *Journal* II, 31.
91. *Id.* at II, 19; Lechford, *loc. cit. supra* n. 54, at 101.
92. Almost as many criminal cases were tried before the assistants between 1640 and 1642 as in the years 1635 to 1640. See *Assistants Records* II, 173 *et seq.*, title "Crimes."
93. E.g., Stats. 1 James I, c. 22, 4 James I, c. 2. See F. C. Dietz, *Economic History of England* (New York, 1942) 257, 259, 269–270. The widespread acceptance of such ideas in the American colonies is discussed by E. A. J. Johnson, *American Economic Thought in the Seventeenth Century* (London, 1932) 142 *et seq.*
94. *Mass. Records* I, 76, 79, 109. See Chaps. III, p. 28; V, pp. 77–78, *supra.*
95. *Mass. Records* I, 257–258, 327; II, 61–62.
96. *Id.* at I, 304.
97. Winthrop, *Journal* II, 31. See also *Mass. Records* I, 322.
98. *Mass. Records* I, 294.
99. *Id.* at I, 327. See also Weeden, *op. cit. supra* n. 81, at I, 173–174.
100. *Mass. Records* I, 344.
101. *Id.* at II, 105–106, 251–252.
102. *Id.* at I, 292.
103. Hugh Peter, *A Dying Fathers Last Legacy* (London, 1660) 101–102. See Winthrop, *Journal* II, 31–32. The mission appears to have accomplished little; see R. P. Stearns, "The Weld-Peter Mission to England," *Col. Soc. Mass. Publ.* XXXII, 188 (1937).
104. Winthrop, *Journal* II, 23–24.
105. *Mass. Records* II, 18, 29, 169, 249. See especially the preamble to the 1646 act (*id.* at II, 169).
106. Winthrop refers to a successful voyage, as early as 1643, "which did much encourage the merchants, and made wine and sugar and cotton very plentiful, and cheap" (Winthrop, *Journal* II, 93).
107. *Johnson's Wonder-Working Providence* (ed. J. F. Jameson: New York, 1910) 247.
108. See the list of trades in Boston in 1647 enumerated *id.* at 247–248. In 1648, two guilds (shoemakers and coopers) were established to promote their respective trades (II, 249, 250). In 1644, owners and shipbuilders were authorized to form a company with power to regulate the building of ships (*id.* at II, 69).

109. *Id.* at II, 69, 109, etc. Cf. W. Aspinwall, *Notarial Records* (Boston, 1903) *passim.*

110. *Mass. Records* III, 193; IV (Part 1), 69.

111. Johnson, *op. cit. supra* n. 107, at 210.

112. See Aspinwall, *op. cit. supra* n. 109, at 394 *et seq.*, especially 417.

113. Weeden, *op. cit. supra* n. 81, at I, 152–153.

114. The sumptuary laws of 1651 should be noted in this connection (*Mass. Records* III, 243–244).

115. For example, John Winthrop, John Humfry, John Cotton, Thomas Weld, and Hugh Peter had all attended Trinity College, Cambridge; Thomas Shepard was a graduate of Emmanuel. For others, see Savage, *loc cit. supra* n. 20, at 247–249.

116. The phrase is from the Massachusetts School Act of 1647 (*Mass. Records* II, 203). It has been observed that one of the fundamental characteristics of all the Puritan states was their concern for education. H. D. Foster, *Collected Papers* (privately printed, 1929) 73. Although the education of Indians had been declared in the charter to be a principal purpose of colonization, little was done in that direction until John Eliot's missionary activities began in 1646. See Morison, *op. cit. supra* n. 6, at Chap. 10.

117. *Mass. Records* II, 6.

118. See, generally, S. E. Morison, *The Puritan Pronaos* (New York, 1936) Chaps. 2–5.

119. *Id.*, at Chap. 5.

120. *Mass. Records* II, 203.

121. Morison, *op. cit. supra* n. 118, at 61, 96–97.

122. Morison, *op. cit. supra* n. 6, at 186. Needless to say, the character and orthodoxy of the schoolmaster were carefully inquired into since godliness was a principal aim of education. See W. H. Small, *Early New England Schools* (Boston, 1914) 87 *et seq.*

123. Morison, *op. cit. supra* n. 118, at 29. See generally, *id., Harvard College in the Seventeenth Century* (Cambridge, Mass., 1936) I, Chaps. 7–13. Although it is clear that Harvard was not intended to be a theological seminary, it should be emphasized that there was no conflict between its secular purposes and the purposes of Christianity. See P. Miller, *The New England Mind: The Seventeenth Century* (New York, 1939) 76.

124. A. L. Lowell, *What a University President Has Learned* (New York, 1938) 27. Harvard's reputation became such that as early as 1645 its degree was regarded by Oxford and Cambridge as the equivalent of their own (Morison, *op. cit. supra* n. 123, at 299–301).

125. See n. 54, *supra.*

126. For a brief survey of libraries and book collections, see Morison, *op. cit. supra* n. 118, at Chap. 6; T. G. Wright, *Literary Culture in Early New England, 1620–1730* (New Haven, 1920) Chap. 2. Inventories of seventeenth century libraries may be found in C. F. and R. Robinson, "Three Early Massachusetts Libraries," *Col. Soc. Mass. Publ.* XXVIII, 107 (1935); A. O. Norton, "Harvard Text-Books and Reference Books of the Seventeenth Century," *loc. cit. ibid.* at 361.

127. K. B. Murdock, *Literature and Theology in Colonial New England* (Cambridge, Mass., 1949) 65. Elsewhere, Professor Murdock has emphasized

that even the Puritan attitude toward music was the same in Massachusetts as in England (*id.*, Book Review, *N.E.Q.* VIII, 433 *et seq.* [1935]).

128. Winthrop, *Journal* II, 36–37.
129. *Id.* at I, 260; II, 304.
130. Miller, *op. cit. supra* n. 123, at Chap. 4.
131. Winthrop, *Journal* II, 354–355.
132. Trevelyan, *op. cit. supra* n. 9, at 58–59. See also Morison, *op. cit. supra* n. 6, at 100–101.

Chapter VIII *THE PATH OF THE LAW*

1. It should be noted, however, that the conception of business affected with a public interest was recognized in the regulation of inns and certain forms of transport, such as ferries.
2. E.g., *Assistants Records* II, 21; Winthrop, *Journal* II, 240, 305.
3. See generally Chap. II, *supra*.
4. See Chap. IV, p. 64, *supra*.
5. Winthrop, *Journal* II, 305. See also Chap. IV, p. 65, *supra*.
6. Winthrop, *Journal* II, 337. See also the petition to Parliament in 1651 expressing the colony's gratitude for stopping appeals. T. Hutchinson, *History of the Colony and Province of Massachusetts Bay* (ed. L. S. Mayo: Cambridge, Mass., 1936) I, 430.
7. Winthrop, *Journal* I, 323–324.
8. *Mass. Records* I, 91.
9. *Id.* at I, 77.
10. *Id.* at I, 92, 140. Trade in gold or silver with the Indians was proscribed, doubtless the result of a tendency among the natives to use the coins as ornaments, thereby taking money out of circulation (*id.* at I, 83).
11. *Id.* at I, 137.
12. *Assistants Records* II, 97. See Chap. X, *infra*.
13. E.g., *Essex Probate Records*, (Essex Institute: Salem, 1916) I, 50, 7, 91–92. See Chap. X, *infra*.
14. E.g., *Mass. Records* I, 179.
15. See Chap. III, *supra*.
16. *Mass. Records* I, 124.
17. E.g., *Laws and Liberties* 38.
18. See Chap. VII, pp. 109 *et seq.*, *supra*.
19. *Mass. Records* I, 196, 228, 241.
20. *Id.* at II, 12–13, 21.
21. E.g., *id.* at II, 109.
22. See Chap. VII, *supra*.
23. *Winthrop Papers* IV, 477.
24. *Id.* at IV, 473.
25. P. S. Reinsch, "The English Common Law in the Early American Colonies," *Select Essays in Anglo-American Legal History* (Boston, 1907) I, 367 at 370.
26. *Mass. Records* I, 74.
27. *Ibid.*

28. *Id.* at I, 129, 169, 239; II, 3, 16, 28, 194.
29. *Id.* at II, 28.
30. E.g., *id.* at I, 77–78, 81, 86.
31. *Id.* at II, 21.
32. E.g., *Essex Records* I, 6, 9, etc. See also *Laws and Liberties* 1.
33. *Essex Records* I, 446–449. Although the terms "debt," "replevin," "trespass," etc., had very technical meanings as applied to the forms of action recognized by the common-law courts, they were also used in the courts of the manor and boroughs in a nontechnical but descriptive sense. See Chap. X, n. 12, *infra.*
34. E.g., see those collected in *Note-Book Kept by Thomas Lechford, Esq.* (Cambridge, Mass., 1885) at 46–47, 161; W. Aspinwall, *Notarial Records* (Boston, 1903) 21, 79, 142–143, etc.
35. See *Laws and Liberties*, Epistle.
36. *Ibid.*
37. See *Winthrop Papers* II, 293.
38. For a discussion of this problem of jurisprudence, see generally R. Pound, *Law and Morals* (Chapel Hill, 1924).
39. See *Doctor and Student*, n. 163, *infra;* J. Fortescue, *De Laudibus Legum Anglie* (ed. S. B. Chrimes: Cambridge, 1942) Chaps xv, xvi.
40. *Winthrop Papers* IV, 468 *et seq.*
41. This point is developed in G. L. Haskins, "Codification of the Law in Colonial Massachusetts: A Study in Comparative Law," *Indiana Law Journal* XXX, 1 at 3 (1954); *id.*, "De la codification du droit en Amérique du Nord au xvii ᵉ siècle: une étude de droit comparé," *Revue d'histoire du droit* XXIII, 311 at 313 (1955).
42. See G. L. Haskins and S. E. Ewing, 3d, "The Spread of Massachusetts Law in the Seventeenth Century," *University of Pennsylvania Law Review* CVI, 413 (1958).
43. See Chap. IV, pp. 36–37, *supra.* Professor Clarence Morris, in "Law, Reason and Sociology," *University of Pennsylvania Law Review* CVII, 147 at 155 (1958), has pertinently observed that "Authoritarians and democrats are likely to prefer what Weber calls 'Khadi justice'–'decisions reached on the basis of concrete, ethical, or political considerations or of feelings oriented toward social justice'–decisions made not on the basis of legal rules inspired by these materials, but on the materials themselves."
44. Winthrop, *Journal* I, 323–324.
45. *Ibid.; Winthrop Papers* IV, 476.
46. H. de Bracton, *Le Legibus et Consuetudinibus Angliae* (ed. T. Twiss: London, 1878–1883) I, fol. 1A.
47. J. Dickinson, "Social Order and Political Authority," *American Political Science Review* XXIII, 293 at 301 (1929).
48. E.g., *Laws and Liberties*, Epistle.
49. See W. S. Holdsworth, *A History of English Law* (London, 1936) II, 591–597; *id.*, at V (1945), 155–214.
50. Dickinson, *loc. cit. supra* n. 47, at 617.
51. G. L. Haskins, "Executive Justice and the Rule of Law," *Speculum* XXX, 529 at 531–532 (1955).
52. See J. Goebel, *Cases and Materials on the Development of Legal Institutions* (Brattleboro, Vermont, 1946) 176.

53. See F. W. Maitland, *The Constitutional History of England* (Cambridge, 1941) 251–275.

54. G. L. Haskins, "The Beginnings of the Recording System in Massachusetts," *Boston University Law Review* XXI, 281 at 296, 301 (1941).

55. Cf. *Historical Manuscripts Commission: Report on the Manuscripts of Lord Montagu of Beaulieu* (London, 1900) LIII, 32, 33. Insistence on fundamental written law was also one of Calvin's tenets. H. D. Foster, *Collected Papers* (privately printed, 1929) 102.

56. Winthrop, *Journal* I, 151; *Mass. Records* I, 147.

57. Although it is possible that the idea of codification was derived from Plymouth, which had enacted a rudimentary code in 1636, it must be emphasized that the movement in Massachusetts antedated the Plymouth effort. Distrust of discretionary justice is also found in England later in the seventeenth century. See C. G. Cock, *English-Law: or Summary Survey of the Household of God on earth, and that both before and under the Law, and that both of Moses and Jesus, with an essay of Christian Government under the regiment of our Lord and King* (London, 1651) I, 165; R. Robinson, "Anticipations Under the Commonwealth of Changes in the Law," *Select Essays in Anglo-American Legal History* (Boston, 1907) I, 467 at 470. Puritan opposition to equity has been the subject of comment by R. Pound, *The Spirit of the Common Law* (Boston, 1921) 53–54.

58. C. M. Bowra, *The Greek Experience* (London, 1957) 67.

59. H. S. Maine, *Ancient Law* (London, 1878) 18.

60. *Mass. Records* I, 147.

61. *Id.* at I, 174–175.

62. Winthrop, *Journal* I, 196.

63. The Cotton Code is known both as "Moses his Judicials" and as "An Abstract of the Laws of New-England." It was printed in London in 1641 and 1655 under the latter title, notwithstanding the fact that it never had any official status. For the text, see *Mass. Hist. Soc. Coll.* (1st ser.) V, 173 *et seq.* (1798). See also W. C. Ford, "Cotton's 'Moses his Judicials,'" *Mass. Hist. Soc. Proc.* (2nd ser.) XVI, 274 *et seq.* (1902).

64. See, for example, the deprecating remarks of J. T. Adams, *The Founding of New England* (Boston, 1921) 211.

65. S. R. Gardiner, *History of the Commonwealth and Protectorate, 1649–1660* (London, 1897) II, 265. See also W. Sheppard, *England's Balme* (London, 1657) 2, 7, who accepts the scriptural foundation of law as a major premise.

Reliance upon the Scriptures as the basis for civil legislation was not peculiar to the New England Puritans; Cartwright had contended that the magistrate had no power to depart from those judicial laws of Moses which had perpetual validity, and among such laws he included the injunctions that death be the penalty for blasphemy, idolatry, adultery, and murder. A. F. S. Pearson, *Church and State: Political Aspects of Sixteenth Century Puritanism* (Cambridge, 1928) 108. Whitgift pointed out that Cartwright's position would mean that all the laws of England contrary to Mosaic Law must be abrogated, that lawyers must throw away their lawbooks and rely on the Pentateuch instead, that the clergy must succeed the lawyers as the arbiters of the law and the latter be dispossessed (*id.*, at 107–108). Cartwright denied that lawbooks must be discarded; they must, however, be brought into harmony with the laws of Moses. He cheerfully advised Archbishop Whitgift that the only valid function of the bishops in Parliament was to see that the laws there enacted should not be repugnant to the Mosaic Laws (*id.*, at 108).

66. I. M. Calder, "John Cotton and the New Haven Colony," *N.E.Q.* III, 82 (1930). On the importance of legislative precedents in the American colonies, see S. A. Riesenfeld, "Law-Making and Legislative Precedent in American Legal History," *Minnesota Law Review* XXXIII, 103 (1949).

67. It should be noted that the cursing and smiting of parents and the rebellious son, provided against in Cotton's draft, do not appear in the *Body of Liberties*. It is possible that the laws relating to prices and wages enacted by the General Court in 1636 may have been inspired by one of the provisions in the Cotton code. Cf. *Mass Records* I, 183, with Cotton's draft, *supra* n. 63, Chap. V.

68. Cotton's draft, *supra* n. 63, *passim.*

69. *Id.* at IX, 4, 5.

70. *Id.* at IX, 1.

71. *Id.* at VII *passim.*

72. *Id.* at VII, 9, 15.

73. *Id.* at I, 5; II, 2, 4; III, 5; IV *passim.*

74. *Id.* at V, 3.

75. *Id.* at IV.

76. *Id.* at IV, 8.

77. *Id.* at IV, 7.

78. E.g., *Mass. Records* I, 111; *Assistants Records* II, 51, 54.

79. See Chap. VI, pp. 90–91, *supra.*

80. Cotton's draft, *supra* n. 63, at V, 3.

81. See J. Dorfman, *The Economic Mind in American Civilization, 1606–1865* (New York, 1946) I, 12.

82. J. T. Adams, *op. cit. supra* n. 64, at 211. Only six of the fourteen pages in the Massachusetts Historical Society text contain references to the Bible, although several provisions on other pages are evidently based thereon.

83. *Mass. Records* I, 174–175.

84. Thomas Hutchinson states that he had seen a copy of that code corrected in Winthrop's hand, which had erased the death penalty for the offenses in the following provisions of Chap. VIII: 11 (profaning the Lord's day), 14 (reviling the magistrates), 18 (defiling a woman espoused), 19 (incest), 20 (sodomy and bestiality), 22 (sexual intercourse with a female in her father's house and kept secret until her marriage to another) (Hutchinson, *op. cit. supra.* n. 6, at I, 373n.).

85. *Mass. Records* I, 222.

86. *Ibid.*

87. See *id.* at I, 262. At least two of the towns, Charlestown and Newberry, acted on the order. *A Report of the Record Commissioners Containing the Charlestown Land Records, 1638–1802* (Boston, 1883) iv; J. J. Currier, *History of Newbury, Massachusetts* (Boston, 1902) 56.

88. Winthrop, *Journal* I, 323.

89. *Ibid.*

90. *Mass. Records* I, 279.

91. *Ibid.*

92. F. C. Gray, "Remarks on the Early Laws of Massachusetts Bay," *Mass. Hist. Soc. Coll.* (3rd ser.) VIII, 191 at 208 (1843).

93. *Mass. Records* I, 279; Lechford, *Note-Book, supra* n. 34, at 237–238.

94. *Winthrop Papers* IV, 162.

95. *Mass. Records* I, 292–293.

96. *Id.* at I, 320.

97. Winthrop, *Journal* II, 48–49.

98. *Mass. Records* I, 346.

99. *Body of Liberties* 96. Farrand is mistaken in expressing doubt in his "Introduction" to the Code of 1648 that the *Body of Liberties* ever became law (*Laws and Liberties* vi). The passage he cites in support of his position relates to Cotton's draft, which was never enacted as law (*ibid.*).

100. *Body of Liberties* 1.

101. *Id.*, Liberties 2, 18, 46, 5–7, 45. Liberty 45 permits torture to extract, after conviction, the names of fellow conspirators.

102. *Id.*, Liberty 91.

103. *Id.*, Liberties 70, 75.

104. *Id.*, Liberty 17.

105. *Id.*, Liberty 46.

106. *Id.*, Liberty 47.

107. *Id.*, Liberties 18, 42, 45.

108. *Id.*, Liberty 10.

109. See, for examples, *Mass. Records* I, 55, 322–323, 326–327.

110. *Body of Liberties* 9.

111. *Id.*, Liberty 33.

112. *Id.*, Liberties 25, 55.

113. E.g., *id.*, Liberties 4, 33, 39, 21, 25, 35, 18, 55, 38, 29, 47.

114. *Id.*, Liberties 11, 53, 24, 83, 84, 81, 82, 85–88, 2, 89, 11, 90.

115. *Id.*, Liberty 94.

116. *Id.*, Liberty 65.

117. See the parallel table in *The Colonial Laws of Massachusetts* (ed. W. H. Whitmore: Boston, 1889), 21–24.

118. See *id.*, at 16–18.

119. *Body of Liberties* 98.

120. See *id.*, Liberty 1; see also *Laws and Liberties* 1.

121. *Mass. Records* II, 22. See the facsimile in *Col. Soc. Mass. Trans.* XVII, at 116 (1915) and in G. L. Haskins, "The Capitall Lawes of New-England," *Harvard Law School Bulletin* (February, 1956) 10–11. Capital laws 10, 11, and 12 there printed were not in the *Body of Liberties* but were enacted in 1642 after the conviction of three men for sexual misconduct with John Humfry's infant daughters. *Mass. Records* II, 12–13, 21–22. For Winthrop's account of the Humfry episode, see J. Winthrop, *History of New England* (ed. J. Savage: Boston, 1826) II, 45–48.

122. Notably theft, which for value over a shilling was punishable by death in England.

123. Chap. III, pp. 36–37, *supra*.

124. *Laws and Liberties*, Epistle.

125. *Mass. Records* II, 39.

126. *Id.*, at II, 61.

127. *Id.*, at II, 109.
128. *Essex Records* I, *passim.*
129. *Mass. Records* II, 128.
130. *Id.*, at II, 157.
131. *Ibid.*
132. *Id.*, at II, 168–169.
133. *Id.*, at II, 169.
134. *Id.*, at II, 196.
135. E.g., *Colonial Laws, supra* n. 117 at 19.
136. D. P. Corey, *The History of Malden, Massachusetts* (Malden, 1899) 180–181. Hills was allowed £10 for his work (*Mass. Records* II, 273). F. Pulton, "a distinguished barrister," was a seventeenth century compiler and classifier of English statutes (P. H. Winfield, *The Chief Sources of English Legal History* [Cambridge, Mass., 1925] 79, 92).

137. Most of the changes made in the legislation of November, 1646, before its incorporation into the Code, were in fact minor. When the Indian paw-waw law was incorporated into the title "Indians" of the *Laws and Liberties,* the phrase subjecting to fine "every assistant countenancing [the paw-waw], by his presence or otherwise," was changed to read "every other"; presumably, "assistant," correctly used in the original law in the sense of "participant," was rejected because of the possibility of confusion with "assistant" in the titular sense as used in the colony. Cf. *Mass. Records* II, 177, with *Laws and Liberties* 29. A statute concerning church attendance was changed by the addition of a sentence to the effect that any single magistrate could hear and determine any offense arising thereunder. Cf. *Mass. Records* II, 178, with *Laws and Liberties* 20. The law establishing the assize of bread was incorporated into the Code without significant change under the title of "Bakers"; a paragraph was added, however, detailing the method of choosing clerks of market for enforcement of the assize and extending the power of such clerks to butter. Cf. *Mass. Records* II, 181, with *Laws and Liberties* 3. The assize of wood was made part of the Code and entitled "Wood," with the addition of prescribed measurements of wood sold by the cord. Cf. *Mass. Records* II, 181, with *Laws and Liberties* 54–55. The statute dealing with contempt of the Word or its ministers provided that a person offending thereunder the second time should be punished by public display, wearing a paper saying "A WANTON GOSPELLER"; in the Code, title "Ecclesiasticall," the statute, otherwise unchanged, provides for a paper saying, "AN OPEN AND OBSTINATE CONTEMNER OF GODS HOLY ORDINANCES." Cf. *Mass. Records* II, 179, with *Laws and Liberties* 19–20. More substantial was the change in the mode of punishment for heresy. Originally, the statute provided that a heretic who continued obstinate after due means of conviction was to pay twenty shillings per month for the first six months, and forty shillings per month thereafter, "& so to continue dureing his obstinacy"; the penalty for seducing others to heresy was five pounds for every offense. As carried over to the code, title "Heresie," the punishment, either for maintaining a heresy or for seducing others to it, was banishment. Cf. *Mass. Records* II, 177, with *Laws and Liberties* 24.

138. *Mass. Records* II, 176 ff.

139. For the meaning of "prudential laws," see *Colonial Laws, supra* n. 117, at 12–13.

140. *Mass. Records* II, 221.
141. *Id.* at II, 117–121.
142. *Laws and Liberties* 39.
143. *Mass. Records* II, 224.
144. Apparently such a draft existed as early as 1646. See *Mass. Records* II, 168–169.
145. See *Laws and Liberties* 4 ("Bills"), 17–18 ("Dowries"), 47–48 ("Secretarie"), 48–49 ("Straies").
146. *Mass. Records* II, 212.
147. *Id.* at II, 209, 217–218, 246, 263; *Laws and Liberties* 38.
148. See n. 117, *supra.*
149. See Chap. IV, p. 62, *supra.*
150. *Laws and Liberties*, Epistle.
151. T. F. T. Plucknett, Book Review, *N.E.Q.* III, 156 (1930).
152. See Chap. X, *infra.*
153. *Laws and Liberties* 23.
154. *Mass. Records* II, 21–22; see *Assistants Records* II, 30 (whipping), *Essex Records* I, 71 (fine and whipping), 80 (fine), 82 (whipping), 180 (fine or whipping, but fine to be remitted if the individuals marry).
155. *Assistants Records* II, 51.
156. *Laws and Liberties* 53–54, 2–3.
157. *Id.*, Epistle.
158. See *Winthrop Papers* II, 282 *et seq.*
159. *Laws and Liberties*, Epistle.
160. *Id.*, at 5–6, 29–31, 24, 25–26, 35–36, 43.
161. *Id.*, Epistle.
162. Cf. O. W. Holmes, Jr., *The Common Law* (Boston, 1881) 1, to the effect that "The life of the law has not been logic: it has been experience."
163. In another connection, Holdsworth has remarked that "the work done elsewhere by the law of nature was done in England by 'reason,'" (Holdsworth, *op. cit. supra* n. 49, at II [1936] 602 *et seq.*). St. Germain, the author of *Doctor and Student [The Dyaloges in Englishe, betwene a Doctour of divinitie and a student in the lawes of England]* (London, 1554), refers to "The lawe of nature . . . which is also called the lawe of reason" (Dialogue I, Chap. ii).
164. This conception in modern law is discussed by J. Dickinson, "The Law Behind Law," *Columbia Law Review* XXIX, 113 (1929). See also E. S. Corwin, *The "Higher Law" Background of American Constitutional Law* (Ithaca, 1955).

Chapter IX *A RULE TO WALK BY*

1. *Winthrop Papers* IV, 472.
2. Quoted in P. Miller and T. H. Johnson, *The Puritans* (New York, 1938) 209.
3. *Mass. Records* I, 174–175.
4. *Laws and Liberties*, Epistle.
5. See *infra*, pp. 146 *et seq.*

6. E.g., P. S. Reinsch, "The English Common Law in the Early American Colonies," *Select Essays in Anglo-American Legal History* (Boston, 1907) I, 367 at 372–376.

7. E.g., T. J. Wertenbaker, *The Puritan Oligarchy* (New York, 1947) Chap. 2.

8. William Tyndale's English translation of the New Testament, printed on the Continent, was circulated in England as early as the late 1520's; Miles Coverdale's translation of the entire Bible was published under a royal license in 1537. See *The Cambridge History of English Literature* (ed. A. W. Ward and A. R. Waller: New York, 1909) 46–49.

9. W. S. Churchill, *A History of the English-Speaking Peoples* (London, 1956) II, 61.

10. H. M. and M. Dexter, *The England and Holland of the Pilgrims* (Boston, 1905) 26.

11. F. A. Inderwick, *The Interregnum* (London, 1891) 126.

12. S. E. Morison, *The Puritan Pronaos* (New York, 1936) 17–21.

13. P. Miller, *Orthodoxy in Massachusetts, 1630–1650* (Cambridge, Mass., 1933) 25.

14. Morison, *op. cit. supra* n. 12, at 41–42; L. I. Newman, *Jewish Influence on Christian Reform Movements* (New York, 1925) 635–636.

15. J. T. McNeill, "Natural Law in the Teaching of the Reformers," *Journal of Religion* XXVI, 168–182 (1946).

16. D. Neal, *History of the Puritans* (London, 1837) I, 76–83.

17. *The Acts of the Parliaments of Scotland* (London, 1814) III, 26 (December 20, 1567).

18. J. Goebel, Jr., "King's Law and Local Custom in Seventeenth Century New England," *Columbia Law Review* XXXI, 416, 424, n. (1931).

19. *Ibid.*

20. See W. S. Holdsworth, *A History of English Law* (London, 1942) IV, 275–276, 279–281, and *id.* V (1942) 266–269, for an account of the influence of the *Doctor and Student* upon the development of equity jurisdiction in England during the sixteenth century.

21. Reniger v. Fogossa, 1 Plowden's Reports 1, 8 (King's Bench 1551).

22. Earl of Oxford's Case, quoted in Z. Chafee, Jr., Introduction, "Records of the Suffolk County Court, 1671–1680," *Col. Soc. Mass. Coll.* XXIX, xxxii (1933).

23. Bradley v. Banks, 1 Bulstrode's Reports 141, 142 (King's Bench 1611).

24. Ratcliff's Case, 3 Coke's Reports 37a, 40a (Queen's Bench 1592).

25. W. Lambarde, *Eirenarcha, or Of the Office of the Iustices of Peace* (London, 1607) 401.

26. T. Lechford, "Plain Dealing: or, Newes from New-England," *Mass. Hist. Soc. Coll.* (3rd. ser.) III, 55, 84 (1833).

27. J. Kitchin, *Jurisdictions: or, The Lawful Authority of Courts Leet, Courts Baron, Court of Marshallseyes, Court of Pypowder, and Ancient Demesne* (London, 1653) 13.

28. A. Fitzherbert, *Loffice Et auctoritie de Iustices de Peace* (London, 1617) iv.

29. Newman, *op. cit. supra* n. 14, at 631–635.

30. *Laws and Liberties*, Epistle.

31. J. Strype, *Life and Acts of John Whitgift* (Oxford, 1822) III, 235, 237.

32. See, e.g., the "Post-Script" printed at the end of *Examen Legum Angliae: or, the Laws of England Examined, By Scripture, Antiquity, and Reason* (London, 1656) No. 5 (blasphemy), No. 16 (disobedient children).

33. *Laws and Liberties* 5–6. See also *id.* at 4–5 (theft).

34. *Id.* at 6.

35. *Id.* at 5.

36. *Ibid.*

37. *Ibid.*

38. *Id.* at 6.

39. *Ibid.*

40. *Id.* at 5–6.

41. E. Coke, *Institutes* (Part III) Chap. X: "If the party buggered be within the age of discretion, it is no felony in him but in the agent only." To the same effect, Sir Matthew Hale: "If buggery be committed upon a man of the age of discretion, both are felons within this law. But if with a man under the age of discretion, *viz.* fourteen years old, then the buggerer only is the felon" (*Historia Placitorum Coronae* [London, 1736] I, 670).

42. *Laws and Liberties* 6; *Mass. Records* II, 179.

43. *Ibid.*

44. *Ibid.*

45. *Body of Liberties* 94.

46. *Laws and Liberties* 5. The amended statute quoted in the text was originally enacted in substantially the same form as it appears in the *Laws and Liberties* on November 4, 1646 (*Mass. Records* II, 176–177).

47. Leviticus 24:16. The preamble to the amended statute of November 4, 1646, justifies the extension of the law to the Indians by reference to natural law (*Mass. Records* II, 176).

48. See Chap. XI, pp. 206 *et seq.*, *infra*.

49. W. Blackstone, *Commentaries on the Laws of England* (Oxford, 1769) IV, 59.

50. Hale, *op. cit. supra* n. 41, at I, 424–434.

51. *Laws and Liberties* 5.

52. Coke, *op. cit supra* n. 41, at 55–56; M. Dalton, *The Countrey Justice* (London, 1622) 222.

53. Dalton, *op. cit. supra* n. 52, at 225.

54. E. S. Morgan, *The Puritan Family* (Boston, 1944) 78–80.

55. The Court of High Commission apparently imposed heavy fines, sometimes exceeding £500, upon offenders of superior rank (J. Stephen, *A History of the Criminal Law of England* [London, 1883] II, 422–423).

56. *Winthrop Papers* IV, 477.

57. *Laws and Liberties* 6.

58. A seventeenth century abridgement of the English ecclesiastical law states that adultery could be committed "in a threefold manner, either *ex parte viri, vel feminae, vel utriusq*, always supposing that one or both are Matrimonaliz'd." J. Godolphin, *Repertorium Canonicum, or an Abridgment of the Ecclesiastical Laws of this Realm*, etc. (London, 1680) 475.

59. Cf. *ibid.* with *Laws and Liberties* 6.

60. *The Hutchinson Papers* (Albany, 1865) I, 199; *Body of Liberties* 94(9). The text of the Cotton draft is also printed in *Mass. Hist. Soc. Coll.* (1st ser.) V, 173 *et seq.* (1798).

61. Deuteronomy 22:28 and 29. See n. 33, *supra.*
62. Coke, *op. cit. supra* n. 41, at Chap. XI.
63. Winthrop, *Journal* II, 38.
64. J. Winthrop, *History of New England* (ed. J. Savage: Boston, 1826) II, 46.
65. *Mass. Records* II, 12–13.
66. *Ibid.*
67. *Mass. Records* II, 21.
68. Winthrop, *Journal* II, 38.
69. *Laws and Liberties* 6.
70. Compare *The Hutchinson Papers, supra* n. 60, at I 196–199, with *Laws and Liberties* 5–6. See T. Hutchinson, *The History of the Colony and Province of Massachusetts Bay* (ed. L. S. Mayo: Cambridge, Mass., 1936) I, 373, note, in which the author states that he saw a copy of the Cotton draft, corrected in John Winthrop's hand, whereon he had erased the death penalty for numerous offenses. Cf. Chap. VIII, n. 84, *supra.*
71. *Examen Legum Angliae, supra* n. 32, at 54.
72. Cf. *Mass. Records* II, 243; *Assistants Records* II, 108, for two situations in which the death penalty was not exacted.
73. Heads of households were required "to teach by themselves or others, their children & apprentices so much learning as may inable them perfectly to read the english tongue, & knowledge of the Capital lawes. . . ." (*Laws and Liberties* 11).
74. *Id.* at 54.
75. J. H. Wigmore, *A Treatise on the Anglo-American System of Evidence in Trials at Common Law* (Boston, 1940) VII, 274.
76. Holdsworth, *op. cit. supra* n. 20, at IX (1944) 203–211.
77. See Winthrop, *Journal* II, 257–258, for an account of the trial of a man and woman for adultery in 1645 which resulted in their acquittal of the capital crime because of scruples of the magistrates and jury about the two-witness requirement. Winthrop, *op. cit. supra* n. 64, at II, 47, for Winthrop's summary of the answers of the New England clergy to the question put to them by Governor Bellingham in 1641, "whether two vocal witnesses be always necessary for conviction and sentencing an offender?" However, William Schooler, was convicted of murder and hanged in 1637 upon circumstantial evidence. Winthrop, *Journal* I, 236–238; *Assistants Records* II, 69.
78. See n. 77 *supra.*
79. *Hutchinson Papers, supra* n. 60, at I, 201–202; *Essex Records* I; *passim.*
80. J. Fortescue, *De Laudibus Legum Anglie* (ed. S. B. Chrimes: Cambridge, 1942) 73.
81. *Laws and Liberties* 50.
82. See. e.g., *Calendar to the Sessions Records, County of Middlesex* (ed. W. Le Hardy: London, 1935) (new ser.) I, 188; *Quarter Sessions Records for the County of Somerset* (ed. E. H. Bates: London, 1907) I, 211.
83. *Laws and Liberties* 23.
84. See the statute of 18 Elizabeth I, c. 3. Study of the Somersetshire quarter sessions records for the early seventeenth century shows that the reputed father was ordinarily ordered to pay six or eight pence each week, and that the mother was ordered to contribute money to the support of the child if she could not keep the child herself. So long as the child's upbringing was

not chargeable to the parish, she was not committed to the workhouse. See *Quarter Sessions Records for the County of Somerset* (ed. E. H. Bates: London, 1907) I, *passim*.

85. Coke, *op. cit. supra* n. 41, at 109.

86. E.g., stats. 37 Henry VIII, c. 6; 7 James I, c. 7. See Chap. X, n. 86, *infra*.

87. Exodus 22:3.

88. See Index to *Assistants Records* II and to *Essex Records* I.

89. E.g., *Assistants Records* II, 94, 99, 118.

90. *Mass. Records* II, 180; *Laws and Liberties* 5.

91. *Assistants Records* II, *passim; Essex Records* I, *passim.*

92. E.g., *Assistants Records* II, 9, 14, 53, 59, 62, 72, 98; *Essex Records* I, 25.

93. E.g., *Assistants Records* II, 53; *Essex Records* I, 110.

94. E.g., *Assistants Records* II, 16, 81; *Essex Records* I, 59.

95. Josias Plastowe, who stole "4 basketts of corne from the Indians," was ordered in 1631 to "returne them 8 basketts againe be ffined V £ & hereafter to be called by the name of Josias & not Mr. as formerly hee vsed to be" (*Assistants Records* II, 19).

96. *Assistants Records* II, *passim; Essex Records* I, *passim.*

97. E.g., *Assistants Records* II, 70, 86, 131, 137; *Essex Records* I, 57, 84.

98. *Mass. Records* II, 180; *Laws and Liberties* 5.

99. See n. 86, *supra.*

100. *Laws and Liberties* 53–54.

101. *Id.* at 4, 52.

102. See Chap. X, notes 76 and 77.

103. *Body of Liberties* 85; *Laws and Liberties* 39.

104. *Body of Liberties* 87; *Laws and Liberties* 39.

105. *Body of Liberties* 88; *Laws and Liberties* 39.

106. Stat. 5 Elizabeth I, c. 4.

107. *Ibid.*

108. *Essex Records* I, 83.

109. *Calendar of the Quarter Sessions Papers* (Worcestershire) (ed. J. W. W. Bund: Worcester, 1900) I, 645.

110. *Assistants Records* II, 101.

111. *Quarter Sessions Records for the County of Somerset* (ed. E. H. B. Harbin: London, 1908) II, 109.

112. *Winthrop Papers* IV, 348.

113. *Two Elizabethan Puritan Diaries (Richard Rogers and Samuel Ward)* (ed. M. M. Knappen: Chicago, 1933) 1–16. The editor of these two early Puritan diaries concludes that "the most striking feature of the Puritan way of life as revealed in these diaries is the overwhelming predominance of the ethical element" (*id.* at 2).

114. P. Miller, *The New England Mind: the Seventeenth Century* (New York, 1939) 384–385.

115. W. Ames, *Conscience With the Power and Cases Thereof* (London, 1639) Book 5, Chap. 1, reprinted in *Puritanism and Liberty* (ed. A. S. P. Woodhouse: Chicago, 1951) 187 at 190–191.

116. J. Dickinson, *Administrative Justice and the Supremacy of Law in the United States* (Cambridge, Mass., 1927) 86–88 and authorities there cited.

117. Ames, *op. cit. supra* n. 115, at 190.

118. *Id.* at 187.

119. *Id.* at 191.
120. *Laws and Liberties*, Epistle.
121. W. C. Ford, "Cotton's 'Moses his Judicials,'" *Mass. Hist. Soc. Proc.* (2nd ser.) XVI, 274, 280–284 (1903).
122. *Winthrop Papers* IV, 486–487.
123. Ford, *loc. cit. supra* n. 121, at 284.
124. *Winthrop Papers* IV, 480.
125. Dickinson, *op. cit. supra* n. 116, at 85–86; G. L. Haskins, *The Statute of York and the Interest of the Commons* (Cambridge, Mass., 1935) 29 *et seq.* The idea is an ancient one and appears in Herodotus, *Histories*, III, 31.
126. *Laws and Liberties*, Epistle.
127. Quoted in *John Calvin on God and Political Duty* (ed. J. T. McNeill: New York, 1950) 62–63.
128. *Winthrop Papers* IV, 478.
129. See note 121 *supra*.
130. Quoted in Miller, *op. cit. supra* note 114, at 189.
131. *Id.* at 188–189.
132. See the penetrating analysis of Professor Miller, *id.* at 89 *et seq.*

Chapter X   *AFTER ENGLISH WAYS*

1. P. S. Reinsch, "The English Common Law in the Early American Colonies," *Select Essays in Anglo-American Legal History* (Boston, 1907) I, 367 at 385.
2. See generally W. S. Holdsworth, *A History of English Law* (London, 1924) IV, 294 *et seq.*; F. I. Schechter, "Popular Law and Common Law in Medieval England," *Columbia Law Review* XXVIII, 269 at 296 (1928).
3. Holdsworth, *op. cit. supra* n. 2, at V (1924) 178 *et seq.* F. W. Maitland, *Collected Papers* (ed. H. A. L. Fisher; Cambridge, 1911) 477 at 487–488.
4. Holdsworth, *op. cit. supra* n. 2 at I (1931) 598 *et seq.*
5. J. F. Stephen, *A History of the Criminal Law of England* (London, 1883) II, 402.
6. S. and B. Webb, *English Local Government from the Revolution to the Municipal Corporations Act: The Manor and the Borough* (London, 1908) I, 17 *et seq.*; Holdsworth, *op. cit. supra* n. 2, at I (1931) 149 *et seq.*
7. J. Goebel, "King's Law and Local Custom in Seventeenth Century New England," *Columbia Law Review* XXXI, 416 at 420–421 (1931); Webb, *op. cit. supra* n. 6, at I, 17 n. 3.
8. See Chap. V, notes 107, 131, *supra*; see, e.g., *Munimenta Gildhallae Londoniensis* (ed. H. T. Riley: London, 1862) III, 86; *MSS., Boston Corporation Minutes* (Boston, England) I, 111, *passim; id.* at II, 167.
9. The assistance of Miss Bridgett E. A. Jones in connection with this search is gratefully acknowledged.
10. *Essex Probate Records* (Salem, 1916) I, 11; E. Coke, *Institutes* 176 b. However, the custom was known in Yorkshire, and was recognized in a limited way by the common law. H. Swinburne, *A Briefe Treatise of Testaments and Last Willes* (London, 1611) 117 *et seq.*; Holdsworth, *op. cit. supra* n. 2, at III (1941) 562.

11. For a partial list of these treatises, see Webb, *op. cit. supra* n. 6, at I, 10, n. 2.

12. E.g., *A Selection from the Prescot Court Leet and Other Records* (ed. F. A. Bailey: Record Society of Lancashire and Cheshire, 1937) 91, 94, 135, 140.
It should be noted that the forty-shilling limit on cases which might come before the commissioners' courts for small causes in Massachusetts parallels the similar limitations imposed by statute on the jurisdiction of manorial courts, and suggests that the colonists may well have thought of the latter as a rough equivalent of their own courts for small causes (Webb, *op. cit. supra* n. 11, at 17; *Laws and Liberties* 8).

13. E.g., *Prescot Records, supra* n. 12, at 212–213.

14. *Id.*, at 229.

15. *Id.*, at 91.

16. *Id.*, at 165.

17. *Id.*, at 253.

18. E.g., *Essex Records* I, v, 64, 115 (case). See Z. Chafee, Jr., Introduction, "Records of the Suffolk County Court, 1671–1680, Part I," *Col. Soc. Mass. Coll.* XXIX, xxxviii–xlv (1933), for a discussion of forms of action, pleading, and practice in the Massachusetts courts during a later period in the seventeenth century.

19. E.g., *Essex Records* I, 12, 154, 171. See also *Laws and Liberties* 32.

20. E.g., *Prescot Records, supra* n. 12, at 87, 135, 143, 189, 205, etc.; *Essex Records* I, 5, 11, 14, 19, 24, 26, 29, 31, 33, etc.; *Winthrop Papers* IV, 294–295, 299, 397; *id.* at V, 233.

21. See Chap. V, n. 108, *supra; Essex Records* I, 7, 174, 39, 113, etc.

22. Goebel, *loc. cit. supra* n. 7, at 431; *Records of the Borough of Leicester* (ed. M. Bateson: London, 1901) II, xxxiii–xxxix.

23. *Body of Liberties* 81, 82; *Laws and Liberties* 53–54. The law is less explicit than as stated in the text, but partibility is implicit in the double portion, and, in any event, the statement is borne out by the distributions made by the courts. Although the law enacted by the General Court appears to prefer male children, the court records demonstrate that daughters and sons took together. See *Assistants Records* II, 97; *Essex Probate Records, supra*, n. 10, at I, 11, 62, 91, 118, 173, 201, 325–326, etc. A detailed study of the intestacy law can be found in G. L. Haskins, "The Beginnings of Partible Inheritance in the American Colonies," *Yale Law Journal* LI, 1280 (1942).

24. Haskins, *loc. cit. supra* n. 23, at 1310–1311.

25. *Id.*, at 1281.

26. It was at one time supposed that the Massachusetts scheme was traceable to the custom of gavelkind in Kent. See Jackson v. Phillips, 14 Allen's Reports 539 at 561 (Massachusetts, 1867). This supposition has no basis. See Haskins, *loc. cit. supra* n. 23, at 1297–1300; *id.*, "Gavelkind and the Charter of Massachusetts Bay," *Col. Soc. Mass. Publ.* XXXIV, 483 (1946).

27. Haskins, *loc. cit. supra* n. 23, at 1303 n. 179.

28. *Id.*, at 1303, notes 180–187.

29. *Id.*, at 1303, notes 188–193.

30. Sympson v. Quinley, 1 Ventris' Reports 88 (King's Bench 1670); Newton v. Shafto, 1 Siderfin's Reports (King's Bench 1665). See C. I. Elton, *Origins of English History* (London, 1882) 193; Haskins, *loc. cit. supra* n. 23, at 1304, notes 195, 196.

31. C. I. Elton, *Tenures of Kent* (London, 1867) 169; *Borough Customs* (ed. M. Bateson: London, 1906) II, 133, notes 1, 2.

32. Haskins, *loc. cit. supra* n. 23, at 1306, n. 209.

33. E.g., T. Blount, *Tenures of Land and Customs of Manors* (London, 1874) 174.

34. Winthrop, *Journal* II, 228.

35. Phillips v. Savage, *Acts of the Privy Council, Colonial Series* (London, 1910) III, 433.

36. "Case of Phillips v. Savage," *Mass. Hist. Soc. Proc.* (1st ser.) V, 64 at 78 (1862).

37. For a detailed study see G. L. Haskins, "The Beginnings of the Recording System in Massachusetts," *Boston University Law Review* XXI, 281 (1941).

38. *Mass. Records* I, 306–307; *Laws and Liberties* 13–14. The imprisonment provision may have been intended to apply only to grantors who remained in possession after the conveyance.

39. See *Massachusetts General Laws* (1932), Chap. 183, secs. 4, 29. In this connection, see the comments of M. Howe, "The Recording of Deeds in the Colony of Massachusetts Bay," *Boston University Law Review* XXVIII, 2 (1948), who argues that the 1640 act was intended to apply only when the grantor remained in possession.

40. Haskins, *loc. sit. supra* n. 37, at 289–291.

41. *Mass. Records* I, 116.

42. Henry VIII's effort to establish such a system subsided in the face of parliamentary opposition. Haskins, *loc. cit. supra* n. 37, at 293. The Statute of Enrolments soon became a dead letter (*id.*, at 291–292).

43. For authorities, see *id.*, at 296, n. 78.

44. *Id.*, at 297, notes 79, 80, 81.

45. *Id.*, at 298, notes 87, 88. For examples of recording at sessions, see *Quarter Sessions Records* (North Riding of the County of York [ed. J. C. Atkinson: London, 1886]) IV, 126–172.

46. See *MSS. Boston Corporation Minutes, supra* n. 8, at II, 110, 236, *passim.* The recorder in an English borough was the chief judicial officer. See Webb, *op. cit. supra* n. 6, at I, 323.

47. E. M. Leonard, *The Early History of English Poor Relief* (Cambridge, 1900) 73 *et seq.*

48. See W. J. Ashley, *Introduction to English Economic History and Theory* (London, 1925) II, Part 2, 274–282; I. S. Leadam, "The Security of Copyholders in the Fifteenth and Sixteenth Centuries," *English Historical Review* VIII, 684 (1893).

49. Holdsworth, *op. cit. supra* n. 2, at II (1936), 379–381.

50. *Id.* at III (1942), 208–209; A. Savine, "Copyhold Cases in Early Chancery Proceedings," *English Historical Review* XVII, 296 (1902).

51. *Select Cases Before the King's Council in the Star Chamber* (ed. I. S. Leadam: London, 1911) II, 28, 33, 38, *et seq.; Select Cases in the Court of Requests* (ed. I. S. Leadam: London, 1898) lix–lx, lxv.

52. Goebel, *loc. cit. supra* n. 7, at 444.

53. See Chap. V, p. 76, *supra.*

54. *Mass. Records* I, 74. See Chap. III, n. 10; Chap. VIII, n. 26, *supra*.

55. See J. Winthrop, *History of New England* (ed. J. Savage: Boston, 1826) II, 344–350, for examples from what appears to be a notebook kept by Winthrop during 1636–1638, in which he noted examinations of suspected offenders in prison and their admission to bail, and the imposition of summary punishment. For a recent survey of the powers of the English magistrates, see W. Notestein, *The English People on the Eve of Colonization, 1603–1630* (New York, 1954) 213 *et seq*. For bibliography, see *id.*, at 276–277, and E. G. Kimball, "A Bibliography of the Printed Records of the Justices of the Peace of Counties," *Univ. of Toronto Law Journal* VI, 401 (1946).

56. M. Dalton, *The Countrey Justice* (London, 1622) 140–175; see also Chap. V, notes 177, 178, *supra*.

57. For instances of branding, see *Mass. Records* I, 99–100, 100–101, *Assistants Records* II, 60; for ear cropping, *Mass. Records* I, 88; see also, for a 1657 case, *Essex Records* II, 48. Justices of the peace in England were authorized to order ear cropping under statutes of 2 & 3 Edward VI, c. 15; 5 & 6 Edward VI, c. 4. See also *West Riding Sessions Records* (ed. J. Lister: Leeds, 1915) II, 226. Branding with a hot iron was expressly authorized under 5 & 6 Edward VI, c. 4, when the guilty party had already lost his ears, and it was resorted to in the seventeenth century for the punishment of rogues and vagabonds. 1 James I, c. 7; *Middlesex Sessions Records* (ed. W. L. Hardy: London, 1936) (new series) II, 26, 108.

58. *Essex Records* I, 18.

59. *York Records, supra* n. 45, at I (1884) 140–141.

60. *Essex Records* I, 88.

61. *Nottinghamshire County Records* (ed. H. H. Copnall: Nottingham, 1915) 45.

62. *Essex Records* I, 274.

63. *York Records, supra* n. 59, at I, 179.

64. A single justice had power to hear, determine, and punish tippling (1 James I, c. 9) and petty pilfering (43 Elizabeth I, c. 7); two justices had power to license keepers of alehouses (5 & 6 Edward VI, c. 25) and to imprison servants who assaulted their masters for a period not to exceed a year (5 Elizabeth I, c. 4).

65. A single magistrate could summon a jury of inquest to investigate a "Death untimely" (*Laws and Liberties* 16) and to hear and determine offenses against the law prohibiting tippling and drunkenness (*id.*, at 29–31); two magistrates could open the votes for assistants brought sealed to them at Boston (*id.*, at 21) and the consent of two magistrates was required if a master wished to sell the services of his servant to another person for more than a year (*id.*, at 39). See generally Chap. III, *supra*.

66. S. and B. Webb, *English Local Government from the Revolution to the Municipal Corporations Act: The Parish and the County* (London, 1906) 302–303; Notestein, *op. cit. supra* n. 55, at 213.

67. Compare the requirement that one of the two justices licensing an alehouse keeper be of the quorum (5 & 6 Edward VI, c. 25) and that one of the two justices who committed a rogue to the house of correction be of the quorum (39 Elizabeth I, c. 4).

68. *Laws and Liberties* 14–15.

69. The "commissioners" who were appointed by the County Courts to hear civil cases (in which the amount claimed was less than forty shillings) in towns where no magistrate was resident, pursuant to *id.*, at 8, should not be confused with the commissioners who shared the bench with the magistrates in the County Court. Cf. Chap. III, p. 33, *supra.*

70. Compare, for example, *Assistants Records* II, *passim*, and *Essex Records* I, *passim*, with *York Records, supra* n. 59, at I, *passim.*

71. Holdsworth, *op. cit. supra* n. 2, at III (1942) 392; See *Nottinghamshire County Records, supra* n. 61, at 24–25.

72. The offense of "contempt in open Court" was nonbailable by a provision of the *Body of Liberties* 18, carried forward into the *Laws and Liberties* 28. For examples of summary punishment, see *Assistants Records* II, 21, 48, 56, and *Essex Records* I, 9, 19, 89. See *Laws and Liberties* 36, requiring that contemners of authority be "lawfully convict," indicating that formal process of indictment was required in cases of contempt committed out of the presence of the court.

73. E.g., *Assistants Records* II, 18, 40, 57; *Essex Records* I, 3, 4, 5, 6, etc.

74. E.g., *Assistants Records* II, 27, 57, 59–60; *Essex Records* I, 9.

75. Stat. 5 Elizabeth I, c. 4. See *Middlesex Sessions Records, supra* n. 57, at 238.

76. *Assistant Records* II, 80, 103; *Quarter Sessions Papers, Worcestershire* (ed. J. W. W. Bund: Worcester, 1900) I, 645; *Nottinghamshire County Records, supra* n. 61, at 128–129.

77. *Assistants Records* II, 92, 101; *Nottingham County Records, supra* n. 61, at 128; *Quarter Sessions for the County of Somerset* (ed. E. H. B. Harbin: London, 1908) II, 109.

78. Chap. III, n. 65 *supra;* Chap. V, n. 98 *supra.*

79. See Notestein, *op. cit. supra* n. 55, at 217–218; Holdsworth, *op. cit. supra* n. 2, at IV (1942) 137–145. The most significant aspect of the "civil" jurisdiction of the justices of the peace was that of one or more justices over the adjustment of disputes between master and servant, or master and apprentice, under the Statute of Labourers (5 Elizabeth I, c. 4) and that of two or more justices to supervise certain partitions between overlords and commoners (35 Henry VIII, c. 17 and 13 Elizabeth I, c. 25).

80. See Notestein, *op. cit. supra* n. 55, at 214, n 7; Holdsworth, *op. cit. supra* n. 2, at I (1956) 297–298.

81. See generally Chap. V, *supra.*

82. *Mass. Records* I, 111.

83. See Chap. V, n. 164 *supra.*

84. Stat. 5 Elizabeth I, c. 4. See notes 73–77, *supra.*

85. Cf. *Mass. Records* II, 180, with stat. 43 Elizabeth I, c. 7.

86. E.g., stats. 37 Henry VIII, c. 6, 5 Elizabeth I, c. 21, 3 James I, c. 13. It is significant that throughout the early period, during which the colonial magistrates set the penalty for theft, single or twofold, but never threefold, restitution was imposed.

87. Chap. VIII, p. 134, *supra.*

88. Cf. *Mass. Records* II, 18 with stat. 1 James I, c. 22.

89. See the declaration of uses in *Winthrop Papers* IV, 370–371.

90. "Governor Thomas Dudley's Library," *New England Historical and Genealogical Register* XII, 355 (1858).

91. W. B. Trask, "Abstracts of the Earliest Wills on Record, or on the Files in the County of Suffolk, Massachusetts," *New England Historical and Genealogical Register* XXX, 432 at 433 (1876).

92. See A. C. Potter, "Catalogue of John Harvard's Library," *Col. Soc. Mass. Publ.* XXI, 190 at 204, 213 (1920).

93. See *Note-Book Kept by Thomas Lechford, Esq.* (Cambridge, Mass., 1885) *passim*. A statute of 1651 expressly provided that standard common-law expressions be employed for creating fees simple and fees tail and also recognized the fee tail male and the fee tail special (*Mass. Records* IV [Part 1] 39).

94. *Essex Records* I, 46, 76, 63, 140, 145.

95. See, e.g., *Winthrop Papers* III, 10, 84, 205–206, etc.

96. Lechford's *Note-Book*, supra n. 93; W. Aspinwall, *Notarial Records* (Boston, 1903).

97. See, e.g., B. Cocker, *Young Clerk's Tutor* (London, 1680); *Compleat Clark and Scrivener's Guide* (London, 1655); E. Henden *et al.*, *Perfect Conveyancer* (London, 1650)); T. Madox, *Formulare Anglicanum* (London, 1702); G. Malynes, *Lex Mercatoria* (London, 1636); T. Phayer, *Booke of Presidents* (London, 1583); W. West, *Symboleography* (London, 1632).

98. See Lechford's *Note-Book*, supra n. 93, at 64, 285, 388; Cocker, *op. cit. supra* n. 97, at 75; *Scrivener's Guide*, supra n. 97, at 445; Madox *op. cit. supra* n. 97, at 319, 323; West, *op. cit. supra* n. 97, at sec. 419.

99. E.g., Lechford's *Note-Book*, supra n. 93, at 386; Aspinwall, *op.· cit. supra* n. 96, *passim*; *Scrivener's Guide*, supra n. 97, at 180; West, *op. cit. supra* n. 97, at secs. 657, 658.

100. E.g., Lechford's *Note-Book*, supra n. 93, *passim*; Aspinwall, *op. cit. supra* n. 96, *passim*; Malynes, *op. cit. supra* n. 97, at 261–262; West, *op. cit. supra* n. 97, at secs. 659, 660.

101. Cf., e.g., Aspinwall, *op. cit. supra* n. 96, at 117, with Madox, *op. cit. supra* n. 97, at 367.

102. Cf., e.g., Lechford's *Note-Book*, supra n. 93, at 262, with West, *op. cit. supra* n. 97, at sec. 428.

103. E.g., the Elizabethan custumal of the manor of Wimbledon, which required that "in pleas reall and myxte" attachments and essoins "shall accorde with the cours of the comen lawe." *Extracts from the Court Rolls of the Manor of Wimbledon*, Part III (London, 1869) 70.

104. Holdsworth, *op. cit. supra* n. 2, at I (1956) 276 *et seq.*

105. *Id.* at I (1956) 284.

106. What follows is based on G. L. Haskins, "A Problem in the Reception of the Common Law in the Colonial Period," *University of Pennsylvania Law Review* XCVII, 842 (1949), which contains detailed references to the authorities.

107. For the early history and development of dower, see *id.*, "The Development of Common Law Dower," *Harvard Law Review* LXII, 42 (1948).

108. Coke, *op. cit. supra* n. 10, at 30 b.

109. *Id.*, at 36 b.

110. *Id.*, at 32 a.

111. *Id.*, at 34 b, 35 b.

112. *Id.*, at 35 a.

113. Haskins, *loc. cit. supra* n. 23, at 1291–1292.

114. *Laws and Liberties* 17–18. In 1641 it was provided that if a man did

not leave his wife a "competent portion" of his estate the General Court might give relief (*Body of Liberties* 79).

115. The dower act also provided that the widow receive a one-third share in the husband's personal estate. This share was subject to creditors' claims (*Laws and Liberties* 18).

116. *Coke, op. cit. supra* n. 10, at 110 b–112 b; *Borough Customs, supra* n. 31, at II, 121–122. The fraction varied, according to custom, from one-fourth, or one-third, to the whole. See C. Watkins, *A Treatise on Copyholds* (London, 1797) II, 87–89. Freebench should be clearly distinguished from dower by special custom under which a widow might take a life interest in one-half, instead of one-third, of the lands of which her husband had been seised during coverture. See Coke, *op. cit. supra* n. 10, at 33 b, 111 a; Baker v. Berisford, 1 Keble Reports 509 (King's Bench 1663).

117. Cf. Gomme, "Widowhood in Manorial Law," *Archaeological Review* II, 184 (1888). In some custumals the wife is explicitly referred to as her husband's heir: H. B. Shillibeer, *Ancient Customs of the Manor of Taunton Deane* (Tiverton, 1821) 42; M. Imber, *The Case, or Abstract of the Customs of the Manor of Merden* (London, 1707) 47; cf. Martin v. Wentworth, Noy's Reports 1 (Queen's Bench 1596). At common law a woman was never her husband's heir except in the rare instances when she was related to him by blood and there was none nearer in degree than herself.

118. See Chap. VIII, *supra*. See also Winthrop *Journal* II, 264–266.

119. *Laws and Liberties* 32.

120. *Id.*, at 51.

121. Holdsworth, *op. cit. supra* n. 2, at IX (1926) 368–369. See in this connection Bacon's orders, printed in G. Spence, *The Equitable Jurisdiction of the Court of Chancery* (Philadelphia, 1846) I, 398–399.

122. *Mass. Records* I, 88; *Assistants Records* II, 16, 19. Cf. Chap. III, p. 28, *supra*.

123. Holdsworth, *op. cit. supra* n. 2, at V (1945), 208 *et seq.*

124. *Les Reportes Del Cases in Camera Stellata* (ed. W. P. Baildon: privately printed, 1894) 177. Emphasis supplied to underscore the similarity to Winthrop's statement that "iudges are Gods vpon earthe."

125. *Mass. Records* I, 88; *Assistants Records* II, 16.

126. Chaps. III, IV, and especially VIII at p. 120, *supra*.

127. Chap. V, p. 83, *supra;* Chap. VI, p. 90, *supra*.

128. The printed selection of sixteenth and seventeenth century records of the Archdiocese of Essex, from which many of the original settlers had come, is especially pertinent. See W. H. Hale, *Precedents and Proceedings in Criminal Causes, 1475–1640* (London, 1847).

129. Goebel, *loc. cit. supra* n. 7, at 425, n. 16.

130. See Chap. VI, notes 38–44, *supra*.

131. See *supra*, notes 58–63. See also Chap. V, notes 149, 152, *supra*, and *Assistants Records* II, 89–90.

132. H. Hall, "Some Elizabethan Penances in the Diocese of Ely," *Transactions of the Royal Historical Society* (3rd ser.) I, 263–277, especially at 272, 273 (1907).

133. *Id.*, at 274.

134. Hale, *op. cit. supra* n. 128, Index, 276, under "Penance (forms of)" and "Public Confession."

135. *Id.*, at 153–154 (CCCCLXIV).
136. *Assistants Records* II, 34, 35, 46, 51, 52, etc.
137. *Essex Probate Records, supra* n. 10, at I, 8, 24, 58; *Mass. Records* III, 199.
138. *Essex Probate Records, supra* n. 10, at I, 44, 50–51, 388–389; II, 81, 90, 122, 190, etc. See *Mass. Records* I, 153.
139. No attempt to set forth these rules was made before 1641. *Body of Liberties* 79, 81, 82. See generally Haskins, *loc. cit. supra* n. 23, at 1284 *et seq.*
140. Haskins, *loc. cit. supra* n. 23, at 1290 *et seq.*
141. *Id.*, at 1293, n. 96.
142. These views have been advanced by Reinsch, *loc. cit. supra* n. 1, at 370; F. L. Paxson, "Influence of Frontier Life on the Development of American Law," *Proceedings of the State Bar Association of Wisconsin* XIII, 477 (1921).
143. See Z. Chafee, Jr., *loc. cit. supra* n. 18, at lv.
144. *Mass. Records* IV (Part 1) 10.
145. See *The Hutchinson Papers* (Albany, 1865) I, 223 *et seq.*
146. See *Examen Legum Angliae* (London, 1656) Chaps. 1, 2, 3, 9. 10.
147. Winthrop, *Journal* II, 271.
148. *Id.*, at II, 314.
149. Quoted in P. Miller and T. H. Johnson, *The Puritans* (New York, 1938) 211, 209.
150. Chap. III, p. 30, *supra.*
151. Winthrop, *Journal* II, 301.

Chapter XI *TOWARD NEW HORIZONS*

1. Winthrop, *Journal* I, 323–324.
2. *Id.* at I, 324.
3. *Id.* at II, 301. The declaration was made in reply to an answer made by the Child petitioners to a charge drawn by the General Court.
4. *Ibid.*
5. *Mass. Records* I, 12.
6. See J. H. Smith, *Appeals to the Privy Council from the American Plantations* (New York, 1950), 465 *et seq.*
7. See *Puritanism and Liberty* (ed. A. S. P. Woodhouse: Chicago, 1951) [43]–[51] for an excellent discussion of the Puritans' reforming instincts.
8. On proposals for law reforms in England during the Interregnum, see generally, F. A. Inderwick, *The Interregnum* (London, 1891), 153–248; R. Robinson, "Anticipations Under the Commonwealth of Changes in the Law," *Select Essays in Anglo-American Legal History* (Boston, 1907) I, 467–491.
9. *Examen Legum Angliae: or, The Lawes of England Examined By Scripture, Antiquity, and Reason* (London, 1656), "A Post-Script," nos. 21, 24, 40, 41, 26.
10. *Id.* at 124.
11. *The Somers Tracts* (ed. W. Scott: London, 1811) VI, 177. See *id.* at 177–245 for draft legislation prepared by the Hale Committee and submitted to Parliament for consideration.
12. 4 Coke's Reports (ed. 1610) "To the Reader."

13. M. Howe, *Readings in American Legal History* (Cambridge, Mass., 1949) 80–81 n. 2.

14. F. Bacon, *Law Tracts* (London, 1741) 3, 9.

15. *Id.* at 10–12.

16. *Id.* at 13–14.

17. The practice of partible inheritance, for instance, was followed in the colony for several years before the enactment of the provision of the *Body of Liberties* providing for the scheme of distribution of intestate property. G. L. Haskins, "The Beginnings of Partible Inheritance in the American Colonies," *Yale Law Journal* LI, 1280 at 1292 (1942).

18. *Laws and Liberties* 26, 23–24. The quotation in the text is from the preamble of the statute dealing with Jesuits, *id.* at 26.

19. See the laws under the title "Ecclesiasticall" in the *Laws and Liberties* 18–20.

20. Quoted in P. Miller and T. H. Johnson, *The Puritans* (New York, 1938) 209.

21. W. Bradford, *Of Plymouth Plantation, 1620–1647* (ed. S. E. Morison: New York, 1952) 86.

22. W. S. Holdsworth, *A History of English Law* (London, 1956) I, 622–623.

23. In England at this time the ecclesiastical courts granted the divorce *a mensa et thoro* upon grounds of adultery and cruelty. They also could pronounce a marriage void *ab initio*, in which case the parties were divorced *a vinculo matrimonii;* they had, however, no power to pronounce a divorce *a vinculo* if there had been a valid marriage (*ibid.*).

24. E. S. Morgan, *The Puritan Family* (Boston, 1944) 78–80.

25. *Body of Liberties* 75; *Laws and Liberties* 45–46.

26. *Ibid.*

27. *Body of Liberties* 70; *Laws and Liberties* 52.

28. *Body of Liberties* 12; *Laws and Liberties* 35.

29. *Body of Liberties* 2; *Laws and Liberties* 32.

30. *Laws and Liberties* 49; *Mass. Records* I, 196.

31. *Body of Liberties* 11; *Laws and Liberties* 1.

32. Holdsworth, *op. cit. supra* n. 22, at IX (1944) 93–96.

33. See note 28 *supra*.

34. J. F. Stephen, *A History of the Criminal Law of England* (London, 1883) I, 233–239. Cf. M. Dalton, *The Countrey Justice* (London, 1622) 278–297.

35. Stephen, *op. cit. supra* n. 34, at I, 233–239.

36. *Ibid.*

37. *Body of Liberties* 18; *Laws and Liberties* 28.

38. *Ibid.*

39. *Laws and Liberties* 2. Cf. the appeals section of the *Body of Liberties* 36, which the foregoing appeals statute superseded. The earlier enactment simply provided that "everie man shall have libertie to complaine to the Generall Court of any injustice done him in any Court of Assistants or other."

40. Stephen, *op. cit. supra* n. 34, at I, 308–310.

41. *Id.* at 308.

42. E. Coke, *Institutes* (Part III) Chap. CI.

43. ". . . no man shall be twice sentenced by civil Justice for one and the

same Crime, Offence or Trespasse" (*Laws and Liberties* 46; see also *Body of Liberties* 42).

44. ". . . in all capital cases all *witnesses* shall be present wheresoever they dwell" (*Laws and Liberties* 54).

45. *Ibid.*

46. Holdsworth, *op. cit. supra* n. 22, at IX (1944) 226–227.

47. *Id.* at IX (1944) 225–227.

48. Quoted in W. Notestein, *The English People on the Eve of Colonization* (New York, 1954) 213.

49. See, *e.g.,* the judicial examination of Joseph Redknape during his trial in 1644 for refusing to allow his child to be baptized. *Essex Records* I, 70. See also, e.g., the references to the two successive examinations of William Schooler by the magistrates of Ipswich upon suspicion of murder in 1636 and 1637 (Winthrop, *Journal I,* 236).

50. J. H. Wigmore, *A Treatise on the Anglo-American System of Evidence in Trials at Common Law* (Boston, 1940) VIII, 293–301.

51. Lilburne's Trial, *Howell's State Trials* III 1315 (Star Chamber, 1637).

52. Winthrop, *Short Story of the Rise, Reign, and Ruine of the Antinomians,* etc. (London, 1644), reprinted in *Antinomianism in the Colony of Massachusetts Bay, 1636–1638* (ed. C. F. Adams: Boston, 1894) 194.

53. *Ibid.*

54. *Id.* at 195.

55. *Ibid.*

56. *Id.* at 194.

57. Winthrop, *History of New England* (ed. J. Savage: Boston, 1826) II, 47.

58. *Ibid.*

59. *Body of Liberties* 3; *Laws and Liberties* 43. Compare the discussion of the colonial privilege against self-crimination in S. A. Riesenfeld, "Law Making and Legislative Precedent in American Legal History," *Minnesota Law Review* XXXIII, 103 at 117–120 (1949), a valuable study which advances the thesis that the colonists of Massachusetts in this period recognized a number of civil rights which, in some respects, went "noticeably beyond the traditional liberties of Englishmen" (*id.* at 116). Professor Riesenfeld's conclusion, from the Bellingham correspondence and the Code provision against the use of torture to extract confessions, that "the privilege against self-incrimination became a recognized civil right long before the adoption of the Constitution," appears to be entirely accurate in the sense that a privilege against forcible self-crimination, similar to that in effect in England after the prohibition of the *ex officio* oath, was recognized at this period of the colony's history. Recognition of the privilege in its modern form, however, appears not to have been a part of the colony's law at this time.

60. *Laws and Liberties* 50.

61. In 1638 John Winthrop threatened a woman who refused to plead to an indictment for murder with the ancient torture of *peine forte et dure,* practiced in England in the seventeenth century to force an accused to plead to an indictment. Winthrop, *Journal* I, 282–283.

62. D. Jardine, *A Reading on the Use of Torture in the Criminal Law of England* (London, 1837) 22–70, 76–109.

63. *Ibid.*

64. *Body of Liberties* 17; *Laws and Liberties* 35.
65. Holdsworth, *op. cit. supra* n. 22, at I (1956) 230.
66. Z. Chafee, Jr., *Three Human Rights in the Constitution of 1787* (Lawrence, Kans., 1956) 163–164.
67. *Id.* at 165–166.
68. *Ibid.*
69. Winthrop, *Journal* I, 151.
70. J. T. McNeill, "Natural Law in the Teaching of the Reformers," *Journal of Religion* XXVI, 174 (1946).
71. Quoted in *id.* at 178.
72. Quoted in P. Miller, *The New England Mind: The Seventeenth Century* (New York, 1939) 198.
73. T. Hooker, "A True Sight of Sin," reprinted in Miller and Johnson, *op. cit. supra* n. 20 at 292 *et seq.*
74. *Id.* at 292.
75. Quoted *id.* at 218.
76. *Mass. Records* II, 241.
77. Winthrop, *Journal* II, 177.
78. See *infra*, pp. 210–211.
79. See *infra*, notes 80–83.
80. *Mass. Records* I, 208–209.
81. *Id.* at I, 157.
82. *Assistants Records* II, 117.
83. *Id.* at II, 95, 99. The records indicate that Jenkins married the girl. *Winthrop Papers* IV, 268.
84. See Chap. VI, *supra.*
85. *Mass. Records* I, 252.
86. Winthrop, *Journal* I, 313.
87. *Ibid.*
88. *Laws and Liberties* 1–2. See also the provision as to neglect of education of children and servants (*id.* at 11); and the "Heresie" statute (*id.* at 24), which also required the application of "due means of conviction" to the offender before he could be sentenced to banishment. Cf. the statutory penalty for contempt of the "Word preached or the Messengers therof" (*id.* at 19–20).
89. *Id.* at 11.
90. *Id.* at 1.
91. *Winthrop Papers* IV, 487.
92. See the frequent appearance of the formula "Unde dominus habita monitione eum dimisit" in the extracts from the act books of the Archdeaconry of Essex for the early seventeenth century in W. H. Hale, *Precedents and Proceedings in Criminal Causes, 1475–1640* (London, 1847).
93. E.g., *id.* at 245, 247–248, 255.
94. E.g. F. W. X. Fineham, "Notes from the Ecclesiastical Court Records at Somerset House," *Royal Historical Soc. Transactions* (4th ser.) IV, 103 at 123, 134 (1921).
95. T. Hooker, *supra* n. 73 at 292.
96. *Winthrop Papers* IV, 476.
97. *Ibid.*

98. *Assistants Records* II, 104.

99. *Essex Records* I, 15.

100. *Assistants Records* II, 65.

101. *Id.* at II, 126.

102. If he refused, he was to "stand at the whipping post half an hour after lecture with a paper in his hat on which in capital letters shall be written, 'For slaunderinge of the Church and for abusinge of the Governor'" (*Essex Records* I, 185).

103. *Assistants Records* II, 108.

104. For examples of "wearing papers," see note 102, *supra; Assistants Records* II, 89, 124; *Essex Records* I, 15, 36. See also *Laws and Liberties* 19–20; *Assistants Records* II, 41, 81.

105. See the Index to *Essex Records* I, *passim.*

106. See note 97 *supra.*

107. *Examen Legum Angliae, supra* n. 9, at 54.

108. F. Bacon, "Certain Articles or Considerations Touching the Union of the Kingdomes of England and Scotland," in *Resuscitatio* (ed. W. Rawley: London, 1671) I, 175.

109. Quoted in Robinson, *loc. cit. supra* n. 8, at 476.

110. *Laws and Liberties* 8. The original limitation of twenty shillings was changed to forty in 1647. See Chap. III, n. 67, *supra.*

111. *Id.* at 2.

112. *Id.* at 1.

113. *Id.* at 12.

114. *Id.* at 1.

115. *Id.* at 2, 4, 16, 49.

116. *Id.* at 47.

117. *Id.* at 32.

118. *Ibid.*

119. *Ibid.*

120. *Ibid.* (emphasis supplied).

121. *Ibid.*

122. Land was exempt from administration unless the testator provided otherwise, as by a direction to the executor to sell land. H. Swinburne, *A Briefe Treatise of Testaments and Last Willes* (London, 1590) 210-213, 221. For the rules governing the descent of land, see Holdsworth, *op. cit. supra* n. 22, at III (1942) 171–174.

123. *Id.* at III (1942) 555–558; Hensloe's Case, 9 *Coke's Reports* 36 b (Queen's Bench 1600); J. Perkins, *A Profitable Booke, Treating of the Lawes of Englande* (London, 1586) 109.

124. Perkins, *op. cit. supra* n. 123, at 109.

125. *The Probate Records of Essex County* (Salem, 1916) I, 82.

126. *Id.* at I, 12, 40, 72, 80, 84, 93–94.

127. *Body of Liberties* 79.

128. T. Atkinson, *Handbook of the Law of Wills* (St. Paul, 1953) 35–36.

129. *Laws and Liberties,* 17–18. The English Statute of Distribution was enacted in 1670 (22 & 23 Charles II, c. 10).

130. *Mass. Records* II, 281.

131. *Essex Probate Records supra* n. 125 at I, 50.

132. *Id.* at I, 106.

133. *Id.* at I, 121.

134. *Id.* at I, 67.

135. *Id.* at I, 162.

136. *E.g., id.* at I, 106 (of £37, widow received entire estate), 121 (of £57, widow received entire estate), 91 (of £88, widow received four-fifths).

137. *E.g., id.* at I, 65 (of £586, widow received one-fourth), 118 (of £108, widow received one-half).

138. *Mass. Records* I, 344–345.

139. *Id.* at I, 74.

140. *Mass. Records* I, 344–345; *Laws and Liberties* 12.

141. *Mass. Records* IV (Part 1), 5.

142. *Id.* at IV (Part 1), 27.

143. *Laws and Liberties* 55. For cases of garnishment see *Essex Records* I, 43, 109, 115.

144. *Laws and Liberties* 34.

145. *Ibid.*

146. *Laws and Liberties* 2.

147. *Ibid.*

148. *Ibid.*

149. At common law the creditor could elect between the *fieri facias*, entitling him to levy on the debtor's goods and chattels, or an *elegit*, entitling him to the debtor's goods and tenancy in half his lands until the debt was paid, or imprisonment of the debtor until the debt was paid. If the creditor chose to proceed by an *elegit* or to arrest the debtor, he could have no other remedy. Only if he began with a *fieri facias* could he move on to arrest or an *elegit*. A fourth alternative, the writ of *levari facias*, entitling the creditor to levy on the debtor's chattels and on the profits of his lands, had fallen into disuse and had been largely supplanted by the *elegit* in the seventeenth century. See Holdsworth, *op. cit. supra* n. 22 at VIII (1937) 230–232.

150. As in England at the time, the colony law does not appear to have provided the debtor with a remedy comparable to the modern discharge in bankruptcy; apparently, also, he could not force a composition of creditors. See *id.* at VIII (1937) 233, 240, 244.

151. *Id.* at VIII (1937) 79–80.

152. *Mass. Records* I, 304.

153. *Id.* at I, 307.

154. *Laws and Liberties* 34; W. Sheppard, *Epitome of the Laws* (London, 1656) 547.

155. *Munimenta Gildhallae Londoniensis: Liber Albus* (ed. H. T. Riley: London, 1859) I, 199–200, 219–220; Holdsworth, *op. cit. supra* n. 22 at IX (1944) 250 n. 2.

156. *Liber Albus, supra* n. 155, at 177.

157. J. H. Beale, "The Exercise of Jurisdiction *In Rem* to Compel Payment of a Debt," *Harvard Law Review* XXVII, 107 at 112, 116 (1913). For cases of garnishment, see *Essex Records* I, 109, 115.

158. *Borough Customs* (ed. M. Bateson: London, 1904) I, 193, 210.

159. R. H. Tawney, *Religion and the Rise of Capitalism* (London, 1926), 231.

160. *Laws and Liberties,* Epistle.

161. R. J. Taylor, *Western Massachusetts in the Revolution* (Providence, 1954) 103–127.
162. G. L. Haskins and S. E. Ewing, III, "The Spread of Massachusetts Law in the Seventeenth Century," *University of Pennsylvania Law Review* CVI, 413 (1958).

Chapter XII *OF LAW AND LIBERTY*

1. Quoted in B. M. Levy, *Preaching in the First Half Century of New England History* (Hartford, 1945) 65.
2. Winthrop, *Journal* II, 239.
3. *Winthrop Papers* IV, 481.
4. J. B. Fordham, *The State Legislative Institution* (Philadelphia, 1959) 87.
5. *Laws and Liberties*, Epistle.
6. R. Pound, "Why Law Day?" *Harvard Law School Bulletin* X, 3 at 7–8 (1958).
7. W. J. Brown, *The Austinian Theory of Law* (London, 1906) 16 *et seq.*
8. F. C. von Savigny, *System des heutigen Römischen Rechts* (Berlin, 1840) I, 14, 16, 38.
9. See references in R. Pound, *Law and Morals* (Chapel Hill, 1924) 92 *et seq.*
10. F. Pollock and F. W. Maitland, *The History of English Law* (Cambridge, 1895) xxv.
11. E. Ehrlich, *Fundamental Principles of the Sociology of Law* (Cambridge, Mass., 1936) Chaps. 3, 5.
12. Cf. R. Pound, *Outline of Lectures on Jurisprudence* (Cambridge, Mass., 1928) 60 *et seq.*
13. *Ibid.*
14. *Ibid.*
15. Cf. G. C. Homans, *English Villagers of the Thirteenth Century* (Cambridge, Mass., 1941) 405 *et seq.*
16. Winthrop, *Journal* II, 238.
17. Quoted in P. Miller and T. H. Johnson, *The Puritans* (New York, 1938) 190.
18. *Id.* at 254.
19. Quoted in C. H. McIlwain, *Constitutionalism and the Changing World* (New York, 1939) 256.
20. Miller and Johnson, *op. cit. supra* n. 17, at 258, 264.
21. *Id.* at 264.
22. *Id.* at 209.
23. *Id.* at 268.
24. *Id.* at 192–193.
25. J. Dickinson, *Administrative Justice and the Supremacy of Law in the United States* (Cambridge, Mass., 1927) 97.
26. *Id.* at 95–96.

Index

289

Salem, Mass., 10, 48, 107, 157, 175
Sales, law of, 114
Saltonstall, Richard, 11, 20, 258
Savigny, F. C., viii
Scholasticism, 17, 45, 143
Scituate, Mass., 187
Scolding, 170, 184
Scotland, 143
Scriveners, 180
Sealers of weights and measures, 75
Searchers of money, 33
Sedition, 183, 196, 200
Selden, John, 165, 170
Selectmen, town, 74–75, 78, 82, 240, 250
Self-crimination, 50, 130, 200–202, 283
Self-defense, 147, 149
Separatism, 16, 19, 24, 47–49, 63–65, 115, 187, 194. *See also* Congregationalism
Sequestration, 219
Sermons, 88, 118
Servants, 79, 81–82, 87, 100–101, 134, 154. *See also* Master and servant
Servitude, 81, 153, 217
Shays' Rebellion, 220
Sheep, 108
Sheldon, G., 73
Shepard, Thomas, 61, 88, 106, 124, 262
Shipbuilding, 108
Ships, sale of, 179
Sicily, xiii
Slander, 169, 183–184, 210. *See aslo* Defamation
Slavery, 81, 101, 129, 154, 259
Smith, Bradford, 97
Smith, John, 66, 247
Social structure, English, 95–97
Social structure, Massachusetts, 96–102
Society, organic theory of, 17–18, 43, 52, 59, 79, 84, 219–220, 224
Sodomy, 125, 145, 147, 266, 271
Somersetshire, 157
Southampton (Long Island), 125
Spain, 109, 166
Speech, freedom of, 74, 130, 196–198, 222
Spencer, William, 127
Sports, Sunday, 78, 178
Statute of Artificers, 81, 178

Statute of Distribution, 215, 285
Statute of Enrolments, 276
Statute of Labourers, 156, 176, 178, 278
Statute of Uses, 178
Stocks, 154, 175
Story, Joseph, 5
Stoughton, Israel, 127, 243
Strangers, 34, 71, 73, 78, 116, 130, 255. *See also* Aliens
Stubborn or rebellious son, 81, 134, 145, 147–148
Suffolk, England, 171
Summons, 34, 212, 216
Sumptuary laws, 33, 52, 77, 89, 102, 177–178, 252
Surveyor of highways, 71, 76
Surveyor of wheat and flour, 75
Swearing, profane, 52, 78, 89–90
Swine, 70
Symonds, Samuel, 133
Synods, church, 88, 246

Tanning and leather trades, 178
Tawney, R. H., 219
Taxation, 29–30, 57, 73, 77, 108, 251, 261
Ten Commandments, 62, 144, 152, 158–159, 161. *See also* Bible; Law, Mosaic
Theft, 28, 89, 134, 153–154, 165, 169, 178, 191, 211, 229, 259, 267, 277
Theocracy, 62–63
Thirty Years' War, 21
Tile earth, 134
Tindale, William, 270
Tippling, 52, 78, 166, 168, 178, 277
Tithingmen, 75
Tobacco smoking, 28, 77, 178
Toleration, religious, 18, 50–51
Torksey, England, 171
Torture, 129, 166, 201–202, 267
Town meeting, 72–74, 85
Towns, 30, 34, 59–60, 68–79, 103, 106–107, 110, 125, 135, 248, 251. *See generally* Chap. V
Trade, 25, 107–109
Trades and crafts, 106–107
Tradesmen, 100
Trading companies, English, 58–59, 76
Treason, 125, 145, 152, 164, 199
Trespass, of cattle, 130